P9-DYE-307

Mormons and the Bible

RELIGION IN AMERICA SERIES

Harry S. Stout
General Editor

A Perfect Babel of Confusion
Dutch Religion and English Culture in the Middle Colonies
Randall Balmer

The Presbyterian Controversy
Fundamentalists, Modernists, and Moderates
Bradley J. Longfield

Mormons and the Bible
The Place of the Latter-day Saints in American Religion
Philip L. Barlow

The Rude Hand of Innovation
Religion and Social Order in Albany, New York 1652–1836
David G. Hackett

Seasons of Grace
Colonial New England's Revival Tradition in Its British Context
Michael J. Crawford

The Muslims of America
edited by Yvonne Yazbeck Haddad

Mormons and the Bible

The Place of the Latter-day Saints
in American Religion

Philip L. Barlow

OXFORD UNIVERSITY PRESS
New York   Oxford

Oxford University Press

Oxford   New York
Athens   Auckland   Bangkok   Bogota   Bombay   Buenos Aires
Calcutta   Cape Town   Dar es Salaam   Delhi   Florence   Hong Kong
Istanbul   Karachi   Kuala Lumpur   Madras   Madrid   Melbourne
Mexico City   Nairobi   Paris   Singapore   Taipei   Tokyo   Toronto

and associated companies in
Berlin   Ibadan

Copyright © 1991 by Philip L. Barlow

First published in 1991 by Oxford University Press, Inc.
198 Madison Avenue, New York, New York 10016

First issued as an Oxford University Press paperback, 1997

Oxford is a registered trademark of Oxford University Press, Inc.

All rights reserved. No part of this publication may be reproduced,
stored in a retrieval system, or transmitted, in any form or by any means,
electronic, mechanical, photocopying, recording or otherwise,
without the prior permission of Oxford University Press.

Library of Congress Cataloging-in-Publication Data
Barlow, Philip L.
    Mormons and the Bible : the place of the Latter-day Saints in
American religion / Philip L. Barlow.
        p.   cm. (Religion in America Series)
    Includes bibliographical references and index.
    ISBN 0-19-506233-7; ISBN 0-19-510971-6 (pbk.)
    1. Bible—Criticism, interpretation, etc.—History.
2. Mormon Church—Doctrines.
3. Church of Jesus Christ of Latter-day Saints—Doctrines.
I. Title.   II. Series: Religion in America series
(Oxford University Press)   .
BS500.B33 1991 220′.08′8283-dc20 90-36034

Portions of this work, in different form, appeared in the *Journal of the American Academy of
Religion*, the *Harvard Theological Review*, and *Dialogue: A Journal of Mormon Thought*.
Permission to incorporate this material here is appreciated.

1   3   5   7   9   8   6   4   2

Printed in the United States of America
on acid-free paper

To
LaMar and Thelma Barlow,
who coaxed from us an enduring reach for
spirituality made relevant

Preface

"No man knows my historiography." Were the corporate Mormon Church articulate, such a self-reflection would barely qualify as hyperbole. Since the mid-twentieth century—from about the time Fawn Brodie published her controversial biography of Joseph Smith[1]— students of Mormonism have produced a veritable flood of scholarship. Although Brodie's book was by no means the sole catalyst for this flood,[2] Moses Rischin, writing in 1969, could reasonably conclude that the great flow of works on the Saints was "unparalleled for any religious group except the Puritans."[3] Rischin noted that scholars of every religious persuasion were contributing to this current. And the tide has increased sharply since he wrote.

There are good reasons for this interest. One is that Joseph Smith's followers have exerted disproportionate influence on national affairs. For instance, the newly formed Republican Party in 1856 built its platform around the abolition of "the twin relics of barbarism": slavery and polygamy. In the twentieth century, Mormons have had substantial impact on such national issues as abortion and the Equal Rights Amendment.

Perhaps a more telling reason for the unusual scrutiny is Mormon-

1. *No Man Knows My History: The Life of Joseph Smith, the Mormon Prophet* (1945). [Apart from convenient exceptions, items listed in the bibliography are cited in the footnotes by short titles only, even at the first reference.]

2. For other influential figures and factors, see Davis Bitton and Leonard J. Arrington, *Mormons and Their Historians* (SLC: University of Utah Press, 1988).

3. "The New Mormon History," *American West* 6 (March 1969): 49.

ism's complex and inherently fascinating nature, which continues to challenge its most able observers. As A. Leland Jamison put it, "The historical evolution of the Mormons furnishes the most thrilling chapter in the whole chronicle of American religion. By comparison, the adventures of the settlers in New England seem tame."[4]

Additionally, the Mormons are accessible for study—both because they are flourishing today and because, from their beginnings, they have been incredibly diligent record-keepers. Furthermore, the Saints were, for much of their history, relatively isolated and socially homogeneous, providing the same sort of laboratory for study that Perry Miller felt he had discovered in the Puritans. Finally, Mormonism has seemed to provide students of culture with an unusual resource in the quest to apprehend America. Tolstoi thought "the Mormon people teach the American religion." In the less poetic words of Sydney Ahlstrom, a careful study of Joseph Smith and his heirs "yields innumerable clues to the religious and social consciousness of the American people."[5] More than mere "denominational history" is at stake in the story of the Latter-day Saints.

Despite all this attention, however, gaps and idiosyncrasies remain in the historiography. Two issues in particular seem fundamental. The first is the persistence of disagreements over Mormonism's very nature: What *is* Mormonism, and how does it relate to the rest of American religion? Although opponents and casual observers have easily pigeonholed the Saints, more careful students have had a tougher time achieving consensus. Some scholars, such as Timothy Smith, have played down Mormon peculiarities, arguing that Mormonism has been essentially part of the religious "mainstream." Others, like Klaus Hansen, feel that in the beginning Mormons really were dissenters who at the turn of the twentieth century underwent a transformation and became consummate conservative Americans. Mark Leone has gone further, asserting that cultural accommodation *is* the story of Mormonism. More recently, Laurence Moore has used the Mormons as a prime illustration of his contention that, in America, self-conscious "outsiders" have been in important ways "insid-

4. In James Ward Smith and A. Leland Jamison, eds., *The Shaping of American Religion,* p. 213; cf. Martin E. Marty's preface to Klaus Hansen, *Mormonism and the American Experience.*

5. Thomas J. Yates, "Count Tolstoi and the American Religion," *IE* 42 (February 1939): 94; Ahlstrom, *A Religious History of the American People,* 1:614.

ers," that dissent itself can be seen as quintessentially American, and dissenters shown to wield influence. And, though she noted her thesis was not wholly new, Jan Shipps caused a stir among both Mormon and non-Mormon scholars with her sustained argument that Mormonism was so different that it quickly matured from an obscure cult into a genuinely new religious tradition, like Islam or Christianity itself. Clearly, these and works of similar stature have made important contributions in relating Mormonism to broader currents in American religion. What is less clear is whether the results of such studies are entirely compatible.[6]

This difficulty leads to a second problem. Rich as the historiography of Mormonism has become, it has yet adequately to address the fundamental issue of Mormon biblical usage. Other concerns, sometimes sensational ones, have monopolized scholarly attention. Yet obviously the Bible has been central to the nation's religious past. Until we can ascertain whether Mormons have tended to use the Bible in ways that are more like or more unlike those of other American religionists, assertions about Mormon similarity or dissimilarity to American religion more generally remain on insecure ground; the scholarly discussion to date simply lacks a dimension too central to ignore.

To some believers, of course, the nature of scripture appears self-evident: scripture is the word of God. Scholars are doomed to find such issues more complex. In many traditions, the very definition of

6. Timothy Smith, "The Book of Mormon in a Biblical Culture"; Hansen, *Mormonism and the American Experience;* Leone, *The Roots of Modern Mormonism;* Moore, *Religious Outsiders and the Making of Americans;* Shipps, *Mormonism: The Story of a New Religious Tradition.* Perplexity about the Saints could, if space permitted, be documented at great length. This perplexity is reflected in the wavering assessments of Mario DePillis, who long described Mormonism as "the fourth American religion," but who more recently has expressed doubts. It is further reflected by the willingness of Edwin Gaustad to give the Mormons separate status, along with Catholics and Protestants, in the large inserted maps of his *Historical Atlas of Religion in America* (New York: Harper & Row, 1976). It is evidenced in the difficulty scholars like Joachim Wach and Catherine Albanese experience in finding an adequate sociological label for the Saints (they finally settle on "independent group"). Perhaps the extraordinary sociological and historical difficulty is best captured by Ahlstrom's eloquent surrender: "One cannot even be sure if the object of our consideration is a sect, a mystery cult, a new religion, a church, a people, a nation, or an American subculture; indeed, at different times and places it is all of these" (*A Religious History,* 1:613).

scripture is difficult,[7] to say nothing of the problematic nature of revelation or inspiration, the relation of inspiration to recorded scripture, the relation of "truth" and culture to either, the various problems of canonicity and textual development, and the diverse perspectives within even single traditions about these matters and their implications. In the case of Mormonism, all this is further complicated by such dimensions as oral scripture, private scripture, noncanonized scripture, temporary scripture, and others. But notwithstanding the difficulty of the task, understanding a people's conception and employment of scripture can contribute much toward comprehending their religious essence. This applies especially to the Latter-day Saints.

A quarter of a century ago, one of Mormonism's most thoughtful analysts lamented that "there is no reliable study of Mormon exegesis. . . ." "I can think of no single area of exploration," wrote Davis Bitton, "which promises to be so fruitful in understanding the dynamics of Mormonism."[8] As this study will suggest, I believe a look at the Mormon relationship with the Bible needs to be more multidimensional than strictly a "study of Mormon exegesis." It must also examine the cultural uses to which the Saints have put the Holy Book. Yet I concur with the general direction of Bitton's observation, and the study for which he called has not heretofore been attempted—at least not any broadly conceived historical study.[9]

Our subject, then, is worth pursuit. Certainly I am not pretending to rewrite Mormon history along severely new lines. But I am pro-

7. See, for example, Denny and Taylor, eds., *The Holy Book in Comparative Perspective* (1985).

8. Davis Bitton, "Anti-intellectualism in Mormon History," *Dialogue* 1 (Autumn 1966): 122.

9. Except for attention to Joseph Smith's use of the Bible, the only serious historical works on the subject are Sherlock's 1979 essay on a Mormon response to a controversial history of Israel published in 1949 ("Faith and History"), Irving's examination of the years 1832–1838 as revealed through Mormon periodicals ("Mormonism and the Bible," 1972), and Underwood's three-page "The Old Testament in the New Dispensation" (1983). These are able treatments but are deliberately restricted in scope, and, for the most part, do not attempt the larger task of relating Mormon biblical usage to Christian usage generally. Hutchinson has contributed significantly to twentieth-century Mormon studies with his "LDS Approaches to the Holy Bible" (1982), but, as he notes, his work is hermeneutical, not historical. Kent P. Jackson summarizes standard official LDS perspectives in "Latter-day Saints: A Dynamic Scriptural Process," in *The Holy Book* (1985), ed. Denny and Taylor.

posing that nothing—not the early pioneer experience of the Saints, not the geography of Mormon headquarters, not Mormon political behavior, not the famous attempts to establish a polygynous or theocratic or communal society, not Mormon millennialism or Mormon social make–up, not the alleged contemporary corporate wealth, not former charges of racism or still-current accusations of sexism, not the quasi-religious interest of some early Mormons in folk magic; in sum, none of the more dramatic aspects of the Mormon experience often spotlighted by observers—captures the evolving but enduring *religious* quintessence of Mormonism and its relationship to the balance of American religion better than a firm, comparative grasp of the Bible's place among the Latter-day Saints. This assertion applies even to Mormon theology and revelation, which, as we shall see, is inextricably enmeshed with and dependent on prior and often unconscious biblical perspectives.

Just how to compare Mormons with others has presented certain difficulties, for much remains to be learned about scripture in American culture. Judging from the best general histories of Catholicism in the United States, for instance, an uninitiated reader would have to be alert to conclude that Catholics were even conscious of the Bible.[10] Gerald Fogarty has accomplished an important advance in this domain with his recent *American Catholic Biblical Scholarship,* but even here we must remember that biblical scholarship is but one dimension of the topic.

Students of Protestantism, especially evangelical Protestantism, have naturally been more attuned to the Bible's cultural role. Since the early 1980s such students have at last begun to press beyond the mere recognition that the Bible has been extremely influential in American culture.[11] For example, we know that the particular ver-

10. One looks in vain for substantial attention to the subject in such generally fine works as John Tracy Ellis, ed., *Documents of American Roman Catholic History* (Milwaukee: Bruce, 1967); Ellis, *American Catholicism,* rev. ed., (Chicago: University of Chicago Press, 1968); Philip Gleason, ed., *Contemporary Catholicism in the United States* (Notre Dame: University of Notre Dame Press, 1969); Thomas McAvoy, *A History of the Catholic Church in the United States* (Notre Dame: University of Notre Dame Press, 1969); James Hennessey, *American Catholics* (New York: Oxford University Press, 1981); or Jay Dolan, *The American Catholic Experience* (Garden City, NY: Doubleday, 1985).

11. Until recently, scholars seemed almost content with sentiments akin to Perry Miller's oft-quoted hyperbole: "The Old Testament is truly so omnipresent in the

sion of the Bible used by various groups can matter greatly. This is illustrated by the two factions in the antinomian controversy in seventeenth-century Massachusetts, whose respective conceptions and arguments were conditioned by the use of two different Bibles, the Geneva and the Authorized.[12] We also know something about modern biblical studies in this country, which first developed in New England as Unitarians were parting company with the Congregationalists.[13] After the Civil War, these studies flourished more widely, helping to incite a national crisis in biblical belief. We have learned much about the shifting intellectual assumptions behind this crisis, which was instrumental in realigning American Protestantism into modernist and fundamentalist camps.[14]

As for current usage, we know that the Bible is widely dispensed in America—not just among evangelicals—with sales totaling an estimated $170 million in 1983. Recent Gallup polls suggest many people actually read the Bible (12 percent once a day, 30 percent once a week), and even more of them (42 percent) believe "the Bible is the word of God and is not mistaken in its statements and teachings." Although it does not appear those who hold the Holy Book in such high esteem necessarily know its contents well (less than 50 percent of either Catholics or Protestants can name even five of the Ten Commandments), it is nonetheless apparent that many Bible-believers are prepared to fight about its interpretation. In the 1970s and 1980s, several Protestant denominations, including the nation's largest, the Southern Baptist Convention, experienced fierce struggles over the role and interpretation of the Bible. Meanwhile, the Lutheran Church–Missouri Synod suffered an actual schism over similar issues.

American culture of 1800 or 1820 that historians have as much difficulty taking cognizance of it as of the air the people breathed" ("The Old Testament," in *Historical Viewpoints,* ed. John A. Garraty, 2 vols. [New York: Harper & Row, 1970], 1:95). Although Miller's statement has merit, it is hardly an excuse for failing to try to grasp just how this omnipresent influence has taken shape. I therefore consider highly significant such recent works as Hatch and Noll, eds., *The Bible in America,* and the ongoing series on the history of biblical studies in America, sponsored by the Society of Biblical Literature.

12. Harry Stout, "Word and Order in Colonial New England," in Hatch and Noll, eds., *The Bible in America.*

13. Brown, *The Rise of Biblical Criticism in America, 1800–1870.*

14. See especially Hutchison, *The Modernist Impulse in American Protestantism,* and Marsden, *Fundamentalism and American Culture.*

Harold Lindsell's *The Battle for the Bible* (1976) is only the most famous of a host of books that continue to appear, arguing different sides of a complex problem.

In addition to this kind of knowledge, philosopher Richard Mouw has sketched "a preliminary taxonomy" of biblical usage among twentieth-century Protestants.[15] He distinguishes four primary tendencies among those who defend the Bible's authority: doctrinalism (intellectual submission to correct beliefs), pietism (devotional emphasis), moralism (the Bible as a sourcebook for personal ethics), and culturalism (the Bible as stimulus for cultural transformation or for interpreting culture). As we shall see, additional categories might be proposed, but Mouw's taxonomy is a helpful beginning.

Comprehensively relating the Mormons to all of this seemed too large a task for a single book, given the current state of the scholarship. A beginning, though, could have been approached in a number of ways. One might have attempted an exhaustive study of the Mormon use of the Bible in a single generation or decade, and then compared this usage to that of other Americans. Or one might have focused on a specific aspect like the public use of the Bible in sermons of Mormon leaders, or the proselytizing use of scripture, or the reaction of Mormonism to modern biblical criticism in the twentieth century.

In light of the historiographical needs explained above, I felt the most helpful course would be to cut a narrow swath through the whole of Mormon history. I therefore chose to explore the use made of the Bible by a series of key individuals who have had particular impact on Mormon scriptural conceptions and who have themselves reflected major LDS tendencies.

Six primary chapters follow. In addition to these, the Introduction considers the Bible's stature in antebellum America (a stature with enormous implications for nascent Mormonism) and the Summary presents conclusions and suggests lines for further research. The overall work conveys a sense of chronological development, but each chapter attempts to present a picture more coherent than possible in a system based on mere sequence in time. Chapters 1 and 2, which center on Joseph Smith before and after 1830, are somewhat different; they do stress sequence. In these cases, special attention to chro-

15. In Hatch and Noll, eds., *The Bible in America,* pp. 139–62.

nology is not simply surrender to convention but is crucial to understanding Smith's unfolding conceptions.

Scrutiny of Smith constitutes the primary exception to the historiographical gap that exists for Mormonism and the Bible, and an examination of his interaction with scripture necessarily owes much to the specialized studies of many talented scholars. Yet a fresh look was important for several reasons. First, a general treatment of the Latter-day Saints and the Bible would be incomprehensible if it did not begin with Mormonism's extraordinary and controversial founder. Second, no one to date has attempted a synthesis of the complex subject, thereby yielding an overall sense of Joseph Smith's biblical connections. Third, significant dimensions of the Prophet's use of traditional scripture have until now remained unexplored. Even on those matters that have been considered before, I have often found myself either arriving at different conclusions than previous analysts or asking different questions of the material. Finally, so far as I can tell, no earlier writer has seriously endeavored to compare Smith's use of the Bible with those of his contemporaries, a necessary exercise if one is to discern what is and is not distinctive about it.

Mormon biblical usage after Smith's death (1844) is nearly as uncharted as the western regions into which the Saints migrated. Chapter 3 asks how Mormon views of revelation developed in the second half of the nineteenth century by exploring the Bible's place in the contrasting thought of two men: Smith's successor, Brigham Young, and Apostle Orson Pratt, the most prominent Mormon intellectual from the 1850s until his death in 1881.

Between the 1880s and the 1920s, the problems of modern biblical studies began to seep from the intellectual treetops, dislocating much of American religious culture in the process. In Mormon historiography, these issues have been overshadowed by attention to the conflicts surrounding Darwinism, thus inverting the real importance of the two issues as challenges to Christian faith. How did the Saints deal with higher criticism? Chapter 4 sketches a spectrum of reactions by focusing on B. H. Roberts (arguably the preeminent religious intellectual in Mormon history), Church President Joseph Fielding Smith (grandnephew of the original Mormon prophet), and William H. Chamberlin (the first prominent Saint to receive a front-rank theological education).

Though few Latter-day Saints are conscious of the change, the King James Version of the Bible underwent a subtle metamorphosis in the corporate Mormon mind between 1867 and 1979. Chapter 5 examines the historical, theological, and emotional reasons for the transformation of the KJV from the common into the official version of English-speaking Mormonism. The discussion centers on J. Reuben Clark Jr., erudite and influential, and longtime member of the Church's First Presidency. By 1956 Clark had appropriated the arguments of Protestant KJV defenders and mingled them with his uniquely Mormon perspectives. In so doing, he made virtually all subsequent Mormon spokesmen for the KJV dependent on his logic.

Chapter 6 completes the study by inquiring how the Bible is used and interpreted in contemporary Mormon ranks. Two Weberian "ideal types" are found in the approaches of the late apostle, Bruce R. McConkie (who may have been correct when he noted that probably no human being of his generation had written and spoken more about Jesus than he had), and the octogenarian philosopher and humanitarian Lowell L. Bennion. The chapter concludes by assessing the significance of the new LDS edition of the Bible (1979), with its "Mormonized" notes, chapter headings, and Bible dictionary.

In approaching the present study, I have tried to attain a proper level of objectivity. However, I do consciously accept a modern notion that absolute objectivity is unattainable—and perhaps only ambiguously desirable. Some recent studies have gone so far as to argue that historical "objectivity" not only is beyond human reach but is an incoherent construct.[16] I do not follow them so far. The concept does retain meaning for me, and, because of the subject matter of this book, invites a brief explanation.

Although perspectives related to the philosophical and literary notion of "deconstruction" have influenced most or every modern discipline, the conversation is colored among students of Mormonism in part by the desire of some participants to protect LDS faith claims. Since 1966, Church leaders and Mormon and non-Mormon scholars have produced more than 150 essays, published speeches, and portions of books attempting to articulate how Mormon history is prop-

---

16. See, for example, Peter Novick, *That Noble Dream: The Objectivity Question and the American Historical Profession* (New York: Cambridge University Press, 1988).

erly approached.[17] Whether objectivity is a possible and appropriate goal is prominently and warmly contested in this literature.

Like all language, the term *objectivity* is ultimately metaphorical and relative; *the word has meaning only in relation to other words.* I use it broadly here as a shorthand to connote a method that embraces such values as balance, fairness, openness, integrity, the willingness to be self-critical, honesty in the attempt to present and follow even difficult or painful evidence, a modesty which respects opposing competent views, an absence of dogmatism, and the ability to produce history which seems responsible to diverse but intelligent and informed people of good will. All this is partially independent from other traits I admire in a scholar, such as intelligence, diligence, or creativity. Hence, for pragmatic purposes, I am prepared to describe as "objective" a historian of religion—whose personal allegiance may be to Hinduism or atheism or Lutheranism or Mormonism—if, in my imperfect judgment, I discern that he or she incorporates such qualities. I am not impressed with the perception that religious believers are by definition less capable of objectivity, thus construed, than nonbelievers. But I am also unsympathetic both with the accusation that those who value such an objectivity are blinded by the vestiges of philosophical positivism, and with some believers' misunderstanding that historians who write in naturalistic terms have, *de facto,* little religious faith or are even doing their subjects harm.

Goethe's equation, in my personal view, is accurate: humankind, divided by reason, leaves a remainder. I am convinced that reality has dimensions far transcending human capacities to ascertain. Perhaps those dimensions impinge on human activity. It may even be, as Richard Lovelace has said, that history, viewed without allowance for spiritual forces, "is as confusing as a football game in which half the players are invisible." If those forces are discernible at all, though, the discernment must come through private intuitions, or the vision of prophets, or the inspiration of poets, or the speculations of metaphysicians. They are not discernible through the tools of historians, strictly speaking, whose more modest task is to deal with things visible. Prophets or metaphysicians may, of course, point to matters of

17. Louis Midgley and David J. Whittaker, "Mapping Contemporary Mormon Historiography: An Annotated Bibliography" (unpublished, 1990) is a nearly exhaustive listing.

history. However, they are not by that motion acting essentially as historians, but as something else.

In Mormon studies, as with the study of other religions in which both believers and nonbelievers participate, much of the discussion over objectivity leads eventually to this problem: Should scripture and religion be viewed from the perspective of culture, or should culture be viewed through the lens of scripture and religious faith? Some insist there can be no middle ground here. But *if* God exists and acts in actual historical circumstances, humans can only know and interpret such events in the context of culturally conditioned experience. This is as true of Mormons as of anyone else, and it applies even to Joseph Smith's claimed revelations, as chapters 1 and 2 illustrate. If Smith's revelations are inauthentic (that is, if there is nothing supernatural about them), then their mundane elements are all that exist, and they invite analysis in order to come to terms with the historical forces shaping our culture. The contrary possibility, that the revelations are authentic, is not compromised by awareness that they are communicated to human beings whose apprehension of reality is necessarily culturally defined. According to Joseph Smith, God himself implied as much.[18] Those who credit such revelations have an *obligation* to study and recognize human limitations as best they can. If God works through imperfect human beings, one danger among others is that human, culturally defined allegiances and perceptions will displace God's work. *Whether or not one is a believer,* the good-faith attempt to critically examine human tendencies ought not induce defensiveness. The historical task can and should be essentially a constructive work for humanity, possibly having as one of its positive goals the distinguishing of moral, spiritual, and intellectual wheat from chaff.

In this enterprise, something less than perfect objectivity is left to the scholar, but something more than utter subjectivity remains. In the case of Mormonism, those who hope to make the church invulnerable to fair and open historical inquiry by asserting the incomprehensibility of "objectivity" seem unaware of the nihilism inherent in their position. If not even approximate, provisional, relative objectivity is possible, no ground whatever exists for human discourse. Shakespeare cannot be preferred to my own doggerel in any but an arbitrary way. Abstractions like wisdom, truth, quality, love, mercy, error, and evil have no meaning. There is no way to gauge them, no

18. D&C 1:24.

basis for making life choices, and no particular virtue in allegiance to God or any form of religion or philosophy. In such a world, the conditions of void described in the Book of Mormon would obtain: "righteousness could not be brought to pass, neither wickedness, neither holiness nor misery, neither good nor bad. Wherefore, all things must needs be a compound in one. . . ."[19]

My respect for objectivity as defined above is not incompatible with an awareness that the very concerns that make history interesting and important to a researcher also affect how the story is told, and even what story gets told. For these and other reasons, an author is in some ways least qualified to warn of his or her biases. Yet it seems prudent to try, and to let others determine how much to allow for personal orientation.

In addition to perspectives already noted, readers have a right to know, first, that I am a practicing Mormon, and second, that I have on many issues a greater personal sympathy for liberal than for conservative religious expressions. Of course, labels can be dangerous, and some of the subjects of my study would be loath to accept them. Moreover, words like *liberal* and *conservative,* applied to Mormons, assume meanings distinct from those the terms convey when applied to other forms of religion (see chapter 6). Still, the concepts hold some measure of cross-denominational utility. Guided in part by advice from the Book of Mormon,[20] my kind of Latter-day Saint is likely to have as much in common with liberals and moderates of other faiths as with staunch conservatives of his or her own church. Helpful attempts to imbue the abstractions *liberal* and *conservative* with meaning in a Mormon context have been initiated by others.[21]

Beyond those personal orientations, my method, like all methods,

19. 2 Nephi 2:11–13.

20. 1 Nephi 29:6–8, 10–12; Alma 29:8; 4 Nephi 15–17. See also *PGP,* Article of Faith #13.

21. Lowell L. Bennion, "Being a 'Liberal,' " in *Do Justly and Love Mercy* (Centerville, UT: Canon Press, 1988), and Richard Poll, "What the Church Means to People Like Me," in *A Thoughtful Faith: Essays on Belief by Mormon Scholars,* ed. Philip L. Barlow (Centerville, UT: Canon Press, 1986). Poll brilliantly discovered alternative and distinctly Mormon symbols for these two religious orientations, but his descriptions approximate liberal and conservative perspectives as I intend them here. Despite recent illuminating and more elaborate efforts at describing LDS social makeup (notably Jeffrey C. Jacob, "Explorations in Mormon Social Character: Beyond the Liahona and Iron Rod," *Dialogue* 22 [Summer 1989]: 44–74), the notions of liberalism and conservatism retain foundational explanatory assets for my purposes here.

has limitations. Critics might argue that one cannot prove anything about general phenomena by selecting a few examples. And they would be right. Like other forms of history, this one requires a measure of trust by the reader to believe that the selected figures and events capture the real spirit of the almost endless relevant data.

One assumption behind my strategy is that we have as much to learn by studying a few crucial individuals in detail, over a long period of time, as we do by studying a more restricted period with more breadth but less depth. In some ways, the logic of my approach is analogous to the arguments of historians like Kenneth Lockridge, who some years ago suggested one could learn more about the history of preindustrial America by studying one town in detail than by knowing a little something about many places.[22]

Even granting the legitimacy of my overall approach, some may wonder why I did not select this or that figure rather than those I did. Furthermore, my study is deliberately restricted to a series of male, English-speaking, American Mormon leaders. It thus does not address the issues of how the Bible might have been put to distinctive uses by Mormon women, by those who did not speak English or who lived outside the United States, or by ordinary Saints who were not part of the intellectual or hierarchical elite. Indeed, it could be argued that the men I have chosen are quite *un*representative of the typical Mormon: Joseph Smith, for example, remains a unique figure; if B. H. Roberts really qualifies as the preeminent intellectual in Mormon history, he is hardly typical of the larger masses of believers; apostles like J. Reuben Clark or Bruce R. McConkie are extraordinary Saints in several senses.

Certainly, more work on women, non-Americans, nonelites, and other elites must be done. We are also in need of more time-concentrated studies. Mine is simply an attempt to make finite a nearly infinite task. Moreover, the figures I have chosen are more representative than they may at first glance seem. Joseph Smith may have been unique in many respects, but in part he gathered disciples

22. *A New England Town: The First Hundred Years: Dedham, Massachusetts, 1636–1736* (New York: Norton, 1970). An approach with more direct similarities to mine is Andrew Greeley's *The Catholic Experience* (Garden City, NY: Doubleday, 1967). Although Greeley's work was based on secondary sources, his study of the Catholic experience in America, as revealed through a series of key individuals, offered an important interpretive handle to a complex subject in a day when American Catholic history was lacking an adequate overall interpretive thesis.

about him precisely because he expressed their inchoate yearnings. Like the others I have treated, he is therefore not so much atypical as *more than typical*. As such, he can in some ways tell us more about his followers than they themselves could. Extreme or unusual manifestations of religiosity often reveal things worth knowing more clearly than milder expressions, as Williams James taught us. And in the religious and metaphysical spheres, "articulate reasons are cogent for us only when our inarticulate feelings of reality have already been impressed in favor of the same conclusion. . . ."[23]

The men examined in the present work not only made conscious the general assumptions or beliefs of many of their peers but also shaped those beliefs. Thus, although the distinctive use made of the Bible by Mormon women (if indeed a distinctive use exists) is an important field for additional research, it probably is not as crucial to an initial understanding of general Mormon perspectives as the views of the reigning patriarchy.

Whether one considers women, the rank and file, or the elite, Mormons are in several ways set apart from others. One of the defining traits of Protestant evangelicalism, for example, is a belief in the Bible as "absolutely authoritative."[24] It is therefore worth noting that modern evangelicals, especially fundamentalists, sometimes chide the Mormons for not *really* being Christians and not *really* believing in the Bible.[25] Mormons have responded aggressively and sometimes defensively. They have insisted they are Christians and in recent years have even given their Book of Mormon a new subtitle: "Another Testament of Jesus Christ."

The present study argues that the Latter-day Saints *are* Bible-believing Christians—but with a difference. In the course of Mormon history this "difference" has proven ambiguous, complex, and evolving. Discovering its essence and implications is the purpose of the pages that follow.

Rochester, New York   P. L. B.
November 1990

23. *The Varieties of Religious Experience* (New York: New American Library, 1958; orig. 1902), pp. ix, 49, 73.

24. Richard Quebedeux, *The Worldly Evangelicals* (San Francisco: Harper & Row, 1978).

25. For example, Anthony A. Hoekema, "Ten Questions to Ask the Mormons," *Christianity Today,* January 19, 1968, pp. 378–82.

Acknowledgments

My native fascination with the study of religion has been heightened and disciplined over time by association with mentors and friends, too numerous to mention individually but treasured privately. For this volume in particular, I hope my debt to previous scholars is symbolized, if not adequately elaborated, in the footnotes. With equal impact, Anne Castleton, Jan Shipps, Richard L. Bushman, Walter L. Barlow, Armand Mauss, and James B. Allen kindly read individual chapters of the dissertation on which this work is based, offering encouragement and valued criticism. Davis Bitton, Leonard J. Arrington, Martin E. Marty, Thomas G. Alexander, Clarissa W. Atkinson, Theodore Hiebert, Jennings G. Olson, Sterling M. McMurrin, Allen R. Barlow, Lowell "Ben" Bennion, and William S. Cottam sacrificed time to scrutinize early drafts of the entire manuscript. They of course bear no responsibility for my final views, but their critiques and interest improved the finished product.

The exacting standards of William R. Hutchison touched the project at almost every stage of its development; to the extent that the study evolved from something of interest into something significant, he deserves special credit. How seriously and ably he has filled the roles of friend, adviser, and scholarly example has influenced my choice to endure in the study of American religion in spite of personal difficulties.

Despite many thousands of hours of research, my relative ignorance of the marvels of modern libraries is laid bare regularly by the encyclopedic knowledge of reference experts throughout the country. I am especially grateful for the cheerful competence of the staff at the LDS Church archives and library. Many thanks also to those at the Utah State Historical Society, and librarians at the University of Utah, Utah State University, Brigham Young University, the Andover-Harvard Theological Library, the University of Rochester, and the Colgate-Rochester Divinity School. David C. Chamberlin went well beyond the bounds of common courtesy in sharing the resources in his private care.

The good judgment and good humor of Cynthia Read, Paul E. Schlotthauer, Betty Seaver, Peter Ohlin, and their colleagues at Oxford University Press have heightened my already substantial respect for excellence in the editorial process. They rescued me from many errors and made the book in its present form possible.

Crucial research support was awarded by the Mellon Foundation, without which this book would have been lesser and later. William Scott Green and his talented colleagues in the Department of Religion and Classics at the University of Rochester provided hospitality, friendship, an interesting place to teach, intellectual stimulation, and supremacy on the softball field against our student challengers.

Barry, Bliss, Brett, Chanelle, and Philip were inspirations in ways they may never guess. Deborah, by existing, made this work and everything else I do seem more worthwhile. She continues to teach me best what cannot be learned through books.

Contents

Abbreviations   xxv

A Note on Mormon Organization and Nomenclature   xxvii

Introduction: The Bible in Antebellum America   3

1. Before Mormonism: Joseph Smith and the Bible, 1820–
   1830   11
2. From the Birth of the Church to the Death
   of the Prophet   43
3. Diversity and Development: The Bible
   Moves West   74
4. The Mormon Response to Higher Criticism   103
5. Why the King James Version?   148
6. The Bible in Contemporary Mormonism   182

Summary: The Ambiguities of a New
Religious Tradition   215

Select Bibliography   229

Index   241

Abbreviations

Many of these abbreviations are used in the text as well as in the notes.

ASV   American Standard Version of the Bible

BYU   Brigham Young University

BYUS   *Brigham Young University Studies* (Provo, UT: BYU, 1925–1937: 1959–present)

CN   *Church News* (SLC: The Church of Jesus Christ of Latter-day Saints, 1931–present)

CT   *The Contributor* (SLC: Mutual Improvement Association of the Church of Jesus Christ of Latter-day Saints, 1878–1896)

D&C   The Doctrine and Covenants of the Church of Jesus Christ of Latter-Day Saints (SLC: The Church of Jesus Christ of Latter-day Saints, 1981 [and other editions as noted])

DN   *Deseret News* or *Deseret Evening News* (SLC: Deseret News Publishing Company [and earlier publishers], 1850–present)

DNTC   *Doctrinal New Testament Commentary,* by Bruce R. McConkie

Dialogue   *Dialogue: A Journal of Mormon Thought* (Logan, UT, and previous locations: Dialogue Foundation, 1966–present)

EMS	*The Evening and Morning Star* (Independence, MO, and Kirtland, OH, 1832–1834)
F.A.R.M.S.	Foundation for Ancient Research and Mormon Studies
HC	*History of the Church of Jesus Christ of Latter-day Saints,* ed. B. H. Roberts, 7 vols. (SLC: Deseret Book [orig. Deseret News Press, 1902])
IE	*The Improvement Era* (SLC: Mutual Improvement Association of the Church of Jesus Christ of Latter-day Saints, 1897–1970)
JD	*Journal of Discourses,* 26 vols. (Liverpool: F. D. Richards and others, 1855–1886)
JI	*Juvenile Instructor* (SLC: The Church of Jesus Christ of Latter-day Saints, 1866–1970)
JMH	*The Journal of Mormon History* (Provo, UT: Mormon History Association, 1974–present)
KJV	King James (or Authorized) Version of the Bible
LDS	Latter-day Saint; equivalent to "Mormon"
LXX	Septuagint
MS	*Millennial Star* (Manchester, Liverpool, and London: European Mission of The Church of Jesus Christ of Latter-day Saints, 1840–1970)
PGP	*The Pearl of Great Price* (SLC: The Church of Jesus Christ of Latter-day Saints, 1981 [and other editions as noted])
RLDS	The Reorganized Church of Jesus Christ of Latter Day Saints
RSV	Revised Standard Version of the Bible
RV	Revised Version of the Bible
SLC	Salt Lake City
TR	*Textus Receptus;* the Greek text from which the KJV New Testament was translated.
TS	*Times and Seasons* (Nauvoo, IL: E. Robinson, and others, 1839–1846)
YWJ	*Young Woman's Journal* (SLC: Mutual Improvement Association of The Church of Jesus Christ of Latter-day Saints, 1889–1929)

A Note on Mormon Organization and Nomenclature

Mormonism functions primarily as a lay organization. Apart from the few thousand professionals who staff the Church's international education system or its departments of welfare, social services, and perhaps two dozen other departments at Church headquarters in Salt Lake City, virtually no one gets paid for the services they render the Church. In lieu of a professional clergy, each worthy male over the age of twelve is "ordained" to the priesthood and carries out distinct duties. The priesthood is divided into the *Aaronic* (lower) and *Melchizedek* (higher) orders. The latter is subdivided into *Elders* (an ecclesiastical term with no reference to age) and *High Priests*. The *Seventies,* a third division, no longer functions as a separate entity at the local level. Women participate in a parallel organization, the *Relief Society,* though the meaning of "parallel" merits further discussion; reflecting Mormon participation in the broader culture, gender roles are in modest flux.

After the family, the most important socio-religious unit for Latter-day Saints is the *ward* (congregation), several of which make up a *stake* (something like a diocese). Most active women and men in each ward accept *callings* (responsibilities) apt to involve several or many hours in any given week. The *bishop* (pastor or minister) who heads each ward typically puts in fifteen to thirty hours of Church service each week in addition to his secular profession. A Relief Society *president* contributes similar time. Such individuals are *called* for a temporary but indefinite duration, often about five years.

Both the professional bureaucratic and the lay ecclesiastical arms of Mormonism are responsible to the Church's *general authorities,* approximately one hundred men (the number is growing) who govern the Church. These are the only ecclesiastical leaders whose assignments entail full-time work, and who thus receive a living allowance. These authorities have specific titles to suit their various offices, but often the term *General Authority* is used as a title in and of itself. Such leaders, sometimes called *the Brethren,* are not theologically trained in any professional sense, but are drawn from the world of business, law, education, and other secular fields.

Among these highly respected people, a few are revered by the Saints as "prophets, seers, and revelators." These are the *Twelve Apostles* and the *First Presidency,* to whom all departments of the Church are ultimately responsible. In addition to their spiritual leadership, both the First Presidency (made up of the Church's president and his [usually two] counselors) and the Twelve Apostles function as two separate quorums or boards, the presidency having executive responsibility for the entire church and the apostles discussing policy matters and supervising the various administrative departments. All fifteen of these leaders meet together regularly. As we shall see, differences of opinion do of course occur, but in recent generations these differences have rarely been allowed to become public knowledge.

The Church's president is also its prophet. His two counselors and the other apostles are likewise held to be prophets, but the honor has unique connotations when applied to the president, who is the spiritual head of the Church on earth. He is the one who receives inspiration for all of Mormonism, though he is not prone to impose his views forcefully without substantial support from other apostles. Position in the Quorum of Apostles (the *Quorum of the Twelve*) is by seniority: once selected as an apostle, one is at the bottom of the ladder; each time someone in this body is removed by death, those below move up one notch. Tenure is for life. When the president of the Church dies, the senior member of the Quorum of the Twelve succeeds to the presidential office. In this system, the president of the Church is inevitably advanced in years (often in his eighties or nineties), which has advantages and disadvantages. Another consequence is that presidential succession tends to be orderly; struggles for the position of ultimate power are minimized.

Latter-day Saints ordinarily address their living prophet and each of his colleagues in the First Presidency by the title *President*—thus, for example, "President McKay" and his counselor, "President Clark." When referred to in the third person, the president is equally likely to be called *the prophet.* (This label applies to Joseph Smith uniquely, and I have reserved upper-case usage, *the Prophet,* to designate Smith alone.) Counselors in the First Presidency are also properly addressed as *Elder,* as are all apostles, other general authorities, and male missionaries. A Mormon is more apt to refer to an apostle as "Elder Brown" or "Elder Smith" than as "Apostle Brown" or "Apostle Smith." To address Stephen Welti, an ordinary elder in an ordinary congregation, as "Elder Welti" would strike local participants as overly formal.

Mormons and the Bible

Introduction

The Bible in Antebellum America

The Christian Bible cast a vast shadow over the pre–Civil War United States. Even those few Americans who rejected the Bible or who may have been unconscious of its impact were affected by it. The nature of this scriptural influence had evolved—changed—during the seventeenth and eighteenth centuries, interacting with diverse social forces. By the onset of the egalitarian age of Jackson, privately interpreted scripture rivaled or surpassed the clergy and the traditional creeds as the preeminent religious authority of the land. The Bible's prominence on this side of the Atlantic peaked in the middle decades of the nineteenth century, exceeding anything Europe had known. The implications of this environment for nascent Mormonism were complex and profound.

The Bible's broad influence in America from the time of the initial English settlements seems intuitively obvious. Scholars are still exploring the composition and ramifications of that biblicism, but whether one thinks of the new social order attempted in New England's "Bible Commonwealths" or of the death penalty prescribed in Virginia's earliest laws for anyone who "shall speake any word, or do any act, which may tend to the derision . . . of Gods holy word," the scriptures were prominent from the first.[1]

---

1. A beginning point for documenting the Bible's cultural impact is Hatch and Noll, eds., *The Bible in America.* For a more global assessment of biblical influence in such realms as law, politics, art, music, literature, everyday speech, education, social wel-

It is true that later, in the early days of the republic, certain deists might ridicule the Bible for its improbable miracles or the suspect morality of its Old Testament heroes. Thomas Paine was more colorful than most: "Whenever we read the obscene stories, the voluptuous debaucheries, the cruel and torturous executions, the unrelenting vindictiveness, with which more than half the Bible is filled, it would be more consistent that we called it the word of a demon, than the word of God."[2] But while such critics received publicity, their numbers remained small and they often served, in fact, as a foil for true believers. Even Thomas Jefferson, who produced a private version of the Bible reduced to what he deemed its simple ethical essence, still opened his pocketbook for the distribution of the traditional Bible among the populace.[3]

And this distribution seems to have been widespread. Mason Weems, Jefferson's contemporary and a traveling Virginia Bible salesman, thanked God that business was booming:

> I tell you this is the very season . . . of the Bible. Bible Dictionaries, Bible tales, Bible stories—Bibles plain or paraphrased, Carey's Bibles, Collin's Bibles, Clark's Bibles, Kimptor's Bibles, no matter what or whose, all, all will go down—so wide is the crater of public appetite at this time.[4]

Moreover, the organized zeal to promote and fill that appetite increased in the nineteenth century. Such zeal spawned diverse Bible societies, like the one in Monroe County, New York, which gave a Bible to each of the county's twelve hundred households that an 1824 census had shown to lack one. Even earlier, in 1816, a national organization had formed in order to—as its constitution put it—"claim our

fare, and, of course, Western religions, consult Sivan, *The Bible and Civilization.* For Virginia, see Article 5 of "Dale's Laws" (1610), in H. Shelton Smith, Robert T. Handy, and Lefferts A. Loetscher, *American Christianity: An Historical Interpretation with Representative Documents,* 2 vols. (New York: Scribner's, 1960), 1: 43. The intense biblicism of the Puritans was apparently the only social force sufficient to make literacy almost universal among adult males. See Kenneth Lockridge, *Literacy in Colonial New England: An Enquiry into the Social Context of Literacy in the Early Modern West* (New York: Norton, 1974), pp. 72–101.

2. *The Age of Reason* (New York: Thomas Paine Foundation, n.d.), pp. 18–20.

3. Jefferson to Samuel Greenhow, January 31, 1814, *The Writings of Thomas Jefferson,* ed. A. A. Lipscomb, 20 vols. (Washington, D.C.: Thomas Jefferson Memorial Association, 1905–1907), 14:81.

4. Quoted in Hatch and Noll, eds., *The Bible in America,* p. 3.

place in the age of Bibles." In less than four years the American Bible Society had distributed nearly one hundred thousand copies of the Holy Book.[5]

In the mid-seventeenth century, John Eliot had labored heroically to translate scripture for native Americans. By 1663 his complete *Mamusee Wunneetapanatamwe Up-Biblum God* was available to the Massachusetts. One and one-half centuries later, Christian missionaries expanded his example by translating the Bible into Sioux, Cherokee, and other Indian tongues.[6]

In 1814 Alden Bradford produced the first American commentary on the New Testament. Cadences from the Authorized Version by this time informed the speech of common folk and educated alike. Noah Webster's 1828 *Dictionary of the English Language,* the first distinctly American dictionary, both reflected and reinforced the Bible's influence on the nation's speech. Even American Jews, lacking the scholars and well-trained teachers of their Continental counterparts, taught the Hebrew Bible to their students by means of the King James translation. Authorities like Isaac Leeser indulged in a new bibliocentrism—a significant departure from European Jewish orthodoxy.[7]

Themes from the Bible suffused the minds of U.S. citizens, whatever their faith. National leaders proclaimed days of fasting and thanksgiving, and on such occasions ministers expounded scriptural texts. Settlers named their towns Zoar and Bethel and Eden and Salem, and christened their children Noah, Sarah, and Abraham.[8] As

5. Whitney R. Cross, *The Burned-Over District: The Social and Intellectual History of Enthusiastic Religion in Western New York, 1800–1850* (New York: Harper & Row, 1965; orig. 1950), p. 127. *Constitution of the American Bible Society . . . May, 1816 . . .* (New York: G. F. Hopkins, 1816), as excerpted in Edwin S. Gaustad, ed., *A Documentary History of Religion in America: To the Civil War* (Grand Rapids, MI.: Eerdmans, 1982), p. 328. Ahlstrom, *A Religious History* 1:515.

6. Henry W. Bowden, *American Indians and Christian Missions* (Chicago: University of Chicago Press, 1981), pp. 117, 137, 175, 189.

7. Rosalie Slater, Foreword to the 1967 facsimile reprint of Webster's 1828 dictionary (San Francisco: Foundation for American Christian Education). Sperling and Levine, *History of Jewish Biblical Scholarship in North America,* chap. 2.

8. Lewis O. Saum, *The Popular Mood of Pre-Civil War America* (Westport, CT: Greenwood Press, 1980), pp. 3–104. John Leighly, "Biblical Place-Names in the United States," *Names* 27 (March 1979): 53, 56. David W. Dumas, "The Naming of Children in New England, 1780–1850," *New England Historical and Genealogical Record* 132 (July 1978): 196–210.

the frequent use of such names implies, the figures and stories of the Old Testament dominated, at least in public usage, until midcentury, though after 1820 or so a shift toward the New Testament was evident, exemplified by the growth of "Christian primitivism."

White evangelical Americans updated the Puritan vision by seeing their country as God's new Israel. Enslaved blacks, among others, did not share this view, but they did share the young nation's bias for the Old Testament. Daniel and David, Joshua and Jonah, Moses and Noah—the heroes of the spirituals—these were delivered in *this* world, and in ways that struck the slaves' imaginations. Harriet Beecher Stowe captured something of the Old Testament spirit of the age when she described the prayers of *Oldtown Folks:*

> They spoke of Zion and Jerusalem, of the God of Israel, the God of Jacob, as much as if my grandfather had been a veritable Jew; and except for the closing phrase, "for the sake of thy Son, our Saviour," might all have been uttered in Palestine by a well-trained Jew in the time of David.

Nevertheless, American interpretation of pre-Christian scripture was everywhere influenced by a Christian consciousness.[9]

A society deeply immersed in the images and language of scripture was no American novelty, of course. A concerted effort to elevate biblical authority and to dispense the Holy Book widely among the populace had existed since the Protestant Reformation.[10] But the

9. For the Old Testament's public predominance through the early nineteenth century, see Noll, "The Image of the United States," in Hatch and Noll, eds., *The Bible in America,* pp. 44–45. For the slaves, see Albert J. Raboteau, *Slave Religion: The "Invisible Institution" in the Antebellum South* (New York: Oxford University Press, 1978) p. 83, and Lawrence W. Levine, *Black Culture and Black Consciousness: Afro-American Folk Thought from Slavery to Freedom* (New York: Oxford University Press, 1977), pp. 50–51. Stowe, cited by Perry Miller, "The Old Testament in Colonial America," in *Historical Viewpoints,* ed. John A. Garraty, 2 vols. (New York: Harper & Row, 1970), 1:101. See also William Haller, *Liberty and Reformation in the Puritan Revolution* (New York: Columbia University Press, 1955), pp. 26–27. The year 1820 as a point when a shift from Old Testament to New Testament dominance is quite noticeable is my own impressionistic estimate, though of course there was some movement earlier. That the shift was pronounced by 1850 is indicated in Donald M. Scott, *From Office to Profession: The New England Ministry, 1750–1850* (Philadelphia: University of Pennsylvania Press, 1978), pp. 138–39.

10. Derek Wilson, *The People and the Book: The Revolutionary Impact of the English Bible, 1380–1611* (London: Barrie & Jenkins, 1976).

Good
nupentss1
00002407446
Mormons and the Bible: The Place o
America)
3/20/2008 11:34:10 AM

slogan *sola scriptura*—such a helpful tool when Reformers were assailing Roman Catholics—became a potentially dangerous weapon when the common people began to use it in earnest. Protestant leaders from Calvin and Luther to Wesley and Whitefield had been forced to fence the concept against the threat of theological anarchy.[11]

During and following America's First Great Awakening, the latent propensity of ordinary men and women to disregard the teachings of the learned and to lean instead on their own scriptural interpretations became increasingly manifest. One could not yet describe the tendency as a fully developed "movement" by 1750, but as the eighteenth century wore on, this growing inclination entwined with a thriving secular democracy. Before and during the Revolutionary War, partisans of independence countered the theory of the divine right of kings with the idea of the divine right of republics, as exemplified in the Old Testament.[12] By the early nineteenth century, the notion of the sovereignty of the people had captured the imagination of the new American nation.

One result of this ascendant democratic mind-set was a general crisis in religious authority. Although the power of the clergy and the old creeds still held sway among some traditionalists, the stronger impulse was to renounce the guidance of any external guides and to elevate an already strong reverence for unmediated scripture.[13] "No creed but the Bible" and "The Bible alone is good enough for me" became the watchwords of the day. For example, Elias Smith, a Massachusetts pastor and an increasingly influential leader among Calvinist Baptists, resolved a personal crisis of authority when he "heard a gentle whisper to my understanding" instructing him to "drop both [Calvinism and Universalism] and search the scriptures [alone]." William Miller, a Vermont freethinker, turned himself into an Adventist leader by removing the "mantle of mysticism" from the scriptures, by rejecting "all commentaries, former views and prepossessions," and by "determining to read and trying to understand [the Bible] for

11. Hatch, "*Sola Scriptura*," in *The Bible in America,* ed. Hatch and Noll, pp. 61–62.

12. E.g., see Samuel Langdon's June 5, 1788 sermon, "The Republic of the Israelites an Example to the American States," excerpted in Morris U. Schappes, *A Documentary History of the Jews in the United States, 1654–1875* (New York: Schocken Books, 1971), pp. 70–71.

13. Hatch, "*Sola Scriptura*," pp. 62–73.

myself." The great revivalist Charles Finney likewise found himself unable to accept doctrine on anyone else's authority: "I had nowhere to go but directly to the Bible, and to the philosophy or workings of my own mind." Thomas Campbell was similarly anxious to defend the "all-sufficiency and the alone-sufficiency of the Holy Scriptures." Examples could be multiplied indefinitely.[14]

Scripture served as a social equalizer. Armed with a Bible, the common man—and occasionally the common woman—could confront the highest temporal authority. After 1800, democratic values and patterns of biblical interpretation flowed together. Although the honor given the Christian scriptures never quite reached the levels achieved by the Qur'an among Muslims, who washed their hands before touching the sacred texts, still, for the first two centuries after English settlement, the Bible played a role in shaping American culture for which there was no European equivalent. The growing prestige of the Holy Book, as interpreted by oneself, reached its apex in the middle years of the nineteenth century.[15]

To be sure, the glorification of a democratically understood scripture did not enchant everyone. Protestant clergymen naturally resisted their waning status, and some denominations, such as the Episcopalians and the Lutherans, remained creedal and formally confessional. Roman Catholics never were mesmerized by chants of "the Bible alone."[16] Most Jews not only found extrabiblical commentary important but actually assigned priority to rabbinic tradition over the Bible—in practice if not in rhetoric.[17] For religious intellectuals, the authority of the popularly interpreted Bible was increasingly undermined by scientific progress in such fields as geology, which suggested a time frame at variance with the account in Genesis.

Even more important, Boston's precocious Joseph Stevens Buck-

14. Elias Smith, *The Life, Conversion, Preaching, Travels and Sufferings of Elias Smith* (Portsmouth, NH: Beck and Foster, 1816). On William Miller, see Joshua V. Himes, *A View of the Prophecies and Prophetic Oracles* (Boston: Moses A. Dow, 1841), pp. 9, 11. Charles G. Finney, *Memoirs* (New York: 1876), pp. 42–46. Thomas Campbell quoted in A. S. Hayden, *Early History of the Disciples in the Western Reserve, Ohio* (1875; reprinted, New York: Arno Press, 1972), pp. 217–18.

15. Marsden, *Fundamentalism and American Culture*, p. 224, and Marsden, "Everyone One's Own Interpreter?" in *The Bible in America*, ed. Hatch and Noll, p. 79.

16. Fogarty, *American Catholic Biblical Scholarship*, pp. 3, 11, and passim.

17. Sperling, "Judaism and Modern Biblical Research"; author's telephone interview with Sperling, May 1988.

minster introduced America, in the first decade of the nineteenth century, to the methods and issues of German biblical criticism. For the first time on these shores, the unity of the Bible and the uniformity of its inspiration were questioned. Buckminster remained confident that the Bible was the final authority in all matters of Christian theology, but he distinguished between the Bible as God's word and the Bible as the *vehicle* of God's word. To learn the real meaning of scripture, he contended, one must apply a rigorous historical method to problems of authorship, date, canonization, inspiration, and varying purposes behind individual texts.[18] Such an approach required scholarly preparation.

Mercersburg Seminary's John W. Nevin was a later dissenter from the notion of the Bible's self-sufficiency. "What are we to think," he wrote,

> when we find such a motley mass of protesting systems all laying claim so vigorously here to one and the same watchword? If the Bible be at once so clear and full as a formulary of Christian doctrine and practice, how does it come to pass that where men are left most free . . . to use it in this way . . . they are flung asunder so perpetually in their religious faith, instead of being brought together, by its influence?[19]

But such protests were mild crosscurrents to the general antebellum stream. In America the Bible had been recanonized—canonized at a new, secondary level—as a symbol of the "Redeemer Nation." To denigrate the Bible was to denigrate the country, and it was no accident that "Battle Hymn of the Republic" echoed scriptural apocalyptic. Catholics and Jews were viewed as "outsiders." John Nevin's complaint about the enthronement of the Bible ran against too many ingrained national attitudes to be generally influential. Progress in science seems, if anything, to have increased the popular cry to rally behind the Bible as the bulwark against secular impiety. And though Joseph Buckminster's efforts were extended by such notables as William Ellery Channing, Andrews Norton, Theodore Parker, and Moses Stuart, biblical criticism in America would not have wide impact until after the Civil War.

Far more representative of the era were the sentiments of an ob-

18. Brown, *The Rise of Biblical Criticism in America, 1800–1870,* pp. 10–26.

19. "Antichrist and the Sect System," in *The Mercersburg Theology,* ed. James Hastings Nichols (New York: Library of Protestant Thought, 1966), pp. 97–99.

scure New England farmer, the Universalist-leaning Asael Smith. Smith championed a Bible unencumbered by "authoritative" interpreters and convoluted theological systems. He uttered the views of thousands of contemporaries when, in a moving testament to his family, "whom I expect ere long to leave," he enjoined his wife and children to give their first allegiance not to any particular form of religion but to "the Scriptures, and . . . sound reason."[20] Smith's son, Joseph Sr., shared his father's sentiments. And Joseph's wife, Lucy Mack Smith, held the Bible in such high esteem that for seventeen years after dedicating her life to the Lord she refused attachment to any congregation; scripture alone was enough: "I . . . determined to examine my Bible, and taking Jesus and the disciples as my guide, to endeavor to obtain from God that which man could neither give nor take away. . . . The Bible I intended should be my guide to life and salvation."[21]

Though baptized a Congregationalist as a child, Joseph Smith Sr. long remained aloof from the churches, content with his dreams and his "scriptures and sound reason." Lucy eventually joined the Presbyterians, adding a particular variety of intense biblicism to the family circle. All their lives the Smiths were a Bible-believing family in a Bible-believing culture. Into such a family, at the turn of the nineteenth century, Joseph Smith Jr., the future Mormon prophet, was born. Had it been otherwise, the genetic constitution of any Mormonism that might have arisen would have differed significantly from the one that actually did.

20. A letter addressed to "My Dear Selfs," holograph in LDS Church Archives; reprinted in Richard L. Anderson, *Joseph Smith's New England Heritage* (SLC: Deseret Book, 1971), pp. 124–29.

21. Lucy Smith, *Biographical Sketches of Joseph Smith, the Prophet,* pp. 37, 46–49.

1

Before Mormonism: Joseph Smith and the Bible, 1820–1830

Joseph Smith grew up in a Bible-drenched society, and he showed it. Like those around him, his religious conceptions and his everyday speech were biblically informed. He shared his era's assumptions about the literality, historicity, and inspiration of the Bible. He read its narratives with presuppositions about the immutability of truth and the direct relevance of prophecy (the imminent millennium; America as chosen) that were common to his place and time. Like others, he viewed the Old Testament through a New Testament lens, was affected by the perspectives of "Christian primitivism," and embraced both a long tradition of typological thought and an emerging train of dispensational thought.

But if Smith participated fully in his culture, he also struggled against it, in some ways outgrew it, and even changed it. He differed from his evangelical contemporaries in that he found the unaided Bible an inadequate religious compass. And unlike the minority who agreed with him on this point, such as Unitarians and Catholics, Smith did not turn to scholarly or ecclesiastical authority to address this lack. Instead, setting himself apart even from other visionaries who used personal revelation as an exegetical guide, he produced more scripture—scripture that at once challenged yet reinforced biblical authority, and that echoed biblical themes, interpreted biblical passages, shared biblical content, corrected biblical errors, filled biblical gaps, was built with biblical language, and restored biblical methods, namely, the prophetic process

11

*itself. In a further departure from Bible-believing convention, Smith
put himself inside the Bible story itself, reading episodes in his own life
as direct fulfillments of biblical prophecy. Well before the twenty-four-
year-old Prophet organized a church in 1830, he was a Bible-believing
Christian with a difference.*

Influential historians sometimes still describe Fawn Brodie's *No
Man Knows My History* as "the standard biography" of Joseph Smith
and "the most influential book on early Mormonism."[1] The assessment is probably accurate so far as Brodie's influence goes, and she
incontestably contributed significantly to modern Mormon studies.
However, recent scholarship argues that her work was fundamentally
flawed.[2] Particularly problematic was Brodie's thesis that Smith descended from a religiously indifferent family and was himself religiously insincere, a conscious fraud who fabricated his first visionary
experience and who only gradually, by a series of wondrous psychological acrobatics, began to take himself seriously as a prophet. More
careful judgment suggests, I think, that Smith's religious quest was
earnest. One way to test this assertion is to ponder Smith's private
writings not intended for publication.[3] Although my purpose here is
to come to terms with the Mormon Prophet's use of the Bible rather
than to pronounce on the legitimacy of his visions, my view of his
sincerity has naturally influenced the tone of my story.

In sharp contrast to writers like Brodie, Mormon apologists have at
times been so anxious to promote their faith that they have lost sight
of some of its most interesting dimensions. Nineteenth-century Apostle Orson Pratt, for example, stressed the originality of Joseph
Smith's prophetic contributions by pointing to Smith's youthful igno-

1. E.g., Ernest R. Sandeen and Frederick Hale, *American Religion and Philosophy*
(Detroit: Gale Research Co., 1978), #774, p. 146.
2. See especially Marvin S. Hill, "Secular or Sectarian History? A Critique of *No
Man Knows My History*," *Church History* 43 (1974): 78–96. Other treatments basically
at odds with Brodie include Hill, *Joseph Smith: The First Mormon*, Bushman, *Joseph
Smith and the Beginnings of Mormonism*, Richard L. Anderson, *Joseph Smith's New
England Heritage* (SLC: Deseret Book, 1971), and Jan Shipps, "The Prophet Puzzle:
Suggestions Leading Toward a More Comprehensive Interpretation of Joseph Smith,"
JMH 1 (1974): 3–20.
3. Dean C. Jessee, ed., *The Personal Writings of Joseph Smith;* Scott H. Faulring,
ed., *An American Prophet's Record: The Diaries and Journals of Joseph Smith.*

rance of the Bible.[4] It was remarkable, Pratt argued, that the Book of Mormon, allegedly produced by Smith, agreed so thoroughly with the Bible, since Smith himself was unschooled in the scriptures at the time the Book of Mormon appeared. Some basis for Pratt's view may be found in the reflections of the Prophet's mother, who remembered her most famous child as never having read the Bible through prior to his first visionary experience as a teenager, and as "less inclined to the perusal of books than any of the rest of our children" but "far more given to meditation and deep study."[5]

We have no reason to doubt such memories, but young Joseph probably knew the Bible better than Pratt and others have guessed. Born in 1805 as the fourth of ten children, Smith spent his youth in New England and religiously volatile upstate New York. As the potent biblicism of those environs had nurtured his parents, so it nurtured Joseph and his siblings. Although Joseph was deprived of any but a rudimentary education, a neighbor, John Stafford, recalled that the Smiths held school in their house and studied the Bible.[6] Stafford's memory is consonant with the various reports of Smith's famous first vision of God and Jesus, which occurred in or near Palmyra, New York, around 1820, that indicate the adolescent Joseph quite naturally "searched the scriptures" in the midst of his religious turmoil.

Preliminary scriptural study was, indeed, a formulaic requirement for those who were, like Joseph, sparked by the revivalistic fires of the surrounding "burnt-over district."[7] In some accounts of his initial vision, Smith says that by the time he prayed in the woods, he was already convinced, by scriptural study, that the contending sects had drifted from pristine New Testament Christianity.[8] Doubtless he was also influenced by similar beliefs of his time; here, as elsewhere, he resembled other Americans who thought the Bible the primary

4. *JD,* 21:169–70.

5. Lucy Smith, *Biographical Sketches,* p. 84.

6. Bushman, *Joseph Smith,* p. 60.

7. For comparative examples, see Neal Lambert and Richard Cracroft, "Literary Form and Historical Understanding: Joseph Smith's First Vision," *JMH* 7 (1980): 31–42.

8. Hill, "The Role of Christian Primitivism," links early Mormonism to the primitive gospel movement, which shared Smith's sentiments about the churches.

source of their ideas when it often functioned as validation for beliefs already held.[9]

The earliest recorded account of the vision (1832) not only documents Smith's explicit concern to search the Bible but is itself, in part unconsciously, laced with biblical expressions, revealing how thoroughly the boy's mind was steeped in the words and rhythms of the Authorized Version. For instance, Joseph describes his prayer in the woods as "my cry in the wilderness," transposing Isaiah's words (40:3) and their messianic application by Matthew (3:3) to a radically new context. Joseph does not say the Lord "spoke to me" but rather, he "spake unto me." The nascent Prophet was telling a sacred story, and this demanded a sacred languague, which for him meant the English of the King James Bible. Groping for words adequate to the glory of his vision, Joseph describes the Lord as appearing in a "pillar of fire" (Exod. 13:21) that was "above the brightness of the Sun" (Acts 26:13). Such a comparison was natural, perhaps intrinsically as well as by biblical precedent. Other visionaries of the time also adopted the imagery of Acts 26:13, as when a teacher in the Palmyra Academy reported in 1825 that he saw Christ descend "in a glare of brightness exceeding tenfold the brilliancy of the meridian Sun."[10]

Reporting the ensuing conversation, Smith quotes and paraphrases Jesus, using uncited expressions from throughout the KJV: "none doeth good no not one" (Ps. 14:1); "they draw near to me with their lips while their hearts are far from me" (Isa. 29:13); "lo I come quickly" (Rev. 3:11); and many others. Referring to the same occasion, Smith later wrote that he "was one day reading the Epistle of James" when he came across a specific passage (1:5) that inspired his first vocal prayer. The casual reference ("I was one day reading . . .") may imply that perusal of the Bible was not an uncommon occupation for him.

9. Cf. Noll, "The Image of the United States as a Biblical Nation," in *The Bible in America*, ed. Hatch and Noll, pp. 41–42.

10. Brodie, *No Man Knows*, p. 22. Cf. Charles Finney, who, in the immediate aftermath of his conversion, was confronted with a light "like the brightness of the sun in every direction." *Charles G. Finney: An Autobiography* (Old Tappan, NJ: Fleming H. Revell Co., n.d.; orig. 1876), p. 34. In Smith's manuscript, "fire" is crossed out and replaced by "light," so that the Lord appears in "a pillar of light."

Furthermore, unlike the official 1838 account, other versions of the vision indicate that it was not just this one passage in James that prompted Smith to pray. The other versions suggest Joseph found inspiration for his theophany in diverse scriptures, such as Matt. 7:7–9. The boy needed knowledge directly from heaven, he felt, for "the teachers of religion of the different sects understood the same passages of scripture so differently as to destroy all confidence in settling the question by an appeal to the Bible."[11] If such recollections portray a boy set apart from his evangelical peers in that he did not find the Bible to be the beginning and end of all religious knowledge, they also depict a boy at least reasonably well versed in holy scripture.

One difficulty with this analysis is that the story of Smith's earliest vision was not recorded until a dozen years after the event. As with the New Testament gospels, the passage of time and the life situation of the author affected the narrative. Subsequent accounts of Smith's vision reveal a man who had grown confident of his prophetic powers and who was established as the leader of a thriving religious movement. The prose of the majestic 1838 version is markedly more restrained, assured, and polished than that of the 1832 rendition. In the 1838 narrative, the earlier resort to ubiquitous biblical phraseology is greatly muted, and the direct citations of the King James Version are fewer and longer, more deliberate and exact. Both Smith's linguistic style and the aspects of the story he chose to highlight were inevitably shaped by the experiences of his progressing career.[12] Capturing the exact nature of his earliest biblical training is therefore difficult.

Nevertheless, it does seem probable that Smith by 1820 had been, like countless others, well exposed to the KJV, that his language and thought patterns had been colored by it, and that he was prepared to find God through scriptural wisdom even though he did not expect the Bible by itself to resolve fully the theological conflicts of the day. When Deity did come, Smith heard him speak in both biblical and Bible-like language.

11. *HC,* 1:4.

12. Lambert and Cracroft, "Literary Form," pp. 31–42. Milton V. Backman, *Joseph Smith's First Vision* (SLC: Bookcraft, 1971), pp. 155–81, reprints the several known accounts of Smith's vision.

The Imperfections of the King James Bible

Those who heard of Joseph Smith's vision in 1820 did not necessarily regard it as unique. A preacher whom Smith reported as showing contempt for the vision probably did so not because visions were unheard of but because "enthusiasm" was a familiar danger with a history harking back to the Great Awakening of the 1740s and even earlier.[13]

What really distinguished Joseph Smith was the 1823 visit of a heavenly messenger, Moroni, who told him of ancient, buried, metallic plates he was eventually to translate into the Book of Mormon. Like Jesus, Moroni cited the Bible version familiar to Smith. He quoted eschatological prophecies from both Testaments, from the third and fourth chapters of Malachi, the third chapter of Acts, and elsewhere. The clergy used such texts to point to the imminent millennium, and the messenger said the prophecies were soon to be realized. Either Joseph by this time knew the Bible quite well, or else the angel's thrice repeated recitation sank deeply into his memory, for he noticed variations in the angel's quotations of Malachi and the way they read in his Bible:[14]

KJV, MALACHI 4	MORONI'S QUOTATIONS
1. For, behold, the day cometh, that shall burn as an oven; and all the proud, yea, and all that do wickedly, shall be stubble; and the day that cometh shall burn them up, saith the Lord of hosts, that it shall leave them neither root nor branch.	For behold the day cometh that shall burn as an oven, and all the proud, yea, and all that do wickedly shall burn as stubble: for they that come shall burn them; saith the Lord of hosts, that it shall leave them neither root nor branch.

The modifications are unspectacular but deserve scrutiny for several reasons. First, the fact of biblical alterations is significant for its own sake. Second, these alterations foreshadow the types of changes later appearing in the biblical sections of the Book of Mor-

---

13. Bushman, *Joseph Smith*, p. 58; D. Michael Quinn, *Early Mormonism and the Magic World View* (SLC: Signature Books, 1987), pp. 7–14.

14. *HC*, 1:12–13. The Prophet did not explain Moroni's alterations of the King James text; he simply reported that the messenger quoted Malachi "with a little variation from the way it reads in our Bibles."

mon and in Smith's revision of the Bible itself in the early 1830s. Finally, the changes reveal ways in which Smith's "restoration" and his view of the Bible were, as early as 1823, distinct from those of his contemporaries.

One change is simply a reduction of excess punctuation.[15] Another heightens the fieriness of the fate of the wicked as distinct from their mere desolation. Also, "the day that cometh" is personalized to "they that come," as though the Lord's avengers are to be people or angels rather than some abstract "day."

Moroni's changes in Mal. 4:5–6 seem more substantial:

KJV	MORONI'S QUOTATIONS
5. Behold, I will send you	Behold, I will reveal unto you the Priesthood, by the hand of
Elijah the prophet before the coming of the great and dreadful day of the Lord:	Elijah the prophet, before the coming of the great and dreadful day of the Lord.
6. And he shall turn the heart of the fathers to the children,	And he shall plant in the hearts of the children the promises made to the fathers,
and the heart of the children to their fathers,	and the hearts of the children shall turn to their fathers;
	if it were not so, the whole
lest I come and smite the earth with a curse.	earth would be utterly wasted at his coming.

Moroni's parallel to verse 5 explicates the role of Elijah, anticipating Smith's later understanding of the "keys" (priesthood authority) given to him by the literal visit of Elijah in the Kirtland, Ohio temple in April 1836.[16] In verse 6 the typical Hebraic parallelism and simple (in this case) chiastic structure are exchanged for an elaboration and reinterpretation. "[He] shall turn the heart of the fathers to the children, and the heart of the children to their fathers" becomes "he shall plant in the hearts of the children the promises made to the fathers," which, it is implied, *will result in* the turning of the hearts of the children to their fathers.[17]

15. Neither the punctuation nor the text of Moroni's quotations in Smith's manuscript history is identical with *HC*, 1:12, which I have used above.

16. *HC*, 2:435–36. These "keys" concerned authority and knowledge to accomplish ordinances (e.g., baptism for the dead) subsequently performed in Mormon temples.

17. Other exegetical matters could detain us here if space did not deter us. For example, the curse of the earth threatened by the Lord at the end of Mal. 4:6 has long

In the altered version there is a sense of "restoration" that is absent in the KJV, namely, the renewing to "the children" of (Old Testament) promises already given to earlier generations. Thus in 1823 the seventeen-year-old Joseph Smith already hinted at a new type of restorationist thought—a "binding up of the generations"—suggesting the Mormon "restoration of all things" was to contrast with other "primitive gospel" movements. For instance, although Mormons may have borrowed the term *restoration* from the Campbellites,[18] from whom they also borrowed a goodly number of converts, their understanding of the concept differed. Campbell essentially meant by *restoration* a return to New Testament Christianity; Mormons meant a restoration of the truths, ordinances, and priesthood of all eras or "dispensations," including Old Testament ones. This distinctive direction bore fundamental implications for Smith's view of the Bible and for future Mormon theology.

Unfortunately, as with the narratives of Smith's first vision, the 1838 account of Moroni's visit postdates by many years not only the experience itself but also the production of the Book of Mormon and the subsequent intense biblical study attendant to Smith's "inspired translation" of the Bible. How much these later events influenced the Prophet's memory of the angel's 1823 use of the Bible is unclear.

Although Moroni's appearance and the events it launched did set Joseph Smith apart, the visionary experiences of contemporaries also sometimes included scriptural recitations.[19] Smith's own mother is representative. During an 1803 illness, she pleaded with the Lord to spare her that she might bring up her children and comfort her hus-

---

bothered certain rabbis, with the result that for public recitation they directed another verse to be repeated after verse 6 to prevent the "twelve prophets" and the Hebrew Bible from ending on such a note (See *The Jerome Biblical Commentary* 2 vols. bound together (Englewood Cliffs, NJ: Prentice-Hall, 1968), 1:401. Moroni's alteration from "lest I come and smite the earth with a curse" to "If it were not so, the whole earth would be utterly wasted at his coming" depersonalizes the cause of the action (just the opposite effect of the change in verse 1), gives more specificity to the result (the earth is not merely cursed, which could mean many things, but would be "utterly wasted"), and also conveys a sense of the futility of earth's existence if Elijah did not come—a sense missing in the KJV (although "wasted" in the 1820s, as now, could also mean "destroyed").

18. Bushman, *Joseph Smith*, pp. 182–83.

19. In addition to the examples I note in the text, Marini, *Radical Sects of Revolutionary New England,* pp. 66, 72–74, provides several striking instances.

band: "During this night I made a solemn covenant with God, that if he would let me live, I would endeavor to serve him according to the best of my abilities. Shortly after this, I heard a voice say to me, 'Seek, and ye shall find; knock, and it shall be opened unto you. Let your heart be comforted, ye believe in God, believe also in me' "— thereby conflating words of comfort from Matt. 7:7–8 and John 14:1.[20]

A more prominent figure, Charles Finney, had a scriptural passage come to his mind "with a flood of light" during his conversion. "Somehow," he wrote of the verses he received, "I knew that that was a passage of Scripture, though I do not think I had ever read it." He then received many promises "both from the Old and the New Testament." Soon Finney was visited by Jesus himself, though he would later qualify the objective reality of the event: "It did not occur to me then, nor did it for some time afterward, that it was wholly a mental state."[21] But although Finney deemphasized the literality of his experience, Smith did just the opposite. In his unpublished history, he reported that when the angel first came to tell him of the plates, he thought it was a dream but later changed his mind.[22] He thereafter seemed to understand his visions in a literal sense, reinforcing his lifelong propensity to understand biblical events similarly. As we shall see, however, what is meant by *literal* deserves additional thought.

By 1823, then, Joseph Smith had been visited by Jesus and by a heavenly messenger, both of whom quoted the Bible in the sacred idiom familiar to him, though alterations in their renditions implied the imperfection of the King James text. Furthermore, the heavenly personages offered literal and specific application of biblical prophecy to Smith and his times. Also, whether or not the young Prophet considered it at this early date, Moroni's message implied the potential not only of ancient extrabiblical scripture but also of new modern scripture: a narrative of the Prophet's early visions and an extract from Moroni's words—events occurring years before translation of the Book of Mormon—were eventually themselves canonized, further distinguishing Mormon scriptural patterns.

In 1824 another in a series of revivals broke out near the Smith's

20. Lucy Smith, *Biographical Sketches*, p. 37.

21. Finney, *An Autobiography*, pp. 16–17, 19–20.

22. Faulring, ed., *An American Prophet's Record: The Diaries and Journals of Joseph Smith,* p. 7.

residence in Palmyra, New York. Joseph's mother was drawn toward the churches as she had been earlier. Like his father, however, Joseph declined to attend them. He told his mother he could learn more in the woods from the Bible than from any number of meetings. His rhetoric was intended to disparage the churches, yet perhaps we may infer from it that he did often study the Bible privately during the crucial period between Moroni's initial visit in 1823 and Smith's possession of the plates four years later. If so, this bears on any attempt to understand the extraordinarily rapid evolution of Smith's mind, a process that does not seem to have abated from our earliest glimpses of his religious concerns in the 1820s until his murder in 1844.

In September 1827 Smith obtained the plates from Moroni and began the process of translation, though he made scant progress during the fall and winter. Poverty, the lack of a scribe, and efforts by others to steal the gold plates all hindered his efforts. Between April and June 1828 he did manage to translate 116 manuscript pages with the scribal help of Martin Harris, later one of the eleven witnesses of the plates themselves.

In February, Harris traveled to New York City and showed a document containing characters Smith had drawn off the plates, first to Professor Samuel L. Mitchell, vice president of Rutgers Medical College, and then to Professor Charles Anthon of Columbia College. Mitchell said he could not read the document, and Anthon—who asked to view the plates themselves rather than the incomplete copy, and who was informed that this would be impossible—told Harris that he cold not read a "sealed book." Harris then returned the document to the "unlearned" Joseph Smith.

At least by 1829 Smith understood this episode as a specific fulfillment of Isa. 29:1–4, 10–12, which prophesied that Jerusalem's voice "shall whisper out of the dust," and spoke of

> the words of a book that is sealed, which men deliver to one that is learned, saying, Read this, I pray thee: and he saith, I cannot; for it is sealed: And the book is delivered to him that is not learned, saying, Read this, I pray thee: and he saith, I am not learned.

Smith's application of Isa. 29 to this incident is important in showing how his early self-consciousness contrasted with that of other Christians, even most who had experienced revelations. Visionaries like Charles Finney and Lucy Mack Smith felt keenly the application of scripture to their own lives, but Joseph Smith did more: he placed himself *inside* the Bible story. Substantially before the organization of Mormonism into a church, Smith had begun to see events in his own life as a continuation of the Bible narrative. It was not simply that the canon was to be extended but that the whole biblical narrative had come to life again, as endings were put on stories that had their beginnings in the scriptural text. As Richard Bushman puts it, "It was as if an old movie, frozen in a frame somewhere, was started up again as new characters came on the screen."[23]

In June of 1828, against the Lord's initial instruction, Smith yielded to Harris's persistent pleas to borrow the completed 116 pages of the Book of Mormon to show to family members. The manuscript was stolen while in Harris's care, never to be recovered. The Smith family was inconsolable, fearful of the Lord's displeasure.[24] Seeking forgiveness and direction, Joseph eventually engaged in "mighty prayer before the Lord."

Modern Revelations in KJV Idiom

Having lost the manuscript, Smith received a divine chastisement, now published as section 3 of the modern Doctrine and Covenants.[25] The document is the earliest extant revelation recorded by the Prophet, and yields the first written example of his prophetic style:

> The works, and the designs, and the purposes of God cannot be frustrated, neither can they come to naught. For God doth not walk in crooked paths, neither doth he turn to the right hand nor to the left,

23. Richard Bushman, correspondence with the author, June 29, 1987. Bushman also points out that the first known Mormon use of Isaiah 29 as a proselytizing tool was in 1836 (*Joseph Smith*, p. 89).

24. Lucy Smith, *Biographical Sketches*, pp. 118–20.

25. The Doctrine and Covenants is a compilation of revelations and proclamations, almost all of which were received, issued, or supervised by Joseph Smith. Mormons accept the D&C as scripture equal in authority to the Bible but assumed to be less obscure, more current, and less damaged in transmission. The early revelations were first published in 1833 as The Book of Commandments with 65 "sections." Some of these were later combined to form single sections. An expanded collection was published in 1835 as the Doctrine and Covenants, comprising 102 sections. Subsequent editions have been added to, but of the 138 sections plus two "official declarations" in the most recent (1981) edition, 135 sections date from the time of Joseph Smith.

neither doth he vary from that which he hath said, therefore his paths are straight, and his course is one eternal round. Remember, remember that it is not the work of God that is frustrated, but the work of men.[26]

Unlike Smith's later canonized narrative of his own life, this is not a report of experiences written in the first person by the author. Instead, the speaker stands emotionally and intellectually exterior to the Prophet, though speaking to and through him. Smith is unabashedly rebuked for yielding to the importunity of Martin Harris:

> Behold, you have been entrusted with these things, but how strict were your commandments; and remember also the promises which were made to you, if you did not transgress them. And behold, how oft you have transgressed the commandments and the laws of God, and have gone on in the persuasions of men. For, behold, you should not have feared man more than God. Although men set at naught the counsels of God, and despise his words—yet you should have been faithful.

After additional rebuke, the Prophet is given hope:

> Behold, thou art Joseph, and thou was chosen to do the work of the Lord, but because of transgression, if thou art not aware thou wilt fall. But remember, God is merciful; therefore, repent . . . and [thou] art again called to the work.

Although the document is too long to reproduce here, its relationship to the Bible begs attention because it set the pattern for dozens of revelations to follow.

The language of the revelation has a biblical ring. The verbs and certain pronouns are cast in King James (sacred) style: "God doth not walk" (D&C 3:2) rather than "God does not walk"; "thou deliveredst" (3:12), not "you delivered." Note also the liberal use of the scriptural "behold" (3:5, 6, 7, 9).

The KJV language runs deeper than this, however. Biblical expressions from the Authorized Version are sprinkled throughout; "mighty works" (D&C 3:4; Matt. 11:20, and throughout the gospels); "God is merciful" (D&C 3:10; 2 Chron. 30:9); "a just God" (D&C 3:4; Isa. 45:4); "for a season" (D&C 3:14; 2 Cor. 7:8) and many others. Some

---

26. Smith received the revelation in July 1828. Because the small portion of the Book of Mormon recorded in March and April 1828 was lost by Martin Harris, this revelation preceded the writing of all of the Book of Mormon as we now know it.

biblical phrases in the revelation go on for six or eight words: "after the dictates of his own will" (D&C 3:4; cf. Eph. 1:11); "the fiery darts of the adversary" (D&C 3:8; Eph. 6:16); "and sets at naught the counsels of God" (D&C 3:4,7; cf. Prov. 1:25). Furthermore, the revelation's ideas are sometimes biblical even when the language is less exactly parallel to the King James text: compare "The works . . . of God cannot . . . come to naught" (D&C 3:1) with its corollary, "if this work be of men, it will come to nought" (Acts 5:38).[27]

Although Smith cast these words in the first person as though the Lord himself were speaking, he does not generally seem to have conceived of his revelations as verbally exact dictations from God that he then recorded in secretarial fashion. More often, the language used is apparently his own attempt to convey the ideas of the revelations he experienced. A misunderstanding of this point has had profound influence throughout Mormon history. It colors Mormonism's twentieth-century insistence on the KJV as its official version, and helps distinguish conservative and fundamentalist from liberal Mormons in the late twentieth century.[28]

By way of cultural inheritance, Smith, at least in his early years, seemed to take it for granted that the words he read in his Bible were, when free of translation and transmission errors, the very words God caused to be written. Whether he ever completely abandoned this assumption or (publicly) reconciled it with his own prophetic practices remains unclear. However, throughout his career he demonstrated that he did not usually think of his own revelations as verbally bound. Indeed, he openly amended their language from time to time, both for clarity and to reflect additional knowledge gained.[29] Although he pre-

27. See also Rasmussen, "Textual Parallels."

28. See chapters 5 and 6. I am referring here to hermeneutical rather than sociological "fundamentalism."

29. See chapter 2 of this work, and Howard, *Restoration Scriptures*. Some of the sections of the D&C went through a series of drafts and are actually the products of multiple authorship. For example, the first canonized revelatory item in the early Church, section 20, is a composite document written by both Oliver Cowdery and Joseph Smith. An earlier (1829) unpublished revelation to Cowdery, which Cowdery himself recorded, bears strong similarities to D&C 20. This provides important context for an argument over Cowdery's insistence that Smith change the wording of a particular verse, which Smith refused to do, asking Cowdery "by what authority he took upon him to command me to alter or erase, to add to or diminish from, a revelation or commandment from Almighty God." See *HC,* 1:104–5; Lyndon W. Cook, *The Revela-*

dictably never produced a learned "Dissertation on Language" exploring the limitations of human communication such as Horace Bushnell
published in 1849, the Prophet nonetheless grew conscious very early
of the difficulties of human discourse: "Oh, Lord," he lamented in
1832, "deliver us in due time from the little, narrow prison, almost as it
were, total darkness of paper, pen and ink;—and a crooked, broken,
scattered and imperfect language."[30]

The generous use of biblical phrases and ideas in his first written
revelation reinforces the notion that the Prophet's mind was by 1828
immersed in biblical language, whether by personal study of scripture, by listening to sermons, by natural participation in the biblical
idioms of family conversation, or by some combination of these. His
religious vocabulary may, in part, gauge how thoroughly biblicized
the vernacular of his culture had become. When recording the impressions of his revelation, he naturally fell into the language accessible to
him.

It would be a mistake, however, to think of Smith's revelation as
merely a pastiche of biblical phrases, just as it would be absurd to
dismiss the New Testament as a huge cut-and-paste plagiarism of the
Old Testament. To the contrary, Smith's revelation has its own intricate structure and integrity. Quite apart from the biblical building
blocks of much of its prose, the revelation is an original religious
creation. Its tone is assertive and authoritative, and Smith is forth-
rightly rebuked. For all the individual biblical phrases found in it, the
revelation as a whole is literarily distinctive; it has no really close
structural parallel in the New Testament, though it is vaguely reminiscent of certain Old Testament prophets, such as Isaiah or Ezekiel,
who confidently represented God as speaking through them in the
first person.[31]

"For although a man may have many revelations," continued the

tions of the Prophet Joseph Smith (Provo, UT: Seventy's Mission Bookstore, 1981), pp.
31, 125; David J. Whittaker, "The 'Articles of Faith' in Early Mormon Literature and
Thought," in *New Views of Mormon History: A Collection of Essays in Honor of
Leonard J. Arrington,* ed. Davis Bitton and Maureen Ursenbach Beecher (SLC: University of Utah Press, 1987), pp. 64–65.

30. *HC,* 1:299.

31. The New Testament writings that come literarily nearest Smith's revelations are
occasional short passages in the Revelation of John (e.g., 2:1–5).

Lord through his spokesman, "and have power to do many mighty works, yet if he boasts in his own strength, and sets at naught the counsels of God, and follows after the dictates of his own will . . . , he must fall and incur the vengeance of a just God upon him." Smith knew, at age twenty-two, how to speak prophetically.[32]

Pressed by economic needs, Smith accomplished little more on the Book of Mormon translation, which he began anew, until April 1829, when he received scribal assistance from Oliver Cowdery, a new acquaintance who showed interest in his revelations. The great bulk of the almost six-hundred-page Book of Mormon (as printed in its first edition) was produced in the astonishingly brief period between April and June as, day after day, Smith dictated and Cowdery wrote.

By the time the translation was complete, Smith had received at least fifteen additional revelations (D&C 4–18). Having varying purposes and contexts, they as a whole show traits similar to those of the first revelation discussed above. They are full of biblical phrases and images, and they echo KJV idiom. The biblicism is sometimes deliberate, with direct allusions to biblical prophecy or concepts, and sometimes (apparently) unconscious—biblical words woven into the fabric of a new narrative having its own coherence.

In some cases, the revelations directly concerned biblical figures. One revelation was a translation of an ancient parchment "written and hid up" by John the Evangelist, and viewed and translated through the Urim and Thummim—the same instrument of divine help through which Smith translated the Book of Mormon. Another was received when the Prophet and Oliver Cowdery acquired the "Aaronic priesthood" (note the Old Testament linkage) at the hands of John the Baptist (New Testament), a heavenly messenger.[33]

Immediately upon receipt of this priesthood, Smith and Cowdery baptized each other and "were filled with the Holy Ghost." So enlightened, they "began to have the Scriptures laid open" to their understanding "in a manner which we never . . . before had thought of." Rapidly progressing with such divine help, they began to proselytize. Their procedure set the pattern for countless Mormon missionaries who followed: they reasoned from the Bible and proclaimed the par-

---

32. Bushman, *Joseph Smith,* p. 94.
33. D&C, 7 and 13.

tially translated Book of Mormon.[34] Their biblically informed audiences were not often apathetic.

The Book of Mormon

The Book of Mormon manuscript was ready for the press by the summer of 1829 and was offered for sale the following March. Smith's earlier revelations may have implied the possibility of extrabiblical scripture, but the published Book of Mormon gave this possibility tangible form. Prepublication rumors already referred to it as Joseph Smith's "gold bible."

To many who resisted it, the Book of Mormon threatened the traditional scriptures. They had to find a way to discredit it without undermining their own defense of the Bible against deists and skeptics.[35] Some Christians dismissed the Mormon book as "a superstitious belief in supernatural happenings"—a precarious posture for heirs of a centuries-long tradition that defended the Bible and Christianity itself on the basis of its miracles.

For others, however, the new scripture affirmed the truth of the old scriptures.[36] The new "gold bible" would have been incomprehensible apart from a biblical context. It was printed in biblical fashion as a collection of books, originally divided into chapters and later into verses. It contained two dozen chapters of material common to the Bible. The subjects of its narrative were originally biblical peoples, many of its episodes paralleled biblical stories,[37] and it purported

34. *HC*, 1:39–44. The principal proselytizing tools among Mormon missionaries after the Church was organized were the Bible, perceived "common sense," and Smith's revelations—in that order (Irving, "Mormonism and the Bible," p. 7).

35. Gordon Wood, "Evangelical America and Early Mormonism," *New York History* 61 (October 1980): 359–86, shows how the fundamental questions introduced during the Reformation and Enlightenment had begun to penetrate every aspect of American popular culture by Joseph Smith's generation. This is true despite strong vestiges of folk-magic, to which historians' attention has been called in recent years. Before the forces of the Second Great Awakening evangelized America, the threat of skepticism seemed real. For the Book of Mormon as a threat to the Bible, see Bushman, *Joseph Smith*, pp. 122–25, 229–30 (n. 25).

36. Timothy Smith, "The Book of Mormon in a Biblical Culture," pp. 9–14.

37. The similar experiences of Alma the Younger (Mosiah 27:8–19) and Paul on the road to Damascus (Acts 9:1–9) are dramatic examples. The most striking parallel theme

both to prophesy of the Bible as a book (from a vantage of 600 B.C.E.) and to be itself a fulfillment of biblical prophecy. Indeed, the Book of Mormon explicitly identified itself as a companion to the Bible, written as a record of "a remnant of the House of Israel," "to the convincing of the Jew and Gentile that Jesus is the Christ."[38] Early Saints readily identified the angel Moroni with the angel from the "midst of Heaven" (Rev. 14:6) who was to have "the everlasting gospel to preach unto them that dwell on the earth."

Like other translators of ancient texts and following the precedent set with earlier revelations, Smith cast the book into seventeenth-century prose, though his own vocabulary and grammar arc evident throughout.[39] Because Jacobean speech was not his native idiom, he sometimes rendered the style inexpertly: "ye" (properly a subject) sometimes lapsed into "you" (object) as the subject of a sentence, as in Mosiah 2:19; an Elizabethan suffix attached to some verbs but was inconsistently omitted from others ("yields . . . putteth," Mosiah 3:19). Much of this strained language was refined in the second edition (Kirtland, Ohio, 1837). The preface, for instance, was changed from its 1830 rendering, ". . . now if there be fault, it be the mistake of men," to "if there be faults, they are the mistakes of men." Similarly, some 227 appearances of "saith" were changed to "said."[40]

Like the revelations that preceded it, and even more extensively than scholars have heretofore guessed, the Book of Mormon narrative bulges with biblical expressions. More than fifty thousand phrases of three or more words, excluding definite and indefinite articles, are common to the Bible and the Book of Mormon. Thus when Sydney Ahlstrom makes the dramatic point that "about 27,000 words of the Book of Mormon were borrowed from [the KJV]," he

is the Exodus, which for three millennia has served as the paradigmatic event in Israel's history and whose pattern has been borrowed by various peoples throughout the ages. Exodus from sin, persecution, bondage, or prophesied destruction looms large in the background of the Book of Mormon from its first pages.

38. For explicit prophecies of the Bible in the Book of Mormon, see 1 Nephi 13, 2 Nephi 3:12, and 2 Nephi 29.

39. Until recent decades, translators of ancient texts have commonly attempted to approximate the lordly style of the KJV, particularly when the text was religious. A good example is Montague James's classic, *The Apocryphal New Testament* (Oxford: Clarendon Press, 1924).

40. For the development of the text of the Book of Mormon from its original dictation to recent editions, see Howard, *Restoration Scriptures*.

underestimates by well over 50 percent.[41] However, many of these word groups, perhaps the majority, appear to be random constructions that happen to occur in both books: "about to do," "for that which," and "after he had" are examples. In part, therefore, the large number of common word groups may simply suggest the influence of biblical word patterns on the speech of ordinary men and women of Joseph Smith's day. Furthermore, a great many common phrases derive from the long Isaiah and Sermon on the Mount sections in the Book of Mormon, skewing the overall statistical picture, though the number of remaining common phrases is still enormous.

Sometimes the Book of Mormon employs KJV phrases far more frequently than the KJV itself. Although the Book of Mormon is only one-third the volume of the Bible, the phrase "all manner of" (disease, precious clothing, work, and so on) is found 31 times in the Old Testament, only 11 times in the New Testament, but 110 times in the Book of Mormon—a per-page frequency almost eightfold that of the Bible. Similarly, "and it came to pass" may be discovered 336 times in the Old Testament, 60 times in the New, but 1,168 times in the Book of Mormon. Occasional longer biblical phrases emerge in the Book of Mormon narrative: "if ye will hear his voice, harden not your hearts" (Jacob 6:6, Heb. 3:15); "who had delivered them out of the hands of . . ." (Mosiah 2:4, Judg. 8:34).[42]

How the Book of Mormon adapts biblical language may be demonstrated by a passage attributed to a Nephite prophet in the sixth century B.C.E. Like the separate revelations Smith had received while the translation was in progress, biblical phrases constitute the vocabulary building blocks of much of the Book of Mormon narrative, yet that narrative maintains an independent coherence:

41. *A Religious History,* 1:608. Cf. the unanalyzed and unpublished computer printout by Kenneth D. Jenkins, "Common Phrases Between the King James Version and the Book of Mormon" (3 vols., 1983; housed in the F.A.R.M.S. collection, BYU).

42. Jenkins, "Common Phrases," lists thirty-two pages of phrases of eight or more words common to the Bible and the Book of Mormon. However, the great bulk are either "and it came to pass" constructions or else occur in passages that parallel biblical chapters in large blocks. Many long verbal parallels not included in the above categories are specific quotations of or allusions to biblical material, such as the quotation of several of the Ten Commandments in Mosiah 12:36. When I use the term *biblical phrases,* I do not imply that the phrases necessarily originated in the Bible, for recent scholarship has demonstrated that many such phrases have extrabiblical parallels or antecedents.

KJV

. . . my words shall not pass away
[Matt. 24:35].
. . . and he which is filthy, let
him be filthy still: and
he that is righteous, let him be
righteous still [Rev. 22:11].

Depart from me, ye cursed,
into everlasting fire,
prepared for the
devil and his angels
[Matt. 25:41].
And the devil . . . was cast into
the lake of fire and
brimstone . . . [Rev. 20:10]

[Jesus] endured the
cross,
despising the shame [Heb. 12:2].

. . . blessed of my Father,
inherit the kingdom
prepared for you
from the foundation
of the world [Matt. 25:34]
. . . that your joy might be full
[John 15:11].

2 NEPHI 9:16

. . . the Lord God hath spoken
it, and it is his eternal
word, which cannot pass away.

that they who are righteous
shall be righteous still, and
they who are filthy shall be
filthy still:
wherefore, they who are filthy
are the devil and his angels
and they shall go away
into everlasting fire
prepared for them;

and their torment is as
a lake of fire and
brimstone. . . .
But behold . . . the Saints
. . . they who have believed
in the Holy One of Israel,
they who have endured the
crosses of the world and
despised the shame of it.

they shall
inherit the kingdom of God,
which was prepared for them
from the foundation
of the world,
and their joy shall be full.

The Book of Mormon not only uses biblical language but provides interpretations of biblical passages: Moroni 8:42–46 seems to explain KJV 1 Cor. 13:3, telling how faith, hope, and charity may transform humans into the likeness of God; Ether 13:3–11 expands and interprets KJV Rev. 21:1-17.[43]

The Book of Mormon intersects the Bible when it prophesies, centuries before the fact, of a prophet who will precede the Messiah, who will "prepare the way of the Lord," "cry in the wilderness," "make his paths straight," and "baptize with water" (1 Nephi 10:8–9).

43. Ostler, "The Book of Mormon," pp. 78–79.

Biblical connections are also explicit when Jesus is recorded in post-Resurrection conversation declaring to his new world hearers that they were those of whom he had prophesied during his earthly ministry (John 10:16; 3 Nephi 15:21).

The most obvious biblical connection is the inclusion in the Book of Mormon of whole blocks of material common to the Bible: twenty-one chapters from Isaiah, three from Matthew, and smaller portions from elsewhere. There are many differences in these passages as they are presented in the Bible and the Book of Mormon.[44] For example, of the 433 verses of Isaiah appearing in the Book of Mormon, 199 are identical to the KJV and 234 have been altered. Many of the changes seem slight, others more significant. In general they remind one of changes made in the KJV by the angel Moroni when he appeared to Joseph Smith in 1823.

Sometimes these changes parallel ancient versions to which Smith may not have had access. To cite one instance, in 2 Nephi 12:16 (compare Isa. 2:16) the Book of Mormon text prefixes eight words not found in the Hebrew or in the KJV. The Septuagint (LXX), however, concurs with the Book of Mormon against the Authorized text in adding the phrase at the beginning of the verse:

> B.M.: And upon all the ships of the sea,
> KJV:
> LXX: And upon every ship of the sea,
>
> B.M.: And upon all the ships of Tarshish,
> KJV: And upon all the ships of Tarshish,
> LXX:
>
> B.M.: and upon all pleasant pictures.
> KJV: and upon all pleasant pictures.
> LXX: and upon every display of fine ships.[45]

---

44. Such differences are discussed apologetically by Sidney B. Sperry, *Book of Mormon Compendium* (SLC: Bookcraft, 1968), pp. 507–12; antagonistically by Walters, "The Use of the Old Testament," pp. 32–92; and most thoughtfully by Stendahl, "The Sermon on the Mount and Third Nephi." John A. Tvedtnes, "The Isaiah Variants in the Book of Mormon" (Provo, UT: F.A.R.M.S., 1989; 140 pp.) classifies into seventeen categories every Isaiah passage in the Book of Mormon differing from the KJV, in light of other Isaiah variants from the Dead Sea Scrolls, Septuagint, Vulgate, and other ancient translations and targums.

45. Sperry, *Book of Mormon Compendium* (Bookcraft, 1968), p. 508.

The Book of Mormon text clearly depends on the KJV for its choice of words, but adds a phrase omitted in the KJV yet paralleled in the LXX. This notwithstanding, there is no evidence that Smith had access to a copy of the Septuagint in 1827–1829. Moreover, the very process and speed by which the Book of Mormon was written—most of it was dictated in sixty to ninety days—militate against a theory that envisions Smith engaged in a careful scholarly process comparing the KJV with ancient manuscripts to produce the complex text.

Although the physical writing of the Book of Mormon was accomplished in so brief a time, some scholars have suggested that Smith, a religious genius, may, like Mozart, have composed his work in his head for some years before writing it.[46] Smith's wife Emma, who acted at times as scribe, thought this impossible. Joseph at that time of his life "could neither write nor dictate a coherent and well worded letter; let alone dictating a book like the Book of Mormon." Nor had he during the translation a book or previously written manuscript to read from. "If he had anything of the kind," she said, "he could not have concealed it from me."[47] Furthermore, the Mozart analogy by itself would not account for parallels to ancient texts such as the one noted above. The most careful student of the literature to which Smith potentially had access during and before the Book of Mormon's production feels Smith was not greatly interested in written materials.[48] Even had he been, and even were it proved that such materials were available to him, the ill-educated Smith would have needed, as a teenage boy, to develop the motive, the capacity, and the time meticulously to research such works—all without his family's awareness. Given family members' intimacy in relationships and usually in living space, and given the poverty that pressed them into perpetual grinding labor, such a scenario seems unlikely.[49] Despite

46. Hansen, citing private conversation with Jan Shipps, in *Mormonism and the American Experience,* p. 16; cf. Marvin S. Hill, who offers no assertion on the matter but allows that in theory Smith could have written the Book of Mormon years before its "translation" (correspondence with author, December 12, 1988).

47. Interview of Emma Smith by her son Joseph Smith III, February 4–10, 1879, published in *Saints Herald* (Plano, IA), October 1, 1879, pp. 289–90.

48. Robert Paul, "Joseph Smith and the Manchester (New York) Library," *BYU Studies* 22 (Summer 1982): pp. 333–56; and Paul, correspondence with the author, March 27, 1989.

49. For family circumstances, see Hill, *Joseph Smith,* pp. 32–40, 61–90; Bushman, *Joseph Smith,* pp. 29–42, 59–113.

scholarly progress on several fronts, considerable mystery yet shrouds the Book of Mormon.

Additional readings of biblical passages in the Book of Mormon vary from the KJV text but are attested in various ancient versions of the Bible.[50] More often, though, the changes have no ancient support. Many, in fact, seem insignificant and traceable often to Joseph Smith's personal taste.[51] Others convey a targumic quality, the feel of a biblically based text that has been expanded and thereby interpreted. One scholar, comparing the Sermon on the Mount as it appears in 3 Nephi and in Matthew, found the Book of Mormon text to be less like the synoptic gospels than like John, using several Johannine verbal traits and tending to cosmologize, targumize, and heighten the divine quality and self-awareness of Christ.[52]

Selective Literalism

There is a certain literalistic understanding of biblical events reflected at the most basic levels in the Book of Mormon. The story of God confounding human language at the Tower of Babel (Gen. 11:1–9) launches one Book of Mormon people on their migration to the new world (Ether 1:33ff.). Jesus' admonition to his disciples ("If ye have faith . . . , ye shall say unto this mountain, Remove hence . . . and it shall remove" [Matt. 17:20]) is elevated to an actual event in Ether 12:30. The earthquakes and general destruction promised before Christ's second coming (Matt. 24) have a literal, physical parallel preceding Christ's first coming to the new world (3 Nephi 8).

This tendency to literalism has been noticed so regularly by commentators on Mormon thought that it has become a truism.[53] It is less

50. Consult the notes to the annotated *Book of Mormon Critical Text*, 2d ed., 3 vols. (Provo, UT: F.A.R.M.S., 1987).

51. H. Grant Vest, "The Problem of Isaiah in the Book of Mormon," (master's thesis, BYU, 1938).

52. Stendahl, "The Sermon on the Mount and Third Nephi." Some adherents of the Book of Mormon hold that so-called Johannine verbal traits are attributable to the historic Jesus, and that Christ's divine self-awareness would naturally sharpen after his resurrection.

53. Sterling McMurrin, foreword to *The Theological Foundations of the Mormon Religion;* Moench, "Nineteenth-Century Mormons," pp. 42–44; Irving, "Mormonism and the Bible," ch. 3; Underwood, "Joseph Smith's Use of the Old Testament." By

often observed that the scriptural literalism is not absolute; it is in fact highly selective. This is also true of modern Christian fundamentalists generally, despite their common label—and self-label—as biblical literalists. As James Barr points out, fundamentalists often forsake *literal* readings of scripture to preserve the principle of *inerrancy.*[54]

Biblical interpretation has little meaning outside the context of a theological system or worldview. Joseph Smith's expanding theological understanding at any given time dictated which biblical conceptions or events he took literally and which he understood less literally, not literally at all, or even as uninspired. Although the Book of Mormon is replete with miraculous events literally conceived, it also includes many passages that could be viewed from outside Joseph Smith's 1830 theological framework as "spiritualized" conceptions. The "chains of hell," for instance, are interpreted not as literal but as metaphorical chains in Alma 12:11. (If the example seems petty, one should remember that literalists of Smith's day often took such images as literal objects.)[55] Similarly, the biblical concept of eternal punishment, mentioned frequently in the Book of Mormon, was assigned nonliteral meaning in a revelation received the same month the Book of Mormon was first offered for sale. Smith occasionally went beyond both a literal and a spiritualized reading, as when he declared the Song of Solomon to be uninspired.[56] It is thus not particularly helpful simply to label Mormonism's founder a biblical literalist.

In fact, the proper meaning of *literalism* has generated a complex conversation in the history of Christian exegesis. Origen, for example, thought the literal sense was what the words of scripture said, independently of the author's intent. Hence if Christ were referred to as "the lion of Judah," the literal sense would suggest that Christ was

contrast, Underwood (correspondence with the author, January 15, 1987), and Alexander, "The Reconstruction of Mormon Doctrine," p. 33, n. 23, have noted the selectivity of the literalism.

54. Barr, *Fundamentalism,* pp. 40–55.

55. Most millenarians, however, were less extreme and were much like Joseph Smith in reading some passages literally and others allegorically. But millenarians in general and many early Mormons in particular often seemed less interested in understanding the intent of the original biblical authors for its own sake than in enjoying the apologetic advantage of biblical literalism in a thoroughly biblical culture. See Sandeen, *The Roots of Fundamentalism,* chap. 5; Irving, "Mormonism and the Bible," pp. 41–43.

56. *HC,* 1:73 (D&C 19), verses 6–10. Matthews, "*A Plainer Translation,*" pp. 87, 215.

an animal. Others have tied the concept to the author's intent, but not necessarily to the historicity of events of which a biblical author writes. The definition adopted here is "the sense which the human author directly intended and which his words convey."[57] Despite his protestations that Mormons alone took the Bible literally, much of Joseph Smith's biblical usage was not literalist in this sense.

Gordon Irving has argued that a crucial dimension of Mormon literalism presupposed that "the meaning of the various books was both clear and consistent," and was "readily understood by any man possessed of an average amount of common sense." He further observes that Joseph Smith carried this notion quite far indeed.[58] Although Irving does not note it, early Mormons shared this belief with the main body of evangelical Protestants, and the belief was based on the broader philosophical assumption of the clarity of truth generally.[59] Irving does a service by establishing such conceptions, but it is important to distinguish how Smith said or thought he understood the Bible from how he used it in practice. For example, the kinds of changes he made in his biblical revision (see chapter 2) reveal that he found the KJV frequently *un*clear, contradictory, and erroneous. He often interpreted scripture metaphorically, and he spoke of the mysterious passages of the Bible whose meanings were opened to him only by revelation.

It is nevertheless essential to recognize the enduring literalistic dimension of his mind. That is, although the Prophet acknowledged metaphorical interpretation and even biblical error, for him, the major events told in the Bible corresponded with external reality. Where the Bible did not err by textual omission, mistranslation, or mistransmission, it was truth: the parting of the Red Sea occurred as reported in Exodus; Lot's wife physically became a pillar of salt. "The first Mormon" was a biblical literalist not because he was incapable of figurative understanding but because he believed the stories of the Bible were history rather than legend. It was his faith that biblical prophecies of future events would surely occur as presented—more likely than not in the nineteenth century.

This potential for both a spiritual/metaphorical and a literal/

57. *The Jerome Biblical Commentary*, 2:606–19.
58. Irving, "Mormonism and the Bible," pp. 40, 42–43.
59. George M. Marsden, "Everyone One's Own Interpreter?" in *The Bible in America*, ed. Hatch and Noll, pp. 80–81.

physical understanding of scripture in Joseph Smith's mind (and in the revelations he received and, for that matter, in the Bible itself) is not merely an interesting fact to observe in passing. It relates to the very essence of the Mormon mentality. The tension between these two ways of thinking in fact helps account for the different ways in which the Mormon movement developed when it splintered into several factions after Joseph Smith's death. The ideas of the "Kingdom" and the "New Israel," for example, were construed more literally as a political kingdom by Joseph Smith late in his career and by the Saints who followed Brigham Young than by the Saints of the "Reorganization" who tended to reject the developments in Nauvoo, Illinois where Smith spent the last six years of his life.[60]

Early critics often dismissed the Book of Mormon on defensive or arbitrary grounds. One of its more thoughtful detractors, however, was Alexander Campbell, leader of a movement urging the return to a "simple and pure New Testament Christianity." What most appalled Campbell about the Mormon book was how it "represents the christian [*sic*] institution as practiced among [the] Israelites" well before the appearance of Christ. Nephites preached "baptism and other Christian usages hundreds of years before Jesus Christ was born!" The Book of Mormon, said Campbell, obliterated any meaningful distinction between the Old and New Testaments.[61]

Campbell's observation was largely true. Just as Jesus had declared that the Hebrew scriptures bore witness of him and that Abraham "rejoiced to see my day," and just as Peter had equated Jesus with the prophet of whom Moses had prophesied in Deuteronomy 18 and further implied that Moses and all the prophets since the time of Samuel understood that Jesus would be the fulfillment of their prophesies,[62] so—and more so—the Book of Mormon "Christianizes" pre-Christian times. The book is filled with concepts many scholars would regard as anachronistic.[63]

60. Shipps, *Mormonism,* pp. 76–77 and passim.

61. Francis W. Kirkham, *A New Witness for Christ in America: The Book of Mormon,* 4th ed., vol. 1 (SLC: Utah Printing Co., 1967); rev. ed., vol. 2 (SLC: Utah Printing Co., 1959). The uniformity of the gospel in all ages was a central theme among the early Saints. See Irving, "Mormonism and the Bible," chap. 1.

62. John 5:39, 8:56; Acts 3:20–24.

63. H. Michael Marquardt, "The Use of the Bible in the Book of Mormon," *Journal of Pastoral Practice* 2, no. 2 (1978): 118–32, lists more than two hundred New Testament quotations found in pre-Christian times in the Book of Mormon.

For believing Latter-day Saints, this "Christianizing" of pre-Christian texts could as easily be attributed to Mormon, the fourth-century prophet and editor of what is now the book named after him, as it can be attributed to Joseph Smith. A careful reading of "The Words of Mormon," verses 4 and 5, suggests the possibility. But the possibility does not affect the *fact* of the Christianizing. Prophecies described as once available to the ancient Israelites but now found only in the Book of Mormon testify of the unborn Messiah in very explicit detail: the Messiah, whose name would be "Jesus Christ," would arrive precisely six hundred years after the Book of Mormon prophet Lehi left Jerusalem; he would be born of a virgin and preceded by a baptizing forerunner; he would be lifted up, crucified, and buried in a sepulcher; three days of darkness in the new world would follow his death.[64] The Book of Mormon not only predicts such messianic particulars but teaches that the Old Testament prophets generally did also. It explains the absence of these unmistakable forecasts in the Old Testament by prophesying that wicked people would systematically remove parts of the scriptures originally containing "the plainness of the gospel of the Lord."[65]

Whether or not that accusation is true, the differences between Old Testament thought and the Book of Mormon have seemed to some scholars too basic to be fully explained thus. They argue that not only is the Book of Mormon replete with "translator's anachronisms," but that the two sets of scriptures offer fundamental contrasts in their theologies—in, for instance, their differing conceptions of a messiah, of God, of the meaning of the Law, and of the nature of the after-

---

64. 1 Nephi 19:10, 10:4–11, 11:13–20; 2 Nephi 25:28, 13:13, 25:19.

65. 1 Nephi 13 implies that designing men in emerging Catholicism were primarily responsible for this scriptural excision, but see also Jacob 4:14–15, which may be read as allowing Jews to share the blame. Early Christian apologists accused the Jews of expunging important texts from the Old Testament to rid it of possible messianic allusions to Jesus. Some of these sayings would have reinforced Joseph Smith's perceptions. To illustrate: Justin Martyr (*Dialogue with Trypho* 72:4) and Irenaeus (*Against Heresies* 3:20:4) quote the alleged Old Testament saying "The Lord God remembered his dead people of Israel who lay in their graves, and he descended to preach to them his own salvation"—a proof-text that fit the logic of Mormon temple work (cf. 1 Peter 3:19) and that Mormons, had they known of it, might have used to reiterate the idea of the "Christian awareness" of pre-Christian Israel. The alleged passage cannot currently be found in any known pre-Christian text.

life.[66] This assessment need not imply either the final authenticity or falsity of the Book of Mormon—issues beyond the scope of this study. But whatever one makes of the complex and controversial Book of Mormon, the evidence suggests Joseph Smith's theological preconceptions and cultural surroundings influenced its production. Brigham Young, among others, allowed as much.[67]

The inclination to Christianize the Old Testament was by no means a monopoly of the Book of Mormon or those who eventually embraced it. It was in fact but one expression of a more basic assumption of antebellum Americans: truth was unchanging throughout the

66. Charles, "The Mormon Christianizing of the Old Testament," pp. 37–39; Walters, "The Use of the Old Testament," pp. 7–16. Recent scholarship, however, emphasizes the difficulties in conceiving of either Judaism or Old Testament thought monolithically. See, for example, Jacob Neusner, William S. Green, and Ernest Frerichs, eds., *Judaisms and Their Messiahs* (Cambridge: Cambridge University Press, 1987).

67. *JD*, 9:311. Coming to terms with the Book of Mormon has proven an extraordinary problem for those who have resisted facile explanations. The relevant literature is expansive and growing. Able writers like Fawn Brodie long ago pointed to Ethan Smith's *View of the Hebrews* as a likely source that Joseph Smith made use of. Equally able scholars like Richard Bushman and Klaus Hansen have argued that *View of the Hebrews* cannot explain the Book of Mormon. Valuable introductions to the subject are: Gary P. Gillum and John W. Welch, *Comprehensive Bibliography of the Book of Mormon* (Provo, UT: Foundation for Ancient Research and Mormon Studies, 1982); David J. Whittaker, "The Mormon Scriptures: A Bibliography of Their History and Textual Development, Part III, the Book of Mormon," *Mormon History Association Newsletter*, June 1983, pp. 14–16; David J. Whittaker, "The Book of Mormon—Attack and Defense, A Bibliographical Essay," Part I, *Mormon History Association Newsletter*, November 1984, pp. 8–10. Examples of especially interesting analyses of the Book of Mormon include: Ostler, "The Book of Mormon as a Modern Expansion of an Ancient Source"; Steven D. Ricks, "Joseph Smith's Means and Methods of Translating the Book of Mormon" (Provo, UT: Foundation for Ancient Research and Mormon Studies, 1984); Sandberg, "Knowing Brother Joseph Again: The Book of Abraham and Joseph Smith as Translator" (the essay's keen insights are applicable to the Book of Mormon despite the focus on the Book of Abraham); B. H. Roberts, *Studies of the Book of Mormon*, ed. Brigham D. Madsen; Howard, *Restoration Scriptures;* John L. Sorenson, *An Ancient Setting for the Book of Mormon* (SLC: Deseret Book, 1985); Hugh Nibley, *Since Cumorah: The Book of Mormon in the Modern World* (SLC: Deseret Book, 1967); Wayne Ham, "Problems in Interpreting the Book of Mormon as History," *Courage: A Journal of History, Thought, and Action* 1 (September 1970): 15–22; David Persuitte, *Joseph Smith and the Origins of the Book of Mormon* (Jefferson, NC: McFarland and Co., 1985); Noel B. Reynolds, *Book of Mormon Authorship: New Light on Ancient Origins* (Provo, UT: BYU Religious Studies Center, 1982).

ages.[68] Granted this, it followed that the gospel, the highest truth, also did not change in essentials. One result of this view was a propensity to see Old Testament figures and theology through a New Testament faith.[69] Yet although many other Americans read Christianity backward into the Old Testament, Joseph Smith and his followers were distinctive in claiming revelation for so doing.

Something New Under the Sun

It should be apparent that by March 1830, before the twenty-four-year-old Prophet had organized his small company of followers into a formal church, Joseph Smith's interactions with the Bible were already complex. In many respects these interactions were typical of his culture. Smith believed the Bible and knew it well. His speech and thought patterns had been profoundly influenced by the common version of the day. He turned naturally to the Bible when in need of divine guidance and he responded to the Bible's counsel with action. He reasoned from the Bible when proselytizing, and he read from the Bible when he worshipped.[70]

He shared with many of his time a special interest in certain biblically inspired themes. He also shared with them an understanding of the history and prophecies of the Bible as true accounts of real events. Like so many of his contemporaries, he interpreted scripture with selectively applied literalism, and showed no awareness of the new critical biblical scholarship practiced at Harvard and at Andover Seminary that would polarize American Protestantism later in the century. Smith believed, like antebellum America generally, in the immutability of truth. Although he gave the notion unique application, he did, like others, extend this idea to the gospel, which he conceived as unchanging and therefore essentially as knowable and

68. Marsden, in Hatch and Noll, ed., *The Bible in America*, pp. 80–81; cf. D&C 93:24.

69. A similar tendency may be seen throughout the New Testament itself. The Gospel of Matthew and the Epistle to the Hebrews are prominent illustrations of the method. Similarly, the Old Testament of Martin Luther's German Bible, the prototype of all vernacular Bibles, included commentary and countless marginal notes reflecting Luther's insistence that "Christ must be the sole object of contemplation."

70. *HC*, 1:188–89.

known in Old Testament times as in New. Finally, Smith shared with his time and place an intense belief in Jesus Christ as divine redeemer.

Yet if Joseph Smith in 1830 was an authentic, nineteenth-century, Bible-believing Christian, he was already a Bible-believing Christian with a difference. Contrary to the dominant current of his day, he was not convinced of the Bible's sufficiency. To the thousands like Charles Beecher, who championed "the Bible, the whole Bible, and nothing but the Bible," the Book of Mormon offered only scorn: "Thou fool, that shall say: A Bible, we have got a Bible, and we need no more Bible."[71]

There was substance behind this Mormon challenge. Although no higher authority existed in antebellum Protestant America than the holy scriptures, those scriptures always needed to be construed by the individual reader. As we have seen, the interpretive authority of formal religious bodies had so long been under fire that by the 1820s no church or creed could assure uniform understanding. The reformer Sarah Moore Grimké was typical of the era in declaring her intentions to "depend solely on the Bible," but she was also typical in insisting on her right "to judge for myself what is the meaning."[72]

If the main body of evangelical Protestants assumed the Bible to speak clearly and without equivocation on essentials, in practice the antiauthoritarian insistence on the right of private interpretation spawned a bewildering diversity of theological tenets even among the well-established denominations. Roman Catholics had warned from the outset of the Reformation that without the church, all people were likely to fancy themselves their own legitimate interpreters; spiritual anarchy seemed assured. In the middle decades of the nineteenth century, even as "the Bible alone" reached its apex as a cultural shibboleth, the dire predictions of Catholicism seemed plausible.

Although with rather a different remedy in mind, Joseph Smith agreed with Catholics and other dissenters from evangelical hegemony who saw that an appeal solely to the Bible could not fill the vacuum in religious authority created by America's democratic ways. Smith had

71. Beecher, *The Bible a Sufficient Creed* (Fort Wayne, IN: Fort Wayne, Times, and Press Office, 1846); 2 Nephi 29:3–10.

72. Sarah Moore Grimké, *Letters on the Equality of the Sexes and the Condition of Women, Addressed to Mary S. Parker* (Boston: I. Knapp, 1838), pp. 4, 126, cited in Marsden, "Everyone One's Own Interpreter?" pp. 79–80.

been dismayed at an early age by the sectarian "war of words and tumult of opinions" he found all around him. He often wondered, "What is to be done? Who of all these parties [is] right? Or, are they all wrong together?" Although he turned to the Bible for guidance during his personal religious crisis, he did not expect it alone to solve his perplexity; diverse authorities read scripture diversely. Not only did the Bible invite conflicting interpretations, parts of it were missing or corrupted—and even if it were not so, the Bible's existence did not preclude God's speaking again. As the Lord himself would ask in the Book of Mormon, "Wherefore murmur ye, because that ye shall receive more of my word?"[73]

But the Bible in which Smith believed did direct him to pray, and the answer he received set him on a course apart from other American Christians. If he differed from evangelicals in finding the unaided Bible an insufficient guide, he differed from the Mercersburg theologians and from Roman Catholics in his solution to that lack. Unlike them, he did not turn to the authority of churchly tradition to interpret sacred scripture. Instead, he produced a third testament—scripture saturated with biblical language and themes but a distinct religious creation nonetheless. The Book of Mormon insisted that there was room in the canon for extrabiblical works; after 1830 this notion of "additional canon" would broaden to "open canon."

Joseph Smith was not alone in feeling the modern churches had evolved far from the untainted purity of New Testament Christianity. In this he was only another voice in a broad protest that included such radicals as the Unitarian Joseph Priestly and the entire Christian primitive movement.[74] But Smith differed from many Christian primitivists by his interest—shared with different Americans—in Israel as well as in Christianity, in the Old Testament as well as the New. Furthermore, where "primitive gospelers" like Elias Smith or Alexander Campbell might arrive at their views (as they thought) by a reasoned study of the Bible, Joseph Smith arrived at his (as he believed) in the role of a Bible-like prophet.[75] This role did include scriptural study, but it was grounded in direct revelation and the receipt of priesthood

73. 2 Nephi 29:8.

74. Hill, "The Role of Christian Primitivism," p. 10.

75. In 1830 the Saints were probably theologically most like the Campbellites. Still, Smith's revelatory foundation is easily contrasted with the rationalistic methods of Alexander Campbell. See Bushman, *Joseph Smith,* ch. 6.

authority at the literal hands of returning biblical figures: John the Baptist, Peter, James and John, and eventually others.[76] Thus Smith went beyond even the radical departure of seeing his life as a continuation of the biblical story; living biblical figures were also a part of his life.

The mere fact of his revelations did not of itself make Smith unique in his use of scripture, for, as I have suggested, even such broadly accepted figures as Charles Finney had their scripturally informed visions. But Finney's religious thought, like Campbell's, was based on self-conscious reason. He would never have understood himself as a prophet, declaring and writing original scripture like Moses or Jeremiah. With his legal brilliance, Charles Finney issued a systematic theology; with his prophetic consciousness, Joseph Smith proffered the Book of Mormon.

Mother Ann Lee, Jemima Wilkinson, and other visionaries[77] were not as rational as Finney, to be sure, but neither did they produce a Book of Mormon. As A. Leland Jamison has put it, "All spiritualist and mystical movements verge in the direction of extra-biblical revelation, but usually the new revelations are kept in spoken form rather than in a written canon." The Book of Mormon remains the only important second Bible produced in this country, and represents biblical connections more elaborate, more intricate, and more influential than the products of any other religious movement native to American shores.[78]

Like the Bible-loving evangelicals surrounding him, Smith believed that scriptural promises were literally and directly applicable to him personally. However, as the evolving accounts of his first vision reveal, he quickly grew away from the merely personal applications of biblical promises. He began to see himself, his scriptures, and his

76. PGP, "Joseph Smith—History," 1:68–72; D&C 110.

77. Marini, *Radical Sects of Revolutionary New England*, chap. 4.

78. Jamison, "Religions on the Perimeter," in *The Shaping of American Religion*, ed. Smith and Jamison, pp. 201–2. Joseph Smith did have his imitators, such as James Strang, who issued written revelations, though they do not remotely compare with the Book of Mormon. In later times, such figures as Mary Baker Eddy (*Science and Health with a Key to the Scriptures*) and the Reverend Sun Myung Moon (*Divine Principle*) produced works that accumulated the aura of at least quasiscripture to adherents, but these are essentially metaphysical treatises that include creative scriptural interpretation. They are fundamentally different in character from the historical-mythological-theological narratives of the Bible and the Book of Mormon.

movement in cosmic terms, as themselves a fulfillment of biblical prophecy: "a marvelous work and a wonder."

Smith's earliest recorded revelations contain a great many biblical building blocks, both conceptually and linguistically, and indeed, they are incomprehensible without a knowledge of the Bible, whether Smith's own or the modern reader's. Yet these documents are new religious creations having their own integrity, and cannot be reduced only to their biblical elements any more than the New Testament as a whole can be dismissed as merely an artificial collage of Old Testament fragments. In both cases, something new emerged out of something old.

But this fact can itself be used as a metaphor for how Joseph Smith's early use of the Bible related to that of other Americans. His biblically informed language, his literalistic bent of mind, the New Testament lens through which he viewed the Old Testament, his millennial preoccupations, even his very dissatisfaction with the biblical text as he received it or with the Bible as a sole and final authority— all these tendencies were theoretically available to him by cultural inheritance. They do not, however, completely explain his distinctive uses of scripture. They are, rather, recognizable bricks with which Smith made a new structure. His uses of the Bible, like the Mormon movement as a whole, drew heavily from the environment in which they took root, but they also struggled against the currents of American culture as they grew to fruition. The social milieu of antebellum upstate New York made such a man as Joseph Smith possible, but in his use of the Bible Smith eventually went well beyond his culture.

In 1830 Joseph Smith was a Bible-believing Christian in that he believed in the reality, authority, and efficacy of Jesus as divine redeemer, as well as in the inspiration, the basic truth, and the controlling stature of the Bible as a historical and prophetic document. But though he shared much with the biblicists of his time (including, in 1830, much of their theology),[79] his complex interactions with the Bible were sufficiently different to set them apart as something new under the (American) sun. Smith would expand these precedents for the remainder of his life. As we shall see, however, these interactions seem less unique if we look beyond American shores and before Enlightenment times for models.

79. Alexander, "The Reconstruction of Mormon Doctrine."

2

From the Birth of the Church to the Death of the Prophet

From the day he organized "the Church of Christ" in 1830 until his death in 1844, Joseph Smith expanded the patterns of biblical usage he began in his teens and early twenties. He thereby set the essential course that would ever after distinguish his eventual followers. As "Mormonism" grew from an idea into a movement, the Prophet's confidence seemed to grow proportionately. He had barely completed the Book of Mormon when he was moved to take another step, just as bold a departure from traditional norms. Adding his own sense of prophetic license to the broad notions of authorship common in his day, Smith undertook a revision of the Bible itself.

Additionally (and, in part, consequently), revelation after revelation flowed through the Prophet. All of them showed traits previously established: they were saturated with biblical themes, phrases, and figures, yet were themselves independent religious creations. Careful attention to these revelations, to Smith's biblical revision, and to his sermons and incidental uses of the Bible shows his conception of scripture to have been expansive when compared to those of his contemporaries. For the Mormon Prophet, scripture was not the static, final, untouchable, once-and-for-all Word of God that it was for many antebellum Christians. Although his allegiance to it was deep, scripture was for him provisional, progressive, relivable, subject to refinement and addition, spoken as well as written, varied in its inspiration, and subordinate to direct experience with God.

The Book of Mormon was advertised for sale March 26, 1830. One year later Alexander Campbell's widely quoted review accused it of resolving all the great issues discussed in New York during the 1820s, including "infant baptism, ordination, the trinity, regeneration . . . even the question of free masonry, republican government, and the rights of man."[1]

Elements in the book did seem to connect with a number of then current issues and to answer psychological needs of its readers; some converts used the book as Campbell suggested.[2] Many, however, did not. In fact, compared to the Bible, the Book of Mormon was used surprisingly little. Converts and even Smith's revelations spoke of the "Book of Mormon and the holy scriptures," reserving the latter term for the Bible.[3] The Lord chided Church members for not valuing the Book of Mormon sufficiently.[4] Mormon editor W. W. Phelps complained that the Saints would rather look for mysteries in the Bible than learn the plain things taught in the Book of Mormon. Mormon periodicals in the 1830s cited the Bible nineteen times as often as the Book of Mormon, and in the 173 discourses given in Nauvoo, Illinois for which contemporary records exist, Smith himself paraphrased the Book of Mormon only twenty-three times but quoted or paraphrased the Bible more than six hundred times.[5] Although he described the Book of Mormon as more correct than any other book and as "the keystone of our religion," there is little evidence that he ever took time to study its contents as he did the Bible's.

The Book of Mormon was valued by its adherents, but it did not become the basis for early Church doctrine and practice—Smith's day-to-day revelations did that. It would remain for a later generation of Saints to adopt as heroes such Book of Mormon figures as Alma, Moroni, and Nephi. The earliest Mormons naturally preferred the Bible on which they had been raised, despite the weaknesses they found in it. Nahum, Zechariah, and Malachi were not obscure figures to them

1. Painesville (OH) *Telegraph,* March 15, 1831; cited in Hill, "Christian Primitivism," p. 101.

2. See, for example, England, *Orson Pratt,* p. 18.

3. Orson Pratt, *JD,* 7:37; Parley Pratt, *Autobiography of Parley Parker Pratt* (SLC: Deseret Book, 1980), p. 42; D&C 33:16.

4. D&C 84:54–57.

5. Phelps in *EMS* 1 (January 1833): 60; Underwood, "Book of Mormon Usage," p. 53; Irving, "Mormonism and the Bible," chap. 4; Ehat and Cook, eds., *The Words of Joseph Smith,* pp. 421–25.

and their contemporaries, as they would become to future Saints and future Americans. For its earliest adherents, the Book of Mormon was important, almost independent of its specific contents, because it existed; it was proof that God had spoken again, just as in biblical times.[6]

The sine qua non of the Mormon message as it was proclaimed in 1830 was its distinctive biblical nature: not the Bible as final authority but, rather, the restoration of the authority, teachings, and prophetic methods reflected in the Bible. Convert after convert reported embracing Mormonism because it satisfied their yearnings for a truly biblical Christianity. The Reverend Orson Spencer was representative when he explained the wrenching sacrifices he made to leave his pulpit and join the Latter-day Saints: "What could I do?" he asked. "Truth had taken possession of my mind—plain, simple Bible truth."[7]

Just as Joseph Smith and Oliver Cowdery had first reasoned out of the scriptures in their attempt to attract acquaintances, so later Mormon elders, claiming divine sanction, gathered a following with the same technique.[8] The *Brookville* (Indiana) *Enquirer* was impressed that Orson Pratt made "no lame attempt" at revealing the plain meaning of the Bible. Sidney Rigdon, preaching in Kirtland, Ohio, presented "plain scripture facts" with great effect. Mormon elders reported that whenever they could appeal their case to the Bible they were sure of success. They confidently asked competing ministers to meet them on "Bible ground."[9] Like those of other faiths,[10] the early

6. Bushman, *Joseph Smith,* pp. 141–42. Underwood, "Book of Mormon Usage," pp. 56–59, correctly points out that the preference for the Bible over the Book of Mormon is not adequately explained as a calculated move to avoid Protestant antipathy to the new scripture, for this theory does not account for the equal lack of Book of Mormon citation *within* the community of Saints. The simple fact seems to be that the first generation of converts knew and loved the Bible better.

7. Spencer, *Letters Exhibiting the Most Prominent Doctrines of the Church of Jesus Christ of Latter-day Saints* (Liverpool, Eng., 1848), p. 9, quoted in Arrington and Bitton, *The Mormon Experience,* p. 30. Additional examples may be found in Hill, "The Role of Christian Primitivism," pp. 53–60.

8. D&C 35:23.

9. Irving, "Mormonism and the Bible," p. 45. Although Arrington and Bitton, *The Mormon Experience,* pp. 27–40, list biblicism as only one of seven major "appeals of Mormonism" attracting early converts, most of the other elements they properly identify (e.g., restorationism, the Book of Mormon, eschatological concerns) were intelligible and convincing largely *because of* their relationship to the Bible.

10. "What we may call *the principle of selective* [scriptural] *emphasis* has accounted for the most extensive proliferation of American religious groups" (Jamison, in *The Shaping of American Religion,* ed. Smith and Jamison, p. 179; see also pp. 177ff.).

Mormons selected their texts carefully, emphasizing those topics that reinforced their perceptions: the primitive church pattern, prophecies of apostasy and subsequent restoration, millennialism, the uniformity of the gospel in all ages, and the special role of Israel.[11]

The Bible Revised

"The Church of Christ," as it was originally called, was formally organized at Fayette, New York, on April 6, 1830, eleven days after the Book of Mormon was offered for sale. In two months membership had grown to twenty-seven, and eight months later the branch in Kirtland, Ohio alone numbered almost one hundred.[12] But Smith had hardly nurtured the Book of Mormon into print and launched his rapidly growing, rapidly evolving, and highly resisted church into existence, when he assumed another major "branch of my calling"— the revision of the Holy Bible.

The Bible's imperfection was not a novel idea to Smith in 1830. Years earlier the messenger Moroni had quoted passages that varied from the KJV, and the Book of Mormon had subsequently reflected similar changes. Neither was the notion of flawed scripture utterly new to other Americans. A generation before Smith ever thought of revising the Bible, Thomas Paine had publicly doubted "whether such of the writings as now appear under the name of the Old and New Testament are in the same state in which . . . collectors say they found them, or whether they added, altered, abridged, or dressed them up."[13] Many of the several hundred editions or partial editions of the scriptures published in America between 1777 and 1830 were

11. Irving, "Mormonism and the Bible," chap. 4, especially pp. 55–57, 63–64.

12. Hill, *Joseph Smith*, p. 110; *HC*, 1:146. In the spring of 1831 Joseph Smith and his New York followers moved to Ohio, joining the approximately one hundred converts who had gathered around the impressive former Campbellite and new Mormon recruit, Sidney Rigdon. For approximately seven years Kirtland was a center of Mormon activity. By the summer of 1835 fifteen hundred to two thousand Saints resided in the vicinity. In the meantime a second center was established in Independence, Jackson County, Missouri. Persecution forced evacuation from Jackson County in 1833–1834, and the Missouri Saints congregated in the northern counties until, in 1839, they were driven from the state. From 1839 to 1846, the Mormons built and flourished in the beautiful city of Nauvoo, Illinois.

13. *The Age of Reason* (New York: Thomas Paine Foundation, n.d.), pp. 18–20.

new translations or revisions of the KJV containing modernizations of language, paraphrases, and alternate readings based on Greek and Hebrew manuscripts.[14] The KJV itself underwent considerable evolution after its first publication: in editions between 1611 and 1870 the number of italicized words—used by translators to identify difficult or ambiguous thoughts from the original languages—increased from 43 to 583 in St. Matthew alone.[15]

Smith was probably aware, at least by year's end, that others were trying to improve the Bible. Several Campbellites, including such key figures as Sidney Rigdon and Parley Pratt, became Mormons late in 1830 and likely informed Smith of Alexander Campbell's 1828 New Testament, which was based on the translations of scholars like J. J. Griesbach.[16] An 1833 editorial in a Mormon periodical showed awareness of new translations and revisions, including Noah Webster's forthcoming Bible with its "corrections of errors in Grammar," "omission of obsolete words and phrases," and "use of euphemisms for such indelicate . . . phrases as are most offensive."[17]

While others set out to correct these imperfections by scholarly means, Smith mended the Bible by revelation. In June 1830 he first turned his attention to the Old Testament. Amid "all the trials . . . we have had to wade through," says his history, "the Lord, who well knew our infantile and delicate situation, . . . granted us 'line upon line of knowledge' . . . of which the following was a precious morsel." Smith then recorded "the words of God, which he spake unto Moses at a time when Moses was caught up into an exceedingly high mountain. . . ." The narrative told of Moses' confrontation with Satan and at least two theophanies, one of which explained God's purpose in creation: "For behold, this is my work and my glory—to bring to pass the immortality and eternal life of man."[18]

14. Margaret T. Hills, *The English Bible in America* (New York: American Bible Society, 1961); Durham, "A History of Joseph Smith's Revision of the Bible," pp. 8–19.

15. P. Marion Sims, *The Bible in America* (New York: Wilson–Erickson, 1936), p. 97.

16. Cecil K. Thomas, *Alexander Campbell and His New Version* (St. Louis: Bethany Press, 1958), p. 42. Writers who have tried to establish that Smith was influenced by the content of Campbell's New Testament through Sidney Rigdon seem to be in error. See Durham, "A History of Joseph Smith's Revision," pp. 17–19.

17. *EMS* 2 (July 1833): 106.

18. *HC,* 1:98–101; *PGP,* Moses 1:1, 39.

Throughout the remainder of the year Smith received extensions of this revelation, extracts of which ultimately appeared as "The Book of Moses" in *The Pearl of Great Price*. The new passages soon blended with the familiar opening of Genesis: "I am the Beginning and the End, the Almighty God; by mine Only Begotten I created these things; yea, in the beginning I created the heaven, and the earth upon which thou standest. And the earth was without form, and void." Thereafter the revision essentially follows the KJV text through Gen. 6:13, changing words and phrases as the Book of Mormon had done in its biblical parallels and occasionally filling in biblical gaps. The two contradictory accounts of the creation (Gen. 1 and 2) are reconciled by presenting the first as a spiritual creation, and the second as physical. Substantial material without biblical parallel was inserted about such figures as Noah and Melchizedek. One extension was particularly elaborate. In a December journal entry the Prophet recorded that

> Much conjecture . . . frequently occurred among the Saints, concerning the books mentioned . . . in various places in the Old and New Testaments, which were now nowhere to be found. The common remark was, "They are *lost books*"; but it seems the Apostolic Church had some of these writings, as Jude mentions . . . the Prophecy of Enoch, the seventh from Adam. To the joy of the little flock . . . did the Lord reveal the following . . . from the prophecy of Enoch.[19]

Mentioned only briefly in the Bible, Enoch was, according to this revelation, an extraordinarily forceful prophet. The ensuing passage included cosmic and apocalyptic dimensions:

> And . . . the Lord showed unto Enoch all the inhabitants of the earth. . . . And . . . the God of heaven looked upon the residue of the people, and he wept; and Enoch bore record of it, saying: How is it that the heavens weep, and shed forth their tears as the rain upon the mountains? . . . How is it that thou canst weep, seeing thou art holy, and from all eternity to all eternity? And were it possible that man could number the particles of the earth, yea, millions of earths like this, it would not be a beginning to the number of thy creations . . . ; how is it thou canst weep?
>
> The Lord said unto Enoch: Behold these thy brethren; they are the workmanship of mine own hands, and I gave unto them their knowl-

19. *HC,* 1:131–33.

edge [and] agency; but behold, they are without affection, and they hate their own blood. . . . And . . . the Lord spake unto Enoch, and told . . . all the doings of the children of men; wherefore Enoch knew, and looked upon their wickedness, and their misery, and wept and stretched forth his arms, and his heart swelled wide as eternity; and his bowels yearned; and all eternity shook. . . . And as Enoch saw this, he had bitterness of soul, and wept over his brethren and said unto the heavens: I will refuse to be comforted.[20]

Expanding on what the Bible only hints at,[21] Smith's revelation says that Enoch's people were called "Zion, because they were of one heart and one mind, and dwelt in righteousness; and there was no poor among them." "Zion," a divinely organized utopia, was thus evermore distinguished in Mormon conceptions from the ancient or typological nation "Israel."

Eventually, Enoch's entire city was taken into heaven without experiencing death, but during the millennial reign it would descend again to be joined with a new holy city, a New Jerusalem, built by a new chosen people.[22] At that point, the sacred past merged with the Mormon present and future. Following the vision, Joseph sent Oliver Cowdery to Missouri to locate a site for the New Jerusalem, where Enoch's society and the Latter-day Saints were to be joined. Eventually, Joseph received a revelation for an economic system, "the Order of Enoch," to equalize property and eradicate poverty. The ancient and the modern Zion were thus to become one.[23]

In time these revelations were largely absorbed into Smith's broad revision or "translation" of the entire Bible, a project on which he worked diligently from 1830 to July 1833, and sporadically thereafter. Despite several attempts, he was unable to find the leisure and means to complete and publish his revision before his death, though excerpts appeared in Mormon periodicals. The whole of his incomplete revision was finally published by the Reorganized LDS Church in 1867

20. *HC*, 1:134–36; *PGP*, Moses 7:28–31, 33, 41, 44.

21. Gen. 5:24; Heb. 11:5; Jude 14.

22. *PGP*, Moses 7:69, 62–63.

23. Bushman, *Joseph Smith*, pp. 186–87. Shipps, *Mormonism*, has provided an insightful analysis of the Mormons' movement "out of the primordial present into the future by replicating the [scriptural, mythological] past." See, e.g., chap. 3, "History as Text," especially pp. 52–53.

under the title *The Holy Scriptures,* which consists of a King James Bible incorporating Smith's changes.[24]

The original documents behind this publication are an 1828 KJV Bible (with the Apocrypha) having various markings in pencil and ink, purchased by Smith and Oliver Cowdery in October 1829, and hundreds of sheets of paper with writing on both sides by various scribes. These documents reveal that Smith's revision progressed in stages; many passages contain not only revisions of the KJV but revisions of revisions of still earlier revisions. Other passages show evidence of revisions that were later discarded in favor of the original KJV reading. Some show later revisions of biblical chapters previously marked "correct." Joseph Smith clearly experimented with the Bible as he sought to bring its text in line with the insights of his revelations and understanding.[25]

The Urim and Thummim, described by Smith as tools in his translation of the Book of Mormon, were not used in the biblical revision. Apparently Smith and a scribe would sit at a table, the KJV open before the Prophet, who then read from the Bible, dictating the revisions to the recording scribe. Knowledge of this work was widespread among both the Saints and their detractors.[26]

In the published Joseph Smith translation 3,410 verses vary from their KJV equivalents. Of these, 1,314 are in the Old Testament, 2,096 in the New. In the Old Testament, the bulk of the changed verses occur in Genesis (687), Psalms (188), and Isaiah (178); in the New Testament, they are found in the gospels (1,554), Romans (118), and Revelation (75).[27] Every book in the Bible received attention, though some were permanently labeled "correct" as they stood or, in

24. On the incompleteness of Smith's translation, see *HC,* 4:137, and Matthews, *"A Plainer Translation",* chap. 10.

25. Matthews, *"A Plainer Translation",* pp. 81–86. The experimental method to which the Prophet was by then accustomed is spelled out explicitly in D&C 9.

26. Matthews, *"A Plainer Translation",* pp. 39–40, 49–52.

27. Ibid., pp. 424–25, 243. Figures exclude spelling and punctuation changes (which are frequent but rarely significant). To the 662 verses changed in Genesis I have added the twenty-five verses of Smith's June 1830 revelation that amount to Genesis chapter "0" in *Holy Scriptures.* As with most statistics, these are indicative only and their use invites caution: not all verses are of the same length, versification in the Joseph Smith translation and the KJV are often not identical, and verses with slight alterations are counted as equal with others having more significant changes.

the case of the Song of Solomon, pronounced uninspired. While there are deletions, the revision as a whole is an expansion of the KJV.

The Nature of the Emendations

Smith made six basic types of changes. The first consists of the long revealed additions that have little or no biblical parallel, such as the visions of Moses and Enoch reviewed earlier. Except in Genesis, these kinds of additions are rare and almost never more than three or four verses in length. They fill historical or theological gaps in the biblical narrative or expand already established themes. An example is Smith's addition of four verses between verses 8 and 9 in Matt. 7, where the disciples are presented as interrupting the Sermon on the Mount with questions, providing an opportunity for Jesus to clarify and elaborate his thoughts.

A second type, which overlaps other categories, is a "common-sense" change, illustrated by Jeremiah 18:8.

KJV	SMITH REVISION
If that nation, against whom I have pronounced, turn from their evil I will repent of the evil that I thought to do unto them.	If that nation, against whom I have pronounced, turn from their evil, I will withhold the evil that I thought to do unto them.

God, who is perfect, needs no repentance. Informed by this logic, Smith changed most of the many places in the Old Testament where God is said to repent. Similarly, Jesus' prayer in Matthew 6:13 is improved from "And lead us not into temptation" (which Smith knew God would never do) to "And suffer us not to be led into temptation." This change is particularly interesting because the Book of Mormon parallel to this verse is identical to the KJV; the fact that he made later alterations shows how Smith sometimes progressively refined a text.

A third category is "interpretive additions," often signaled by the phrase "or in other words," which the Prophet appended to a passage he wished to clarify. Thus, to Jesus' counsel to turn one's other cheek if smitten (Luke 6:29), Smith added "or, in other words, it is better to offer the other [cheek], than to revile again." The interpretive phrase "or in other words" (often shortened to "in other words" or simply "or") is common in Smith's sermons as well as in the Book of Mormon, the Doctrine and Covenants, and the revision of the Bible.

"Harmonization" represents a fourth type of change. Because scripture was truth from God and therefore could not be self-contradictory, Smith reconciled passages that seemed to conflict with other passages. For instance, in the revision of Matt. 27:3–8, which tells of the death of Judas Iscariot and seems at variance with the anecdote of Judas's death in Acts 1:18–19, Smith conflated the two accounts and eliminated the discrepancy. In addition to harmonizing the Bible internally, Smith rendered it compatible with his own experience and revelations. Thus John 1:18—"No man hath seen God at any time; the only begotten Son, which is in the bosom of the Father, he hath declared him"—could not be allowed to stand untouched, for Smith himself had seen God, as had Moses, "face to face" (Exod. 33:11). Therefore, John 1:18 was changed to "And no man hath seen God at any time, except he hath borne record of the Son; for except it is through him no man can be saved."

Many changes Smith made are not easily classified; one can observe only that frequently the meaning of a given text has been changed, often idiosyncratically. Proverbs 18:22 is an example of this fifth, miscellaneous type, though it does reflect Smith's tendency to eliminate the KJV's italicized expansions:

KJV	SMITH REVISION
whoso findeth a wife findeth a good *thing,* and obtaineth favour of the Lord.	whoso findeth a wife hath obtained favor of the Lord.

The purposes behind other miscellaneous changes are more easily discerned, but these purposes are too diverse to examine in detail here. One example is Smith's inclination to heighten the miraculous dimension in reported events. Hence when Matt. 2:13, 19 reports an angel appearing to Mary's husband in a "dream," Joseph Smith elevates "dream" to "vision." Likewise, Matt. 8:10 reports that Jesus "marvelled" at a centurion's faith, but Smith altered the passage to read that the multitude, not Jesus, marveled (presumably on the grounds that the divine Savior, who knew all, had no occasion to be surprised).

The final and by far most common type of change the Prophet made in the Bible includes grammatical improvements, technical clarifications, and modernization of terms; the archaic word "meat" in Matt. 3:4 (John the Baptist's "meat was locusts and wild honey") was changed to "food"; "thy Father which seeth in secret" (Matt. 6:4) was changed to "thy Father who seeth in secret"; "such trust have we through Christ to God-ward" became "such trust have we through Christ toward God" (2 Cor. 3:4). More than the previous categories, this sort of alteration had much in common with Webster's and others' revisions.

Certain doctrinal themes were stressed in Smith's revision. These include the Kingdom (where the KJV tends to imply that the Kingdom is to be had for the finding or will "break in" of its own accord, Smith's revision emphasizes that the Kingdom must be "built up" by disciples), eschatological concerns (the entire twenty-fourth chapter of Matthew received extensive revision), priesthood, the plan of salvation, the mission of Jesus, and the nature of God, humans, and Satan or evil. As in the Book of Mormon, the revised Bible stresses that the gospel of Jesus Christ was taught among the ancient patriarchs, beginning with Adam.[28]

No evidence exists that the Prophet ever explained exactly how he understood his "translation." Much of the revision is clearly no more than a "commonsense" (or commonsense made uncommon by inspiration) commentary on the Authorized Version and a reconciliation of apparent internal conflicts. When Smith used the term *translation* to describe his Bible work, he did not mean a scholarly translation from one language to another. Through 1833, when most of the work on the revision was accomplished, the Prophet knew no foreign or ancient language, though he later studied Hebrew and perhaps other languages and in a few instances incorporated insights from this exposure into changes in the KJV (sometimes only orally in his sermons). But Smith's real work was to engage in a "translation" of religious truth, as he understood it, into terms understandable to those of his time, through the medium of the Holy Bible. Much as a modern biblical commentator might rephrase a passage after providing a thorough exegesis, Smith offered interpretive expansions. The differences are that Smith claimed prophetic rather than scholarly authority, and

28. Matthews, *"A Plainer Translation"*, pp. 283–389.

he actually interpolated the text rather than placing his additions as marginal notes.

However, the way in which he presented his changes—as an integral part of the biblical narrative—often conveys the impression that Smith felt he was actually restoring or repairing lost or corrupted material that once existed in the pristine scriptural record. That Smith thought the Bible *needed* such restoration had already been established by such Book of Mormon passages as 1 Nephi 13:20–29, 34, which spoke of "plain and precious things" taken away from the original record. That he believed such supernatural restoration was *possible* was established by the existence of the Book of Mormon itself. He once said, "I believe the Bible as it read when it came from the pen of the original writers."[29] He also spoke of "lost books" such as the Prophecy of Enoch, and then received revelations supplying some of this "lost" material. All these facts imply the Prophet believed many of his changes were inspired restorations of the original biblical text.

On the other hand, Smith's belief in the corruptions of the KJV text could sometimes be combined with an awareness of his own authority *and* his own logic to produce changes that did not necessarily claim divine inspiration. For instance, in October 1843 Smith renewed his oft-stated assertion that ignorant "translators, careless transcribers, or designing and corrupt priests have committed many errors" in transmitting the Bible. He then pointed to what he felt was a logical inconsistency:

> Look at Heb. 6:1 for contradictions—"Therefore leaving the principles of the doctrine of Christ, let us go on unto perfection." If a man leaves the principles of the doctrine of Christ, how can he be saved in the principles? This is a contradiction. I don't believe it. I will render it as it

29. Joseph Fielding Smith, ed., *The Teachings of the Prophet Joseph Smith,* p. 327. Such a statement by Joseph Smith in 1843 (which in turn follows implications in the Book of Mormon at least as early as 1829) suggests that Ernest Sandeen and his followers are incorrect when arguing (e.g., *The Roots of Fundamentalism,* pp. 127–30) that inerrancy of the original biblical manuscripts was a creation of the retreating Princeton theologians between 1860 and 1879. Joseph Smith's attitude constitutes additional evidence that George Marsden and other scholars are correct in insisting that discussion of the autographs was commonplace in earlier nineteenth-century religious literature. See Marsden, "Everyone One's Own Interpreter?" in *The Bible in America,* ed. Hatch and Noll, p. 98, n. 28.

should be—"Therefore *not* leaving the principles of the doctrine of Christ, let us go on unto perfection. . . ."[30]

That Smith felt free to make the change cannot be divorced from his overall sense of prophetic authority. Yet here he made the change by logical assertion and claimed no revealed insight.

Smith also may have felt that some of his additions reflected historical events never included as part of the written collection we know as the Bible. In 1832, during the years of his most intense work on the revision, he said, "From sundry revelations which had been received, it was apparent that many important points touching the salvation of men had been taken from the Bible, *or lost before it was compiled.*"[31] One example of a restored text Smith did not suggest was originally part of the Bible has already been referred to in chapter 1: D&C 7, a translation of a record viewed through the Urim and Thummim, "made on parchment by John [the Apostle] and hidden up by himself."

Though the examples discovered so far are not so impressive as instances in the Book of Mormon, some LDS scholars feel there is limited but significant ancient textual support for a few of Smith's changes, or literary characteristics that suggest the ancient character of some changes.[32] The examples these scholars cite seem to me better explained by Smith's effort to remove difficulties in the KJV— to harmonize scripture with itself, with "common sense," and with his own revelations—than by an actual restoration of ancient texts.[33] Ancient copyists had similar motives to harmonize apparent inconsistencies and may occasionally have produced results similar to Smith's.

Yet if his alterations do not seem to be restorations of ancient texts

30. *HC,* 6:58.
31. *HC,* 1:245; emphasis added.
32. Matthews, *"A Plainer Translation",* chap. 12; Paul R. Cheesman and C. Wilfred Griggs, eds. *Scriptures for the Modern World* (Provo, UT: Religious Studies Center, 1984), pp. 79–83; Nyman and Millet, eds., *The Joseph Smith Translation: The Restoration of Plain and Precious Things,* pp. 42–45 and passim; and Millet, "Joseph Smith's Translation of the Bible and the Synoptic Problem."
33. Cf. Hutchinson, "The Joseph Smith Revision and the Synoptic Problem: An Alternative View"; Hutchinson, "A Mormon Midrash? LDS Creation Narratives Reconsidered"'; and Barney, "The Joseph Smith Translation and Ancient Texts of the Bible."

recoverable by scholarly means, neither are they the pretensions of a madman. There are, of course, those who would assign some form of insanity to recipients of visions almost by definition. But this is a decidedly subjective exercise: one would have to be prepared to write off the mental competence of a vast array of characters, from Jesus and his disciples to St. Francis and mystics of sundry world religions to Charles Finney and other figures of Joseph Smith's own time. Fawn Brodie, who saw no providence in the Book of Mormon, nonetheless recognized something important in the book that is also relevant to Smith's biblical revision. Said she: "Recent critics who insist that Joseph Smith suffered from delusions [early in his career] have ignored in the Book of Mormon contrary evidence difficult to override. Its very coherence belies their claims. . . . [The book is dull] . . . but not formless, aimless, or absurd. Its structure shows elaborate design, its narrative is spun coherently, and it demonstrates throughout a unity of purpose."[34] This coherence is also characteristic of Smith's Bible revision. His expansions tend to reveal either an understandable, "commonsense" motivation behind the changes or else, as with the longer and more original passages, they contain their own literary and religious integrity capable of inspiring large groups of people.[35]

But this puts the modern interpreter in a quandary. If, as I have argued, Joseph Smith was religiously sincere, and if his unusual work on the Bible cannot be dismissed as the delusions of a madman, and yet if his revisions cannot in general be seen as restorations of lost biblical materials recoverable by scholarly means, how are we to understand the Mormon Prophet?

34. Brodie, *No Man Knows*, pp. 68, 69.

35. Ahlstrom (following Brodie) is correct in noting that such writings as the Book of Mormon, which show the impact of the antebellum American setting in which they were produced, cannot engage readers in quite the same way they did in the 1830s (*A Religious History*, 1:608; *No Man Knows*, p. 69). However, Brodie and Ahlstrom underestimate the continuing power of the Book of Mormon on its several million adherents and its influence in attracting the more than two hundred thousand converts who join Mormon ranks each year. This is far too large and rapidly growing a group to dismiss as a "few isolated, atypical individuals" who can still read the book as a religious testimony. The Book of Mormon and Smith's other works are not the only, and perhaps not even the primary, attraction to many of these converts, but they are still highly significant.

A Theory of Joseph Smith's "Inspired Translation"

It is apparent that Joseph Smith had a much freer notion of scripture than most of his contemporaries. Although most or all early Mormon asssertions could be (and were) supported by biblical proof-texts, Smith did not feel obliged to accept the Bible in its current authorized version as a rigid constraint on the unfolding doctrines of his church. He once observed that "there are many things in the Bible which do not, as they now stand, accord with the revelations of the Holy Ghost to me."[36]

Such a statement implies that, for Smith, it was not so much that his revelations needed to be tailored absolutely to biblical data but, rather, that an imperfect Bible ought to conform to his more current and direct revelations. This tendency could be easily overstated, for, in general, Smith believed his revelations and the correctly recorded Bible were parts of one truth. As he once said, after reconciling a conflict in two biblical passages, "If any man will prove to me, by one passage of Holy Writ, one item I believe to be false, I will renounce and disclaim it as far as I [have promulgated] it."[37] But Smith did not see fit to leave the old scriptures as he found them, simply asserting the superiority of his revelations to corrupt, outmoded, or erroneous portions of the Bible. Instead, his belief that truth cannot conflict with itself[38] led him to bring the Bible into better harmony with the truths he felt he had received from God. If Smith received revelations conveying truths given anciently to Enoch or Noah but not recorded in the Bible, or, sometimes, even if he received revelations having little to do with ancient settings, he felt no qualms about adding the material as though it were part of the scriptural record, thereby appropriating the Bible's prestige. The apparent (and perhaps partially unconscious) logic behind such an action was: If certain truths were not originally included in the Bible, they are truths nonetheless and readers will be edified by studying them; it is not the text of the Bible as such, but rather the truths of God that are sacred.

36. *HC,* 5:425.
37. *HC,* 6:57.
38. Later in his career he may have allowed more room for paradox (depending on how one interprets his meaning). For example, three weeks before his death he observed that "by proving contraries, truth is made manifest" (*HC,* 6:428).

Some critics may find such presumptions quaint or outrageous. Some Latter-day Saints, on the other hand, may feel they threaten the authenticity of their founding prophet. Neither conclusion is inevitable. However, it is not my intent here to pass judgment on either Smith's revelations or the legitimacy of his use of the Bible. I simply wish to help make the Mormon prophet more historically understandable: How is it that a sane and religiously sincere man in antebellum America could intrude so radically upon the biblical text that he himself revered by presenting the perceived truths of his own inspiration in an ancient context, as though they had been spoken by ancient prophets?

A consideration of two factors may be useful. The first is the notion of "authorship." "Not too long ago," writes Ernest R. May, "topical indexes contained the reference: 'Ghost Writing—see Forgery'; now the searcher is referred . . . to '—Authorship; Collaboration.' " May lamented that the pace of modern life in the two decades before he wrote had forced an increase in ghost writing for public figures that in turn caused problems for historians in their handling of "primary sources":

> If, on the basis of letters and speeches, a scholar should try to analyze Franklin Roosevelt's mind, he would emerge with a figure made up of Roosevelt and the fragments of Roosevelt's ghosts [=ghostwriters]— Rosenman, Sherwood, Michelson, Grace Tully, Missy Le Hand, even the sprightly apparition of Harold Ickes.[39]

May's historical concerns could be broadened both topically and temporally. Before the last quarter of the nineteenth century, historical methodology operated under different assumptions than it does today. The editorial efforts of the Reverend Jared Sparks, president of Harvard College, were representative of the earlier era. Sparks was a talented man of letters, "the first great compiler of national records," who edited, in twelve volumes, the *Writings of George Washington*. However, when his work was much later compared with the original manuscripts, it was clear that Sparks had rewritten portions of letters, deleted or altered offensive passages, changed irregularities of style and awkward expressions, and greatly magnified Washing-

39. May, "Ghost Writing and History," *American Scholar* 22 (Autumn 1953): 459–65.

ton's laudable qualities—all in Washington's name, without editorial explanation.

Yet while the demands for precision of a later period find Sparks's edition of Washington's writings unacceptable as primary source material, no one rightly questions Sparks's integrity. As his biographer properly observed, Sparks adapted his work "to the then needs of the American people, and to the literary taste of the times in which he lived."[40] Similarly, several generations of scholars have bickered about the meaning of Washington's Farewell Address because no one knows whether Washington himself or Alexander Hamilton was its actual author.[41] Nathaniel Hawthorne's wife rewrote his journals before publication. Ralph Waldo Emerson's *Journal and Miscellaneous Notebooks* were changed to enhance his image as a "gentlemanly sage." Numerous examples from the eighteenth and nineteenth centuries would show that editorial tampering was frequent, that what we now think of as plagiarism was a fairly widespread practice, that indirect discourse was commonly changed to direct "as a means of imparting more life to the narration," and that "quotation marks were not so essential a part of nineteenth century scholarly decorum as they later became."[42]

Dean Jessee has demonstrated that Joseph Smith and the early Saints participated in the editorial practices of their day.[43] In particular, the six-volume *History of the Church,* which even in current editions is subtitled *History of Joseph Smith, the Prophet, by Himself,* is actually of complex authorship, though it is presented as the work of Smith alone. In *History,* narrative gaps were bridged using other sources, indirect discourse was changed to direct, and accounts of episodes about which Smith left no record were supplied by the jour-

40. Herbert B. Adams, *The Life and Writings of Jared Sparks . . .* , 2 vols., (Boston and New York: Houghton, Mifflin, 1893), 2:271.

41. May, "Ghost Writing," p. 461.

42. Bert James Loewenberg, *American History in American Thought* (New York: Simon & Schuster, 1972), p. 186; L. H. Butterfield and Julian Boyd, *Historical Editing in the United States* (Worcester, MA: American Antiquarian Society, 1963), pp. 1–28. The notion of authorship, even in cases where individual writers do not consciously base their work on that of others, could be fruitfully explored at much greater length. See the thoughtful essays by Roland Barthes and others in *Theories of Authorship: A Reader,* ed. John Caughie (London: Routledge & Kegan Paul, 1981).

43. Jessee, "The Reliability of Joseph Smith's History," *Journal of Mormon History* 3 (1976): 23–46.

nals of other participants in the events and then put into Smith's
mouth. The history continued to be compiled for years after the
Prophet's death.[44]

These editorial-authorial practices are well documented for the
writing of history or personal memoirs during the nineteenth century,
but few seem to have noticed that they are also relevant to Joseph
Smith's production of scripture. The Mormon Prophet simply applied
the practices creatively. However, if his willingness to intrude upon
earlier documents was consonant with his era's broad concept of
authorship, in other respects Smith's work was singular. The documents to which he added were, after all, part of previously published
sacred writ enjoying unique status and exposure in America. The
versions of the Bible current in Smith's day were produced by scholars who translated from ancient languages or who slightly amended
the Authorized Version to improve clarity of speech and small points
of theology. They did not claim divine revelation in their efforts.
Smith, by contrast, claimed a divine appointment and worked from
the KJV to produce thousands of changes, some of them major ones,
including long passages of material that can be found nowhere else.
In nineteenth-century America, Smith's Bible was distinctive in conception, procedure, and content.

This brings us to the second factor that must be considered if we are
to understand Smith's revision of the Bible: his own prophetic consciousness. For the historian, what is probably the nearest model for
Smith's expansions of scripture is to be found not among his contemporaries but among biblical writers themselves. After all, the broad
conceptions of authorship discussed above were not novelties of the
eighteenth and nineteenth centuries; they existed anciently.[45]

Thousands of years ago these conceptions of authorship were sometimes coupled with a sense of prophetic license: writers understood
themselves to possess godly authority and insight more or less as great

44. Fawn Brodie, unaware that Smith was not the direct and sole author of the
History of the Church, correctly noticed that these volumes reveal very little about the
Prophet's inner self. With a fine intuition that unfortunately was based on a false
premise, she was thus moved to borrow the Prophet's words by entitling her biography
of Smith, *No Man Knows My History,* writing that "few men . . . have written so much
and told so little about themselves" (*No Man Knows,* p. vii).

45. Anciently, such broad conceptions of authorship existed side by side with instances of genuine forgery, as cautioned against, for example, in 2 Thess. 2:2.

as a given text before them, in a context where the notion of individual authorship was not especially important (though the borrowed prestige of some prior figure often was). This was typically as true of what became the accepted canon as it was of apocryphal and pseudepigraphous works. Biblical scholar Raymond Brown explains:

> In considering biblical books, many times we have to distinguish between the *author* whose ideas the book expresses and the *writer*. The writers run the gamut from recording secretaries who slavishly copied down the author's dictation to highly independent collaborators who, working from a sketch of the author's ideas, gave their own literary style to the final work. . . . Even if we confine authorship to responsibility for the basic ideas that appear in the book, the principles that determine the attribution of authorship in the Bible are fairly broad. If a particular author is surrounded by a group of disciples who carry on his thought even after his death, their works may be attributed to him as the author. The Book of Isaiah was the work of at least three principal contributors, and its compositions covered a period of over 200 years. . . . In a similar way, David is spoken of as author of the Psalms, and Moses [as] the author of the Pentateuch, even though parts of these works were composed many hundreds of years after the traditional author's death.[46]

Joseph Smith, like many of the biblical writers, felt he had received revelation and inspiration from God. With his broad sense of authorship *and* his strong sense of prophetic license, he felt the authority—indeed, the calling[47]—to inculcate his insights into his revision of scripture, much as prophetic writers in ancient times had done. As discussed above, he may also have believed, at least in some instances, that he was actually restoring ancient biblical texts lost in transmission. His dominating concern, however, was not with textual precision but with enlightening the world through revealed truth. He thus did not feel bound by what he took to be the original writings in the Bible, and yet he continued to revere the Bible. The results of his practices are sharply distinctive in antebellum America.

46. Raymond S. Brown, *The Gospel According to John* (New York: Doubleday, 1966), p. lxxxvii. New Testament scholarship has, of course, demonstrated a similar process.

47. E.g., D&C 35:18, 20, 37:1, 41:7, 42:56–58, 45:60–61. For further exploration of the nature of Smith's revelations, see Sandberg, "Knowing Brother Joseph Again," which provides common ground for discussion between Mormon and non-Mormon scholars.

More Revelations

Smith's revision of the Bible was significant for its own sake, but also because it was the stimulus for several important revelations that now constitute the Doctrine and Covenants. For example, during the course of the revision, Smith examined John 5:29, which indicates that both good and evil people will be resurrected. After encountering this passage, Smith and Sidney Rigdon jointly received a clarifying vision, whose essential contents are now published as Doctrine and Covenants 76, detailing the requirements and rewards for souls attaining various degrees of glory in the resurrection. Other D&C sections containing material probably resulting from Smith's Bible revision are 74, 77, 84, 86, 88, 93, 102, 104, 107, 113, and 132. In addition, Smith was told (section 91) that the Apocrypha contains many true and many false "things," and that it was unnecessary for him to translate it.

Although Mormon theology grew ever more distinctive during the 1830s and early 1840s, the dozens of revelations Smith continued to receive remained intimately linked to the Bible.[48] Some dealt directly with biblical themes, and quoted or closely paraphrased traditional scripture. All were saturated with KJV words, phrases, and concepts: for every two verses of the revelations recorded in the Doctrine and Covenants, approximately three phrases or clauses parallel some KJV phrase or clause.[49] The revelations reiterate, fulfill, clarify, or reinterpret biblical events and prophecies. Often, however, the parallel phraseology has little to do with the original biblical context and appears to function essentially as an unconscious connection between Smith and the Bible. These parallel phrases are not merely a small number of stock phrases but represent a very broadly based connection between the Bible and the Doctrine and Covenants. As with the

48. See, for example, David J. Whittaker's perceptive exploration, "By Study and Also By Faith: The Book of Daniel in Early Mormon Thought" (unpublished; copy in author's possession), which illuminates how Daniel helped give focus and meaning to Joseph Smith's understanding of his mission, and puts the (in)famous and widely misunderstood "Danites" in comprehensible historical perspective.

49. I.e., phrases of at least three but often more words, excluding definite and indefinite articles. Rasmussen, "Textual Parallels," p. 360. As with Smith's largely impromptu sermons, the language and subject matter of the revelations are much more dependent on the New Testament than the Old.

earlier revelations, the later ones are not a mere conglomeration of biblical texts but original religious creations.

One revelation particularly demonstrates the striking contrast between Smith's conception of scripture and that of most Americans. In November 1831 the Prophet received a revelation in behalf of several elders about to leave Ohio to proclaim the Mormon message. The revelation instructed the missionaries to expound the scriptures to listeners, and declared that "whatsoever [the elders] shall speak when moved upon by the Holy Ghost shall [itself] be scripture, shall be the will . . . [and] mind . . . [and]word of the Lord. . . ."[50] This revelation introduces two new elements that further distinguish Smith's notion of sacred texts: the idea of oral scripture, and the belief that others besides himself, if appropriately inspired, could utter it.

Etymologically, *oral* scripture is an oxymoron and *written* scripture a redundancy. The intended meaning of *scripture* here is its broader sense of inspired, authoritative "word(s) of God." Noting the separate, oral dimension is important in this context because it further demonstrates the primacy, for Joseph Smith, not of the Bible in particular but of revelation in general. The direct experience of revelation, in turn, took precedence over either an oral or written recounting of revelation. Said Smith, "Reading the experience of others, or the revelation given to *them,* can never give *us* a comprehensive view of our condition. . . . Could you gaze into heaven five minutes, you would know more than you would by reading all that ever was written on the subject."[51]

The idea of oral scripture may have been unusual in antebellum American society but was hardly unknown in the world's religious history. Much of the material of the early Christian gospels, for example, seems to have existed originally only in oral form. The Hindu Vedas have been orally transmitted for three millennia, often in explicit preference to writing. In fact, sacred "texts" in most major traditions were initially transmitted orally and written down only much later, if at all.[52]

The breadth of Smith's conception of scripture is suggested by

50. D&C 68:1–12.

51. Joseph Fielding Smith, ed., *Teachings of the Prophet Joseph Smith*, p. 324.

52. The specifically oral dimension of the written scriptural text receives able treatment in William A. Graham, *Beyond the Written Word: Oral Aspects of Scripture in the History of Religion* (New York: Cambridge University Press, 1987).

many Mormon practices that he instituted, such as "patriarchal blessings" and "fathers' blessings," both of which include an implicit dimension of "private scripture" to those who give and receive them.
Another example: "The Prophet was one day advising the elders all
to keep daily journals, for, said he, 'Your journals will be sought after
as history and scripture. That is the way the New Testament came,
what we have of it, though much of the matter therein was written by
the apostles from their memory of what had been done because they
were not prompt in keeping daily journals.' "[53]

The belief in oral scripture and the fact that potentially anyone
could utter it, in combination with Smith's propensity to alter previously written sacred texts (including his own), raise the additional
issue of levels or degrees of authority and inspiration. The matter was
never comprehensively addressed in Smith's lifetime, though he did
indicate preference for certain texts over others and did show belief in
the unevenness of inspiration in the Bible, in his own revelations, and
among his followers. "Scripturality" arises not intrinsically from a
given text itself but because some person or community comes to
revere the text as sacred. Early Mormons (as well as modern ones)
might abstractly accept "the Bible to be the word of God as far as it is
translated correctly," but they clearly developed a deeper reverence
for some pasasges than for others.

Smith's sermons and writings between 1830 and 1844 show a number of characteristics already seen in his handling of biblical material
in the Book of Mormon, in his revision of the Bible, and in his
revelations. The most salient of these traits include his biblically conditioned language, a certain fluidity in his interpretations, and his
qualified or inconsistent literalism.[54] What Robert M. Grant has written of Paul is also largely true of Joseph Smith: "[His] mind moves
allusively, intuitively, by verbal association rather than by any
[strictly] logical process." "The most striking feature" of Paul's
method is "its verbalism, its emphasis on single words at the expense
of contexts," and especially its "air of freedom." Smith's not entirely
conscious hermeneutic was similarly random or "occasional," not sys-

53. Diary of Oliver B. Huntington, quoted in *YWJ* 2:466.
54. Underwood examines the Prophet's use of the Old Testament in sermons and
everyday speech in "Joseph Smith's Use of the Old Testament."

tematic. Sometimes he was quite literalistic and in the next sentence highly figurative without leaving the topic at hand. However, his tendency to ignore context was just that: a tendency. On some occasions he was sensitive to context: "I have [a] Key by which I understand the scripture—I enquire what was the question which drew out the answer [given by Jesus]."[55]

The selectively applied literalism I have pointed to in Smith's early career remained evident throughout his life, and often fostered new avenues of theological development. For instance, he interpreted the Lord's question to Job, "Where wast thou when I laid the foundation of the Earth?" (38:4) not merely as a rhetorical question to a mythical man to emphasize human ignorance but as implied proof that the historical man Job was existing *somewhere* at the earth's creation, and this in turn was eventually seen as scriptural support for the spiritual "pre-existence" of all human beings.[56] A literalistic view of scripture also helped predispose the Prophet to instigate the restoration of several Israelite practices, most notably polygamy. The revelation on polygamy illustrates the link between the Old Testament and the Mormons' controversial custom:

> Verily, thus saith the Lord unto you my servant Joseph, that inasmuch as you have inquired of my hand to know and understand wherein I, the Lord, justified my servants Abraham, Isaac, and Jacob, as also Moses, David, and Solomon, my servants, as touching the principle and doctrine of their having many wives and concubines—Behold, and lo, I am the Lord thy God, and will answer thee as touching this matter.[57]

This literalistic frame of mind informed Joseph Smith's entire character. When the Bible reported that God spoke with Moses face to face and that angels appeared to human beings, that was the way it was. Smith knew it to be so because he too had been visited by God and angels. Indeed, his literal mind set may have helped make such divine appearances possible for him.

55. Grant, *The Bible in the Church: A Short History of Interpretation* (New York: Macmillan, 1948), pp. 18, 28, 31; Ehat and Cook, eds., *The Words of Joseph Smith,* p. 161.

56. Ehat and Cook, eds., *The Words of Joseph Smith,* p. 68.

57. D&C 132:1–2.

Typology

Many biblical literalists have also tended to interpret scripture typologically: a biblical event is viewed as foreshadowing a later "antitype," or a later event is seen as a recapitulation of a biblical one. In
actual usage by historical figures, the technical denotation of the
word *type* (that is, *prefiguration*) often blurs, so that a "type" may be
seen either as a literal event to be relived or primarily as a mere
allegorical allusion or an example to be followed. This is especially
true of Joseph Smith.

Typological approaches to scripture have a long history. Indeed,
Jesus, Paul, and other biblical figures thought in such terms when
citing episodes in Israel's past.[58] However, typology has often been
attacked either as an illegitimate method of scriptural interpretation
or because "types" are often found where critics think they do not
exist. Very early in modern American history, Roger Williams—who
interpreted the Bible typologically himself—was expelled from Massachusetts partly because he so forcefully rejected the colony's claim
to be in special covenant with God, an antitype of ancient Israel. At
about the same time Thomas Shepard complained that "men's wits
in imagining types and allegories [from the Bible] are very sinfully
luxuriant."

Sinful or not, the tendency did not lessen in later years. During the
Revolution, the patriot victory at Saratoga became, in clerical sermons, the triumph of Hezekiah over the Assyrians. At Washington's
death, ministers likened the fallen general to Abel, Jacob, Moses,
Joshua, Othniel, Samuel, Abner, Elijah, David, Mordecai, Daniel,
Stephen, and others. Millennial themes during the nineteenth century
heightened already lofty perceptions of America as God's modern
chosen nation. And the Exodus from Egypt, of course, continued to
be the type above all types, whether antitypical status was being
claimed by the colonies (God's new Israel) against England (Pharaoh), or by the Southern states against the Northern ones, or by the
slaves against their Southern masters. Typological thought in America before the twentieth century was thus exceedingly common, with

58. "We may say that the New Testament method of interpreting the Old was generally that of typology." Robert M. Grant and David Tracy, *A Short History of the
Interpretation of the Bible,* (Philadelphia: Fortress Press, 1984), p. 36.

biblical events lending meaning to the antitypical events and people of the United States.[59]

Joseph Smith was well versed in the use of types. The Book of Mormon described the law of Moses as a type of Christ's coming, and the fiery execution of the Book of Mormon prophet Abinadi was a type of the future destruction of those who put him to death. One of Smith's most important modern revelations also made use of typology.[60] And when the Prophet heard that his followers had been brutally expelled from Jackson County, Missouri, he wrote, with characteristically innovative spelling and syntax, that "the cloud is gathering around us with great fury and all pharohs host or in other words all hell and the combined powrs of Earth are Marsheling their forces to overthrow us and we like the chilldren of Issarel with the red Sea before them and the Egyptions ready to fall upon them to distroy them and no arm could diliver but the arm of God and this is the case with us. . . ."[61]

Types for Smith were more than suggestive metaphors, however; they were also models for conduct. For example, Smith found the burial practices near the conclusion of Genesis to be a type or example to be followed by the people of God in his own age. Similarly, he could matter of factly reply to a letter of one of his followers thus: "You quoted a passage in Jeremiah with regard to journeying to Zion; the word of the Lord stands sure, so let it be done"—as if, in the

59. On typology, see Sacvan Bercovitch, "Introduction," and Thomas M. Davis, "The Traditions of American Typology," in *Typology and Early American Literature*, ed. Bercovitch (Amherst: University of Massachusetts Press, 1972). Shepard, quoted in Hatch and Noll, eds., *The Bible in America*, p. 11. On Saratoga-Hezekiah, see Timothy Dwight's 1778 thanksgiving sermon, quoted in James West Davidson, *The Logic of Millennial Thought: Eighteenth-Century New England* (New Haven: Yale University Press, 1977), p. 20. See also Tuveson, *Redeemer Nation: The Idea of America's Millennial Role* (Chicago: University of Chicago Press, 1968). On Washington, see Noll, "The Image of the United States," in Hatch and Noll, eds., *The Bible in America*, p. 44. On the Exodus as the archetype for political and cultural revolution in the Western world for the past two millennia, see Michael Walzer, *Exodus and Revolution* (New York: Basic Books, 1985).

60. D&C 76:70. For typology in the Book of Mormon, see Mosiah 13:10, 17:18, 19:20; Alma 13:16, 25:7–12, 15, 33:19, 37:45; Ether 13:6. As a matter of space and convenience, I have placed this discussion in the present chapter. However, the existence of typology in the Book of Mormon demonstrates that Smith was acquainted with this mode of thought well before 1830.

61. Jessee, ed., *The Personal Writings of Joseph Smith*, p. 285.

words of one scholar, the passage were "an actual script delineating exactly how the divine drama was to be played out centuries after Jeremiah spoke."[62]

Typological thinking for Smith could also go quite beyond prescriptive examples, approaching more clearly the classical meaning of the term type. Probably not since the arrival of the Plymouth and Massachusetts Bay colonists in the 1620s and 1630s had any people so deeply identified themselves with biblical peoples as did Joseph Smith and his followers. In an era witnessing the decline of Old Testament influence and the rise of the New, the Latter-day Saints combined in unique fashion elements of the Christian primitivism movement of their day with a Puritan-like Hebrew self-consciousness that developed in ways that seemed to surprise even Joseph Smith.

Even as Smith proclaimed his belief "in the same organization that existed in the Primitive Church," Mormons conceived of themselves as the new and chosen (Christian) Israel. Evangelical Christians, of course, also felt themselves chosen, but for them this was an abstraction with less immediacy than the salvation experience. For the Latter-day Saints, the sense of chosenness was central to their self-identity and very existence.[63] Freely mixing conceptions from both Testaments, they sought to establish a theocratic Zion with a New American Jerusalem, complete with a spectacular temple at its center and having, like the believers in the Book of Acts, "all things in common." Mormon "Patriarchs" pronounced "blessings" upon modern *Saints,* much as Jacob had blessed his sons, the heads of the twelve tribes of Israel. Joseph Smith himself "filled the Old Testament roles of deliverer (Moses), military commander (Joshua), prophet (Isaiah), high priest (Eli), king (Solomon), and the New Testament positions of church founder (Peter) and apostle to the Gentiles (Paul)."[64]

The Mormon leader and his followers were not merely looking

62. Underwood, "Joseph Smith's Use," pp. 383–88; Ehat and Cook, eds., *The Words of Joseph Smith,* pp. 111, 195; *HC,* 1:338–39.

63. Shipps, *Mormonism,* p. 119; Noll, "The Image of the United States," in *The Bible in America,* ed. Hatch and Noll, pp. 44–51.

64. Shipps, *Mormonism,* p. 37; cf. Davis Bitton, "Competing Images of Joseph Smith," (unpublished paper presented at the meetings of the Mormon History Association, Logan, UT, May 1988).

back to the Bible as example or doctrinal authority. Nor were they simply re-creating biblical events by conscious ritual, though they did of course do this. They were actually recapitulating, *living through,* the stories of Israel and early Christianity—reestablishing the covenant, gathering the Lord's elect, separating Israel from the Gentiles, organizing the Church, preaching the gospel, building up the kingdom, living in sacred space and time. As earliest Christianity appropriated and transformed Jewish history, so the Latter-day Saints appropriated and transformed the Old Testament story *and re*appropriated the New Testament appropriation of the same story.[65]

In the fall of 1835 Smith began the study of Hebrew, first on his own, later under the tutelage of Professor Joshua Seixas at the recently organized "School of the Prophets" in Kirtland, Ohio. Smith's interest in languages and his reputation as a restorer of ancient writings led the Church to purchase certain Egyptian mummies and scrolls in 1835, some of which the Prophet identified as a record of Abraham in Egypt. He spent several weeks attempting to translate the scrolls, and returned to the task again in 1842. The Book of Abraham was first published that same year and later appeared in *The Pearl of Great Price.*[66]

Like the preceding Book of Moses, the five chapters of the Book of Abraham overlap with Genesis and include an account of the creation. The book also contains original and creative ideas about human beings, their relation to the universe, and God's purpose for them on earth. Mormon perceptions evolved with astonishing rapidity through the 1830s and 1840s, and the developing theology clearly interacted with Smith's study of Hebrew. This is apparent, for example, when one compares the creation account in Smith's 1830 revision

65. Shipps, *Mormonism,* pp. 34–39, 51–65, 74–83.

66. The precise relationship between the scrolls and the published Book of Abraham has been controversial. The scrolls were lost after Smith's death, but fragments were rediscovered in 1967. Translations of the fragments assure that they were not part of the Abraham text printed in *PGP,* but part of a well-known Egyptian funerary text. Some Mormon scholars have observed that only eleven fragments of the original scrolls exist, and that in any case the scrolls were not translated by scholarly means but may simply have served as a catalyst that turned Smith's highly intuitive mind back to ancient Egypt and opened it to revelation. The most promising direction for future study, whether for skeptics or believing Mormons, is along the lines laid out by Sandberg, "Knowing Brother Joseph Again."

of Genesis in the Book of Moses and the later account in the Book of Abraham (both in *The Pearl of Great Price*).

> And again, I, God, said; Let there be a firmament in the midst of the water, and it was so, even as I spake; and I said: Let it divide the waters from the waters; and it was done [Moses 2:6].

> And the gods also said: Let there be an expanse in the midst of the waters, and it shall divide the waters from the waters [Abraham 4:6].

A literal translation of the Hebrew would read:

> And *Elohim* said, Let there be an expanse in the midst of the waters, and let it divide between the waters and the waters [Gen. 1:6].[67]

Smith's Book of Abraham rendition more nearly resembles the Hebrew and the KJV (which is here a quite literal translation of the Hebrew) than it does the earlier Book of Moses account. In the Book of Abraham, Smith renders the plural noun *Elohim* and its singular verb as "the Gods . . . said," emphasizing the polytheism that was interacting with other ideas to produce an ever more distinctive LDS theology during the Prophet's Kirtland and Nauvoo years. Page 85 of Seixas's *Grammar* described *Elohim* as "a singular noun with a plural form." The word translated as "firmament" in the KJV (and the Book of Moses) means literally "expanse" in Hebrew, which Seixas noted and which Smith used in the Book of Abraham.

But Smith was not really attempting to be a meticulous Hebraist for the sake of scholarship. Rather, as one non-Mormon Hebrew scholar aptly observes, the Prophet commonly "theologized" with his Hebrew. He was not trying necessarily to discover what the original author was saying so much as he was using Hebrew "as he chose, as an artist, inside his frame of reference, in accordance with his taste, according to the effect he wanted to produce, as a foundation for theological innovations."[68] It is certainly inaccurate to say that his study of languages of themselves sponsored his theological innovations, but his linguistic study did interact in a kind of ongoing dialectic with his creative theological expansions.

67. The general form of the literal Hebrew translation follows Walton, "Professor Seixas," pp. 41–42.

68. Zucker, "Joseph Smith as a Student of Hebrew," p. 53.

Biblicism—With a Difference

Among historians it goes without saying that all historical figures are conditioned and made possible by their era. This may be especially true of Joseph Smith, who drew deeply from the religious tensions and resources of his culture. In his attitude toward the Bible in particular, Smith shared much with his non-Mormon contemporaries. Like most of them, he took the scriptures very seriously, as a base line for religious thought. Like them, he believed the events and prophecies recorded in the Bible—where they had not been lost or ruined—were real events that had actually happened or would yet occur.

Smith's speech and thought, like those of his neighbors, were profoundly influenced by the patterns of the King James Bible. His everyday metaphors and images were almost as laced with the language of the Authorized Version as the terms in which he couched his revelations. He continued and enhanced a long tradition of typological interpretation. For him, as for others, Jesus Christ was virtually as much the focus of the Old Testament as of the New Testament, a focus reflected in the Book of Mormon. Biblical motifs such as the millennium and the organizational pattern of the primitive church were themes that interested others as much as they did the Prophet. Assumptions about the dispensational structure of history and about the unchanging nature of truth and the gospel were shared by many American Christians, including the Latter-day Saints. The peculiar biblicism of early Mormonism attracted sympathetic souls; this fact helps explain its survival and growth.

But though Smith was decidedly a man of his time and place, neither his use of the Bible nor his life as a whole is easily explained as the sum total of the historical forces acting upon him. Joseph Smith was uniquely Joseph Smith; he not only participated in his culture but with unusual energy and innovation struggled against it.

For Smith, the Bible was fundamentally important, but it was not *all*-important. Indeed, by itself it was an insufficient guide. It was subject to human error and the corruptions of transmission over the centuries. Others were aware of an imperfect Bible, of course, but, unlike them, Smith's broad conceptions of authorship and strong sense of divine authority led him to reconstruct its contents with enormous confidence. His scriptural perspective was sharply at odds with biblical apologists like millenarian Alexander Carson: "If the Bible is a book partly human and partly divine, it cannot, as a whole, be the word of God, nor be justly ascribed to Him as its sole author. . . . To be God's book, it must be His in matter and in words, in substance and in form."[69]

Even where the meaning of the original text had not, in Smith's view, been altered in the precarious course of its transmission, his belief in progressive, conceptual revelation and his faith in his own prophetic insight induced him, in contrast to the conscious intent of most Christians, to subordinate the inherited text to the truth as he saw it—and he believed he saw it well.[70] Like many who wrote the Bible, and unlike his nineteenth-century antagonists, he felt his access to Deity was more direct than the written word itself; his authority was therefore at least as great as the text's. If Sydney Ahlstrom's and Fawn Brodie's label of "megalomania" serves any useful purpose in describing such attitudes and practices, we must also remember it is equally applicable to many biblical writers and prophets, with whom Smith himself identified.

We have noticed that Smith's conception of scripture was capacious when compared with those of his contemporaries. Scripture was, for him, subject to recapitulation and expansion and correction, not necessarily confined to written form, adapted to human capacity, and sometimes of only temporary applicability. Some early Saints went further than this, perhaps with Smith's approbation. W. W. Phelps, for instance, editorialized that many parts of the Bible, applicable anciently, had little value for nineteenth-century affairs.[71] The Bible fundamentally shaped Joseph Smith's developing thought, and he in turn reshaped biblical theology for himself and for those who followed him. As distinct from his evangelical rivals, he did not seek to enthrone the Bible as final authority; he sought rather to restore the authority, truth, and prophetic gifts recorded in the Bible.

Perhaps Joseph Smith's creative use of the Hebrew language best

69. Quoted in Sandeen, *The Roots of Fundamentalism,* p. 111.

70. He thought he saw it so well that he was sometimes oblivious to the fact that he and his people were also confined by culture. The Mormons, he once declared, really believe what the Bible foretells, while "the sects" hold only to "interpretations" of the book. *Elders' Journal* (July 1838): 42–43; cited in Irving, "Mormonism and the Bible," pp. 42–43.

71. *EMS* 1 (July 1832): 13.

symbolizes his approach to the Bible as a whole. He "delight[ed] in reading the word of the Lord in the original," he said, but he did not devote himself with careful precision to determining by erudition the intent of the ancient authors. Joseph Smith used the Bible less as a scholar than as a poet—or a prophet.

3

Diversity and Development: The Bible Moves West

The uses to which Latter-day Saints put the Bible during the balance of the nineteenth century after Joseph Smith's death have not drawn great attention from students of Mormonism. However, in the long run these distinctive uses may prove a more enduring legacy separating the Saints from other Christians than more sensational but transitory affairs, such as polygamy or the Mormon attempt to establish a political theocracy.

Brigham Young and Orson Pratt, key figures in the unfolding of Mormon scriptural perspectives, shared a fundamental assumption of biblical harmony with Mormon views. Nevertheless, their emphases differed. In the three and one-half decades between Joseph Smith's death and their own, Pratt worked hard to hold Mormon theology together with the traditional Bible, and Young subordinated the Holy Book even more than had Smith.

After noting how deeply biblical the Mormon consciousness remained as the Saints migrated to the Rocky Mountains, this chapter contrasts the Church's president with its chief apologist, showing how their scriptural understandings represented both internal Mormon diversity, and development in Mormon thought following Joseph Smith's era. Comparisons with non-Mormon contemporaries are made along the way and summarized at the chapter's conclusion to suggest that, for all their similarities with others, Mormon approaches to the Bible helped keep the Saints "a peculiar people" into the 1880s.

The June 1844 murder of Joseph Smith subdued the thousands who had followed him, but tensions between the Saints and their neighbors abated only briefly. Soon it was clear that the series of moves that had taken the Saints from New York to Ohio, then to Missouri, and finally to Illinois, would have to continue.

But the Mormon movement did not wilt as its enemies had hoped.[1] If anything, Mormonism's self-conception as a Christianized antitype of biblical Israel may have grown even more intense for the major body of Saints. New England's well-studied Puritans provide an analogue. Scholars have traced a process of secularization over the course of several generations among the first American Puritans.[2] However, this trend was not unrelenting and not unambiguous. Robert Middlekauf has shown how in some ways the children of the founders were more representative of the heart of the Puritan experiment than were their parents.[3] So it was with the Mormons. Through the tragic murder of Joseph Smith, the Saints were furnished a martyr. Doctrine and Covenants 135:3 attests that the biblical precedent was not lost on the mourners. Hardly more than a year later, under mounting harassment from hostile neighbors, Brigham Young announced "the exodus of the nation of the only true Israel from these United States," thus launching one of the most dramatic chapters in American history.

It is true that the theocratic enterprise in the West, begun outside the bounds of the United States upon the Mormon arrival in the Great Basin in 1847, was rather quickly mitigated: first by the 1848 acquisition of Utah Territory by the U.S. government by means of the war with Mexico, and later by the completion in 1869 of the transcontinental railroad, which brought an increased and diversified population to the Mormon kingdom. Nevertheless, the Exodus under Brigham Young and the quasi-biblical colonization effort he directed were

1. For the conflicts that led to Smith's death, the departure of the Saints from the United States, and their journey to the Great Basin, see Arrington and Bitton, *The Mormon Experience*, chaps. 3 and 4, and the sources cited therein.

2. E.g., Joseph Haroutunian, *Piety versus Moralism: The Passing of the New England Theology* (reprint, New York: Harper & Row, 1970); Richard L. Bushman, *From Puritan to Yankee: Character and the Social Order in Connecticut, 1690–1765* (Cambridge: Harvard University Press, 1970).

3. *The Mathers: Three Generations of Puritan Intellectuals, 1596–1728* (New York: Oxford University Press, 1971).

of a scope far more vast than anything accomplished during Joseph Smith's lifetime. Mormon Israel in the American West took shape on a grand scale.

Of course, Christians of all sorts continued to identify with Bible peoples metaphorically; no one seemed to think it remarkable when some Methodist exhorter spoke of himself as "a teacher in Israel." But the Mormon bond with Israel was of a different order—again like that of the seventeenth-century New England Puritans.

Like the Puritans, those who followed Brigham Young westward felt they actually recapitulated key biblical episodes. In their own eyes, Mormons became the "Camp of Israel," organized, like those of the original Exodus, into companies of tens, fifties, and hundreds, with captains over each.

As they departed scenes of bloodshed and "bondage" in Illinois, the first Saints to begin their journey faced a treacherous February crossing of the frigid Mississippi River, which, though neither so broad nor so deep as the Red Sea, is nevertheless at Nauvoo more than a mile wide, and during that winter season was laced with "running ice." But within a few days, a providential cold spell descended, allowing the main body of Saints to cross the river on an ice bridge without wetting their feet. Several bands of the starving and desperate emigrants reported miracles in which easily captured quail and a mannalike substance called honeydew allowed their survival. En route to their Promised Land, the migrating Mormons encamped at such places as "Mount Pisgah," so named by Parley Pratt, who pronounced it as beautiful as Bible terrain.

After wintering (1846–1847) in what is now Nebraska, a vanguard of 144 men—the number corresponding to the "twelve times twelve" cited in the Book of Revelation—pushed on ahead of the main body to prepare the way. Months later, near the end of their thousand-mile trek, the exhausted Chosen People shouted, "Hosanna! Hosanna! Hosanna!" at the first sight of their final destination. Moreover, they soon discovered that the physical setting of their new kingdom was more than an alluvial basin bounded by the peaks of the Wasatch Mountains. It was "Palestine turned around," a portentous territorial echo of mountainous Israel, with a river they named "Jordan" flowing north from a fresh to a dead sea (from Utah Lake, the "western Galilee," to the Great Salt Lake).

The Latter-day errand into the western wilderness enabled the

Saints to build up a theocratic kingdom of Zion. From the Mormon perspective, their endeavor was a direct fulfillment of Isaianic prophecy: "It [was coming] to pass in the last days that the mountain of the Lord's house [was being established] in the top of the mountains." Following Hebraic custom, Brigham Young provided for the poor by instructing grain owners to allow gleaners to follow the rakers and binders. Whenever difficulties arose among the Saints, modern Israel's leaders reasoned, like Old Testament prophets, that the problems were rooted in disobedience and unrighteousness. Many Mormons saw their trials as an inevitable prelude to the millennium.

The gathering and building of Zion were literal and physical, just as the Saints were sure the reestablishment of the nation of Israel, centered at Jerusalem, would be. In Zion's midst was to be a new temple, carefully patterned, in certain respects, after Solomon's own. Here the desert was to "blossom as the rose." Here the Saints went public with their polygynous "patriarchal order" of marriage. Here they lived in forced exile from their former country, now become Egypt. One day, they knew, they would return.[4]

Brigham Young

The Moses/Joshua/Solomon who presided over this neobiblical enterprise was Brigham Young, whose importance in shaping Mormonism and assuring its survival is legendary. Like Joseph Smith and thousands of others in the new United States, Brigham began life in New England (Vermont, 1801) and in his youth was taken by his family to upstate New York in search of economic improvement. His family's near-subsistence living meant he enjoyed little formal schooling. His only intellectual improvement came from reading scripture, and his

4. D&C 20:11; Moench, "Nineteenth-Century Mormons: The New Israel"; England, *The Life and Thought of Orson Pratt,* pp. 115, 134; Gates, with Widtsoe, *The Life Story of Brigham Young,* p. 235; Shipps, *Mormonism,* pp. 58–65; Paul H. Peterson, "The Mormon Reformation of 1856–1857: The Rhetoric and the Reality," *Journal of Mormon History* 15 (1989): 63, 75, 83 n. 45. For examples of Old Testament prophecies, precedents, and "types" of these Mormon experiences, see Deut. 1:15; Exod. 14:22, 16:13, 15, 35; Lev. 19:10; Num. 11:9, 31; Isa. 2:2–5, 35:1; Mic. 4:1–3.

parents taught their children "all the time . . . to reverence the holy Book. . . ."[5]

The Bible continued as a controlling religious force in Young's early adulthood. When he returned home from his day's carpentry, he typically cooked the evening meal, cleaned up, and read from the Bible to his invalid wife, Miriam, who had contracted tuberculosis. He joined the Reformed Methodists in 1823 but was dissatisfied with their scriptural illumination: "As I became acquainted with smart, intelligent, literary priests . . . I would begin to ask questions on certain texts of Scripture; but they would always leave me as they found me, in the dark." "I did not read the Bible as they read it," he said, and he yearned for religion that conformed to the scriptures and appealed to his reason.[6]

In 1830 a missionary presented the Book of Mormon to Young's brother as a supplement to the Bible. His father, brothers, and sisters were, somewhat to their surprise, quickly won over. Brigham declared himself more cautious: "I watched to see whether good common sense was manifest; and if they had that, I wanted them to present it in accordance with the Scriptures. . . ."[7] Two years after his introduction to Mormonism he was baptized—drawn to the Book of Mormon by its plain, biblical style, its answers to questions of life and afterlife, and its clarification of obscure passages in Isaiah, Revelation, and elsewhere.

Although in future years Young would so qualify his allegiance that his assertions of biblical loyalty sometimes appear inconsistent, his position cannot really be understood unless one grasps how thoroughly the Bible influenced his formative religious conceptions. Despite his extraordinarily eventful and busy career, he commonly studied the Holy Book in the evenings and on Sundays throughout his life. A typical journal entry during a proselytizing mission reads, "I preached in the evening upon the evidences of the authenticity of the Bible and the Book of Mormon." He regularly urged his followers to read the Bible, and certain of his sermons reveal the breadth of his own study. He took for granted the need for sinners to be "dealt with according to [biblical prescriptions]." He commended the efforts of

5. Arrington, *Brigham Young*, p. 21; *JD*, 6:290.
6. *JD*, 5:73; 15:164–65; 11:254.
7. Ibid., 8:38.

the American Bible Society in the territory of Utah, and castigated the nation for removing the Bible from its schools. From his first years until his death in 1877 he reverenced the Bible, and professed astonishment at the perpetual hearsay that questioned Mormons's biblical belief. For him, "the Bible, when it is understood, is one of the simplest books in the world, for, as far as it is translated correctly, it is nothing but truth. . . ."[8]

Once Young's enduring and fundamental belief in the Bible is comprehended, one can examine the bounds he gradually put on scriptural authority without undue distortion. Following Joseph Smith, Young felt the Bible was in places mistranslated. The Bible was a fountain of truth, to be sure, but for Young it came to be but one source of truth among others. And the other sources were not simply additional Mormon scriptures:

> "Shall I sit down and read the Bible, the Book of Mormon, and the book of Covenants all the time?" says one. "Yes . . . and when you have done so, you may be nothing but a sectarian after all." It is your duty to study . . . everything upon the face of the earth in addition to reading those books.[9]

Scripture was essential, but not even biblical authority could substitute for wisdom born of actual experience. Young also insisted that although there was no real contradiction between the revelations of the Bible and modern Mormon scriptures, apparent conflicts would surface unless readers read "with the Spirit." Without revelation, some might think they believed the Bible but in reality fail because belief without understanding was nonsense:

> There is not one of us who professed to be Christians before we embraced this Gospel could have borne to be told that we did not believe all that is written in the Old and New Testaments. We should have deemed such a statement very unwarranted and past enduring; yet such was the fact.

8. Eldon J. Watson, ed., *Manuscript History of Brigham Young, 1801–1844,* 2 vols. (SLC: Eldon J. Watson), p. 84; Gates, with Widtsoe, *The Life Story,* pp. 281, 75; *JD,* 1:47, 237; 8:27–31; Watson, ed., *A Chronological Compilation of Known Addresses of Brigham Young,* 1:45, 3:3. A sampling of Young's public sermons demonstrates his explicit and permanent reverence for the Bible: *JD,* 1:243 (1853); 3:335–36 (1856); 9:297 (1862); 14:113, 135–36, 226–27 (1871); 16:71–77 (1873).

9. Gates, with Widtsoe, *The Life Story,* p. 281; *JD,* 14:208.

In time, Young came to limit the Holy Book more severely:

> I cannot say what a minister once said to me. I asked him if he believed
> [all] the Bible, and he replied, "Yes, every word of it." . . . "Well,"
> said I, "you can beat me at believing, that's certain. As I read the Bible
> it contains the words of the Father and Son, angels, good and bad,
> Lucifer, the devil, of wicked men and of good men, and some are lying
> and some . . . are telling the truth; and if you believe it all to be the
> word of God you can go beyond me.

The ancient prophets, Young thought, sometimes acted foolishly, and
not all parts of the Bible were of equal value. Despite his people's
experiential links with Old Testament events, Young preferred the
New Testament, treasuring the sayings of Jesus in particular.[10]

Young's belief that scripture was written according to human ability
to receive and convey divine truth had important implications when
placed in the Mormon theological context of progressive revelation.
Thus the author of any scripture that seemed to conflict with his own
new insights was either being misinterpreted or was to be excused for
having a more limited view than Young had. New conceptions sometimes supersede old ones. The revelations of the Bible were given to
ancient people and therefore did not necessarily apply altogether to
current circumstances; in the same way, "what is now required of the
people may not be required a hundred years hence." In limited and
sometimes inconsistent ways, Young's pre–Civil War views anticipated the shifting notions of later nineteenth-century America: from
truth conceived as "unchanging evermore" to "change" as itself
among the most basic of truths.[11]

Young meant no disrespect to the Bible, but he differed from
most American religious leaders in that he was sometimes openly
amused by the exaggerated, almost idolatrous, veneration it received, just as he was amused by the near-adoration given early
Mormon leaders now grown old, like Parley Pratt or himself, by

10. *JD,* 7:332; 14:208, 74; 1:237; 12:309.

11. Watson, ed., *A Chronological Compilation,* 1:iii; *JD,* 7:332. Of the two reigning
conceptions of the nature of "truth"—its accessibility and its immutability—immutability was under more immediate challenge in America in the middle of the nineteenth
century. Most people seem to have thought they could see truth clearly, but the sense of
a new age and the rejection of old authorities encouraged the belief that truth (or one's
perceptions of it) was changing. See Marsden, in *The Bible in America,* ed. Hatch and
Noll, p. 81.

those who "felt that should they come into [the] presence [of the famed leaders] they would have to pull off their shoes, as the ground would be so holy upon which they trod." Speaking more particularly of the Bible, he asked, "Do you know what distance and age accomplish? They produce in people the most reverential awe that can be imagined." The truths contained in the Bible are plain, "but send [them] abroad and give [them] antiquity, and [they are] at once clothed with mystery" in human minds. Biblical truth is to be revered, certainly, but no more than modern truth. Young noted that any of his discourses, all given extempore, were, "when . . . copied and approved by me . . . as good Scripture as is couched in this Bible. . . ."[12]

Young's inclination to emphasize the primacy of "living oracles" over written scripture contributed to an increasing tendency among Mormon leaders to reduce the Bible's relative status. Although the Bible remained basic to Mormon thought, of course, the trend to limit its authority, muted under Joseph Smith, grew stronger from the 1850s to the 1870s. Thus Apostle Orson Hyde (1854): "The words contained in this Bible are merely a history of what is gone by; . . . the words . . . of God, given to a generation under one set of circumstances, [will not] serve for another generation under another set of circumstances. . . . The Bible is not a sufficient guide." John Taylor, who succeeded Young as Church president, offered similar sentiments. As one Mormon elder put it, if a certain doctrine declared by the current Prophet "cannot be proved by the Bible, it is alright."[13]

Orson Pratt

The tendency to reduce the Bible's relative status was countered in some quarters—most strongly, among those of influence, by Apostle Orson Pratt. Far less well remembered today than Brigham Young, Pratt was in his own day "the St. Paul of Mormondom." He was among the foremost intellectuals in the Mormonism of his time. His fifteen pamphlets on Mormon doctrine rank among the most signifi-

---

12. *JD*, 3:335–36; 13:264, 95.
13. *JD*, 2:75; *MS* 9:323–24; David John Buerger, "The Adam–God Doctrine," *Dialogue* 15 (Spring 1982): 20.

cant contributions to LDS theology in the nineteenth century, and were considered important enough to be reviewed in the leading literary and philosophical journals of Europe. At the popular level, his writings and those of his brother, Parley, made them for many Americans and Europeans the best-known Saints other than Brigham Young and Joseph Smith.

Pratt was one of the original Twelve Apostles chosen in 1835, later became the official Church Historian, and was the first Mormon to enter the Salt Lake Valley—dedicating the site of modern Salt Lake City before Brigham Young ever saw it. He was for a time the president of all branches of the Church in Great Britain "and adjacent countries," and, had he not been briefly excommunicated in 1842, might have succeeded Young as president of the entire Church. Most significant for present purposes, he was the leading Mormon scripturist.[14]

Pratt's ancestors had followed Thomas Hooker to Connecticut in the 1630s to escape the hegemony of John Cotton and Massachusetts Puritanism. Later Pratts forsook both New England and the orthodox church during the eighteenth century, moving west to New York State, where Orson, born in 1811, lived as a boy in several locations along the Hudson Valley.

Bible doctrines of morality and honesty were "diligently instilled" in young Orson from the first. Connecticut law had required all heads of families to teach religion in the home, "leading in family prayer, catechizing their children . . . teaching . . . [them] to read so that they might study the Bible." This was one Puritan injunction the Pratts did not surrender.[15]

Orson was eventually singed by the fires of New York's "burnt-over district." He lived in nearby Canaan at the time of the famous New Lebanon conference in 1827, when Lyman Beecher battled Charles Finney over "new measures" in revivalism. Between ages ten and

14. For appraisals of Pratt's intellectual stature among early Mormon leaders, see Lyon, "Orson Pratt," p. 125; England, *Pratt*, pp. xv–xvi; Leonard Arrington, "The Intellectual Tradition of the Latter-day Saints," *Dialogue* 4 (Spring 1969): 13–26; and the essays by Crawley, Whittaker, and Paul in *Dialogue* 15 (Autumn 1982). As an articulator of theology in Mormonism's earliest years, Orson was not so important as his brother, Parley, but for the last twenty-five years of his life Orson was considered the Saints' intellectual champion.

15. Bushman, *From Puritan to Yankee*, p. 14; England, *Pratt*, pp. 4, 8–9.

nineteen, Pratt felt "a great anxiety to be prepared for a future state." Like most of his father's family, however, he did not formally join a church until he encountered Mormon elders in September 1830. "[As] soon as [their preaching] penetrated my ears, I knew that if the Bible was true, their doctrine was true."[16]

Belief in the Book of Mormon did not necessarily mean that Pratt preferred it over the traditional scriptures. When he was not explicitly demonstrating the Book of Mormon's superiority, he tended, like most first-generation Saints, to use the familiar Bible, particularly early in his career. During his proselytizing missions between 1833 and 1837, for example, Pratt cited Bible passages ten times as often as he cited the Book of Mormon.[17]

Like other Saints, Pratt identified deeply with biblical figures and events. When in 1834 Joseph Smith (acting as Joshua) organized "Zion's Camp" (a quasi-military expedition to help defend his flock against those modern Canaanites, the mobs of Missouri), Pratt naturally reported his participation in biblical terms: "Behold the presence of the Lord was with us by day and by night and his Angel went before us to prepare the way." Years later, caught up by the numbers and sacrifices of European converts whose passage to America he supervised, his prose waxed prophetic, laden with biblical images:

> The poor trust in Zion for a place of deliverance, see them come from the islands and from the nations afar off! See mighty ships spread forth their sails to the winds of heaven, filled with Zion's children! Hear their cheerful songs, as they are swiftly carried up the rolling current of the broad majestic rivers of Zion's land. . . . These are the pastures of the Lord . . . bespangled with the flowers of Eden! . . . Here they gradually ascend the great highway of the redeemed, til they gain the mountaintops . . . the lovely vales of Ephraim.[18]

Pratt's sacrifices for the cause helped him think in Old Testament terms, and his witness of the miracles of "the Restoration" led him to repeat Joseph Smith's belief that the journals of the modern-day

---

16. *JD,* 7:177.

17. Underwood, "Book of Mormon Usage," p. 53 n. 49.

18. Watson, comp. *Pratt Journals,* May 6, 1834; Pratt, *Latter-day Kingdom, or, The Preparations for the Second Advent* (London: L.D.S. Book and Star Depot, 1857), p. 125.

apostles would later prove as valuable as the records of the New Testament.[19]

Pratt's most prominent trait when using the Bible was his lifelone zeal to apply prophecies to the events of the Mormon restoration. His early diaries set the pattern and show that when proselytizing he emphasized the millennium, gifts of the spirit, the need of more revelations and miracles, the scattering and gathering of Israel, the fulfillment of Ezekiel 37 and Isaiah 29 in the arrival of the Book of Mormon, and the establishment of Zion.

How literally, specifically, and confidently he applied biblical prophecy to Mormon settings is suggested by an 1872 sermon: "I will read . . . the 11th verse of the 85th Psalm: 'Truth shall spring out of the earth, and righteousness shall look down from heaven.' Forty-five years ago this morning this prophecy, so far as it relates to 'truth springing out of the earth,' was fulfilled. Forty-five years ago, early this morning, plates resembling gold were taken from the earth. . . ." This literalism and specificity also applied to more than mere abstract theology, as when, taking scriptural precedent seriously, the twenty-year-old Pratt electrified Orleans County, New Hampshire, by healing a woman on her deathbed.[20]

In Joseph Smith's day, Mormons were best known for their extrabiblical scripture. In the era of Brigham Young, however, they gained their notoriety from the practice of polygamy. Until it was officially abandoned in 1890, many Mormon leaders defended the practice with scripture. Orson Pratt—once greatly troubled by the doctrine—was the master in this arena. Other apologists rarely found biblical justification not already mined by him.[21] When in 1852 Brigham Young chose to announce the practice publicly, he quite naturally turned to Pratt. Thereafter Pratt spoke and wrote more in defense of "the peculiar institution" than any other Latter-day Saint.

19. *JD*, 7:36.

20. *JD*, 15:178–79; England, *Pratt*, p. 30. For another example of healing, see Watson, comp. *Pratt Journals*, July 4, 1833, p. 19.

21. For examples of scriptural defenses of polygamy by Mormon leaders, see *JD*, 2:78–79; 13:38–42, 197–200; 23:225–30; 25:89–90; 26:117–27. For additional samples of Pratt's position, see 6:35–64; 13:188–89; 16:171–85. Pratt's arguments, which were well established by 1854, combined scriptural with historical-social and constitutional arguments. Consult Whittaker, "Early Mormon Pamphleteering," pp. 333–43, and Whittaker, "The Bone in the Throat: Orson Pratt and the Public Announcement of Plural Marriage," *Western Historical Quarterly* 18 (April 1987): 294–314.

His scriptural apology climaxed in an 1870 debate with Dr. J. P. Newman, chaplain of the United States Senate, who, followed by the nation's press, invaded Salt Lake City to champion the cause of an indignant evangelical America. The three-day debate ("Does the Bible Sanction Polygamy?") drew front-page coverage in the East as well as in Zion.[22]

In some ways the logic used by the two antagonists paralleled that of opposing sides in an earlier national debate. When the slavery question began to tear the nation apart in the first half of the century, the Bible's authority was so taken for granted by most Americans that both pro- and antislavery pamphleteers commonly turned to it to buttress their arguments.[23]

Pratt's biblical rationale for polygamy resembled the South's scriptural defense of slavery. Focusing on a dozen or so Old Testament texts,[24] Pratt argued that polygamy, far from being condemned in Israel, was assumed as legitimate and merely governed as a matter of course. He pointed out that some of the most righteous men in the Old Testament, such as Abraham, had been polygamists with God's approbation. In what was perhaps a lost cause, Newman contested the proper contextual interpretation of the passages, and eventually hinged his entire case on a marginal and improper reading of Leviticus 18:18.[25]

What is most interesting about the debate is not the actual content of the tedious exegetical straining but the fact that both combatants found it necessary to structure the discussion as they did: Does the

22. The debate was published in 1874 as *The Bible & Polygamy*. All references to the debate not otherwise noted derive from this document.

23. The logic probably most universally employed by slavery's defenders was biblically derived. For a typical example, see H. Shelton Smith, et al, eds., *American Christianity: An Historical Interpretation with Representative Documents*, 2 vols. (New York: Scribner's, 1963), 2:201–5.

24. He was especially fond of such passages as Gen. 1:28 (what better way than polygamy to obey God's call to "multiply and replenish the earth"?); Deut. 21:10–17, 25:5–10; Exod. 21:7–11; Num. 31:15–18. To a lesser extent, Pratt also called on New Testament support, even arguing on some occasions that Jesus probably engaged in plural marriage.

25. At least Newman failed in his attempt to demonstrate that the Bible as a whole condemned polygamy, a form of marriage that was in fact taken for granted in much of the Old Testament.

Bible Sanction Polygamy? As the August 14, 1870 *New York Times*
put it:

> The factitious importance which the discussion will give to the Mormon
> views . . . is greatly to be depreciated [*sic*]. By engaging in it Dr.
> Newman virtually admits that the laws prohibiting polygamy are based
> upon an interpretation, which may be right or wrong, of the Sacred
> Scriptures. . . . That the tournament of quotations now in progress at
> Salt Lake will not in the least affect the marriage laws of the states is
> but trifling consolation in view of the mischief which may be done to
> weak-minded people, who would repudiate the plainest dictum of com-
> mon sense in the nineteenth century, if they were once convinced that it
> did not hold good in the time of the Flood.

Clearly, Newman was convinced of the illegitimacy of polygamous
marriages on cultural and personal grounds, quite apart from the
biblical position. This is suggested by his nonbiblical arguments,
which occupied one-third of his remarks. Polygamy was seen as a
threat to Victorian values. But Newman went on to use the Bible in
an attempt to legitimate these more fundamental concerns to a Bible-
believing American public: the Mormons could thereby be exposed
as unbiblical, hence unchristian, and therefore a threat to the nation.

Some of Pratt's claims were equally oblique to the issue of biblical
sanction. There were, he said, thousands of prostitutes and mistresses
walking the streets of officially monogamous New York—sins not to
be found among polygamous nations. Moreover, accusing his accuser
of cultural conceit, he noted that polygamy had been far more widespread than monogamy in human societies.[26] However, for the most
part Pratt was forthright about the Bible's relationship to Mormon
marriage customs. Although he did insist that his people embraced
the Bible as a rule of faith, he also frankly insisted that the Saints
practiced polygamy not because the Bible allowed it but because
God, through Joseph Smith, had commanded them. In resorting to
biblical justification, therefore, he did so in part as an effort at public
relations: If the Bible itself sanctioned polygamy, why, he reasoned,
should the Mormons' critics not leave them in peace?

During the course of the debate, Pratt revealed several of his life-

26. His point was historically accurate, if not altogether germane. See Reay
Tannahill, *Sex in History* (New York: Stein & Day, Scarborough Books edition, 1982),
p. 20.

long biblical perspectives. His literalism—or occasionally hyperliteralism, for at times he seemed to take scriptural images more literally than the biblical authors themselves—was easily a match for Newman's. For example, both men, in contrast to Brigham Young, took the creation of Eve from Adam's rib at face value. Both also accepted Bishop Ussher's chronology and the Genesis account of the Flood. Their arguments were full of phrases like "God says in the 37th Psalm" rather than "The author of the 37th Psalm says." Newman expressed his hermeneutic explicitly:

> [God] has spoken to us in terms by which we can understand. . . . But . . . all that is written in the Bible is neither approved by the Almighty, nor was it written for our imitation. . . . We are to read Bible history as we read . . . Hume, Gibbon and Bancroft, with this distinction—when we read [secular historians] we are not always sure that what we read is true. . . . The Bible is true, whether it be prophetic truth . . . or historic truth. We should therefore make a distinction, according to the kind of composition we are reading. If we are reading history, read it as history, and make a distinction between what is simply recorded as part and parcel of the record of a great nation . . . and that which is recorded there for our imitation. . . .

Pratt would generally have concurred. He specifically agreed that many practices of the Bible were simply historical facts, not necessarily given as moral models. Brigham Young would not have acknowledged with Newman that everything in the Bible was true, but, for all his urging of biblical literalism, he did insist with both men that not all accurately recorded biblical behavior was intended for imitation.[27]

Unity and Diversity in Mormon Approaches to the Bible

Beyond the scriptural defense of polygamy, Pratt's use of the Bible had much in common with Brigham Young's use, as well as significant points of contrast. Seen together, the two men reveal two major thrusts of Mormon scriptural usage through the bulk of the nineteenth century.

Both Young and Pratt had been attracted to Mormonism by what they saw as its compatibility with the Bible and its fulfillment of

27. *JD,* 14:208, 74.

biblical prophecy. Both in turn gathered converts to Mormon ranks by reasoning from the Bible with a quiver full of literally interpreted proof-texts. Although they agreed the Bible was an insufficient guide to religious life, they reacted aggressively to accusations that Mormonism had thrown the Book out. Young went on to echo Joseph Smith's innocent assertion that others "interpret" the Bible; Mormons alone take it just as it stands. Apparently not conscious of how well his description applied to himself and his people, Young ridiculed the outside "Christian world" for using the Bible selectively, for altering its sense to suit private tastes, for saying it was made for people under different circumstances, and for failing to believe it in its literal sense.[28]

As noted earlier, Pratt and Young also shared a sense of equality and role identification with biblical authors, Pratt going so far as to offer "the First Epistle of Orson Pratt" in his periodical, *The Seer*. Even more than Young, he emphasized the Bible's transmission difficulties, translation errors, and the haphazard process by which it was canonized. He also joined Young in declaring that scripture was not the sole source of God's truth.[29] Both men stressed that the "fruits" of Joseph Smith's labors, when measured against biblical criteria, proved the authenticity of Smith's call from God. Smith's life conformed to the prophetic pattern seen in Daniel, Isaiah, and John's Revelation. Mormon organization matched every feature of the New Testament church.[30]

Like Pratt, Young held to the theoretical superiority of the Book of Mormon, but in actual use he preferred the Bible. What historian Grant Underwood noticed implicitly in his study of the Saints' public Book of Mormon usage from 1830 to 1846, Young observed explicitly of himself thirty years later:

> I was brought up a Christian, very strictly, and was taught to read the Bible, consequently it is natural for me to believe it—it is according to my traditions, and also from the spirit of revelation from God unto myself. In all my teachings, I have taught the gospel from the Bible. I

28. Ibid., 1:237–45; 13:213–14, 235–41.

29. Ibid., 7:22–38, 14:257–60, 16:218, 17:268–70. An 1849 pamphlet, published under Pratt's direction, asserts that "all good books" are possible sources of God's Word.

30. *JD*, 16:71–77; Pratt, *Divine Authority, or The Question, Was Joseph Smith Sent of God?* (Liverpool: R. James, 1848), pp. 16–17.

found therein every doctrine . . . the Latter-day Saints believe in . . .
therefore I do not refer to the Book of Mormon as often as I otherwise
should.[31]

Despite the many similarities, Young's use of the Bible was not, of
course, identical with Pratt's. The reactions of the two to the en-
croachments of science, for example, reveal a more ambiguous relationship in their usage. Pratt, like many contemporary Protestant
theologians, held his religious beliefs to be as empirical as his scientific observations. He shared with other American thinkers the assumptions that truth was accessible to anyone possessed of common
sense and that God revealed himself equally obviously in nature and
in scripture. Like his non-Mormon contemporaries, he spoke easily
of "plain scripture facts" that could be mined like a storehouse.[32] If he
arrived at different theological results than they did, it was largely
because he began with different theological premises.

However, unlike Joseph Smith and Brigham Young, who proclaimed the gospel on their own prophetic authority, Pratt shared the
scholarly, scientific temperament of many evangelical apologists for
the Bible. Perhaps because his scientific work was focused in the
physical sciences, he died (1881) before seriously engaging the challenge of Darwinian evolution. Throughout his life he demonstrated
his belief that science and Mormon theology supported each other.
This dimension of Pratt's work and the Scottish Common Sense Philosophy on which it rested have been examined by other scholars.[33]

Brigham Young was equally devoted to common sense, but not the
philosophical kind. Yet he was sometimes remarkably open to new
knowledge. He was, for example, quite aware of the controversial
"new geology" that had been developing for decades in Great Britain, calling into question the biblical account of creation.

In America the clash between geology and religion was softened
because the nation's most prominent geologist, Benjamin Silliman,

31. *JD,* 16:73. Cf. Underwood, "Book of Mormon Usage," pp. 56–61.

32. *JD,* 15:241–42.

33. For the scientific outlook and its relation to the Bible in America, see the good
brief discussion by George Marsden in *The Bible in America,* ed. Hatch and Noll, pp.
81–95, and the more extended treatments by Hovenkamp, *Science and Religion in
America,* and Bozeman, *Protestants in the Age of Science.* For Pratt specifically, see
Whittaker, "Orson Pratt," pp. 29–32, 38 n. 28, and England, *Pratt,* chaps. 5, 8, 11,
especially pp. 66–67, 152–53, 167–68, 290, 295.

sought to harmonize conflicting views. The Bible, Silliman insisted, was not a scientific textbook. The Hebrew word for "day" in the creation account should properly be understood loosely as "aeon." His student, Edward Hitchcock, went on to explain the earth's long history as a further revelation of God's work. This solution provided welcome relief to some Americans but was sharply contested by others because it implicitly challenged one of the basic assumptions of the Common Sense philosophy that dominated American thought before the Civil War: the self-evident clarity of truth. From the Common Sense perspective, the meaning of scripture, like truth generally, must be plain. If God wished to reveal himself, he must have done so in plain language that could be understood by the common people. Andover Theological Seminary's Moses Stuart, for example, thought the attempt to interpret the "days" of Genesis as long, indefinite periods of time was a perverse attempt to wrest the plain meaning of scripture to soothe the itching ears of scientifically informed modern readers. "I am unable to see," he wrote, "how the discoveries of modern science . . . can determine the meaning of Moses' words." Persuaded that Moses thought the days of Genesis were twenty-four-hour periods, Stuart, probably the leading American biblical scholar of the era, was willing to choose the perspicuity of scripture over the perspicuity of nature; he dismissed the findings of geology and insisted that the earth was only six thousand years old.

The Silliman-Hitchcock and Stuart camps each had followers, but many—perhaps most—Americans knew and cared little about scientific method. The discoveries of geology remained only a vague threat to traditional faith. The forces alienating broad sectors of American Protestantism from the newer forms of modern thought, long powered by anti-intellectual revivalism, gathered new momentum at mid-century.[34]

Brigham Young's position was in one sense more "liberal" even than that of Hitchcock and his students. Not a scholar himself and easily put off by what he saw as scholars' (including Pratt's) pretentious ways, Young still wished to distance the Mormon response to science from what he took to be the common Christian reaction. Widespread infidel-

---

34. Stuart, "On the Alleged Obscurity of Prophecy," *Biblical Repository* 2 (April 1832): 217–45; "Examination of Genesis I, in reference to Geology," *Biblical Repository and Quarterly Observer* 7 (January 1836): 49; cited by Marsden, in *The Bible in America,* ed. Hatch and Noll, pp. 90–95; Conrad Wright, "The Religion of Geology," *New England Quarterly* 14 (1941): 335–58.

ity in the world did not surprise him, he said, because religious teachers often advanced notions "in opposition to . . . facts demonstrated by science," making it difficult for honest, informed people to embrace the claims of religion. Geology, to take a specific instance, "is a true science; not that I would say for a moment that all the conclusions and deductions of its professors are true, but its leading principles are; they are facts. . . ." "[Our] geologists . . . tell us that this earth has been in existence for thousands and millions of years . . . [and Mormonism] differ[s] from the Christian world, for our religion will not clash with the facts of science. . . ."[35]

What, then, of the biblical timetable? In addressing the issue, Young did not simply attack those who flatly chose the Bible over science; he also went quite beyond those who maintained that the Bible, though "not a scientific textbook," still never contradicted scientific fact. In a statement that would not altogether have displeased some future "higher critic," the Mormon prophet said:

> As for the Bible account of the creation we may say that the Lord gave it to Moses, or rather Moses obtained the history and traditions of the fathers, and from these picked out what he considered necessary, and that account has been handed down from age to age, and we have got it, no matter whether it is correct or not, and whether the Lord found the earth empty and void, whether he made it out of nothing or out of the rude elements; or whether he made it in six days or in as many millions of years, is and will remain a matter of speculation . . . unless he give revelation on the subject.[36]

Because of the distractions of the Civil War and its aftermath (among other reasons), Darwinism did not have a wide impact in America until the 1870s, 1880s, and, among many Americans, even decades later. Thus, like Orson Pratt, Young, who died in 1877, had little to say about evolutionary theory. He nevertheless implied the earth was peopled before Adam.[37] Moreover, speaking years before

35. *JD*, 14:115–17.

36. Ibid., 14:114–18.

37. In an 1876 letter to a son, Young did indicate a general antagonism to Darwinism (Jessee, ed., *"My Dear Son": Letters of Brigham Young to His Sons*, p. 199). In 1854 Apostle Orson Hyde preached that the world was inhabited before Adam. Young, who often and freely corrected the talks of Church leaders when they displeased him, stood and commended Hyde's "splendid address," from which he did not "wish to eradicate any items" (*JD*, 2:79, 88, 90).

German biblical scholarship was widely recognized in America as a threat to traditional faith, and possessing no category like the modern technical term *myth,* Young simply dismissed parts of the Genesis creation account as "baby stories" that should naturally be out-grown—this despite his frequent insistence on literally understood scripture. A free-flowing rendition of stenographic notes from an unpublished sermon of October 8, 1854 provides a useful example:

> When the Lord had organized the world, and filled the earth with animal and vegetable life, then he created man. . . . Moses made the Bible to say his wife was taken out of his side—was made of one of his ribs. As far as I know my ribs are equal on each side. The Lord knows if I had lost a rib for each wife I have, I should have had none left long ago. . . . As for the Lord taking a rib out of Adam's side to make a woman of, it would be just as true to say he took one out of my side.
>
> "But, Brother Brigham, would you make it appear that Moses did not tell the truth?"
>
> No, not a particle more than I would that your mother did not tell the truth when she told you that little Billy came from a hollow toad-stool. I would not accuse your mother of lying any more than I would Moses. The people in the days of Moses wanted to know things that [were] not for them, the same as your children do when they want to know where their little brother came from, and he answered them according to the level of their understandings, the same as mothers do their children.[38]

Such views did not please Orson Pratt.

One may focus on this displeasure to grasp a fundamental difference between the two men. This difference, with others, symbolizes the real diversity that existed among the Saints. Despite the many qualifications that must be made, it may be generalized that when the chips were down, Pratt felt obliged to reconcile all Mormon revelation and speculative theology with the Bible; Young instead urged the primacy of living seers and "common sense" and, if pushed to choose, was prepared to subordinate or even abandon parts of the Bible or other Mormon scriptures. On several occasions both before and after Joseph Smith's death, when some Mormon elder proclaimed that the Saints must be bound by the written word of God, Young responded that "compared with the living oracles those books are nothing to

38. The rendition of the notes is by Arrington, *Brigham Young,* pp. 197–98.

me." "I would not give the ashes of a rye straw for all those books . . . without the living oracles. . . ."

Pratt, though he too argued in the abstract for the superiority of modern revelation and though he felt forced to defer to Young, was never fully reconciled to this view. He felt he could disprove his leader's assertions by the scriptures. For example, Young ridiculed the Genesis notion that Adam was literally created from dust and Eve from Adam's rib. He went on to speculate that Adam and Eve were resurrected, celestial beings from another world who had fallen to an earthly state. Pratt thought it preposterous that resurrected personages should "fall" and become mortal again. He preferred the Genesis account.[39]

Conversely, much to Young's displeasure, Pratt preached that the one God of the Bible was really a complex of traits shared by many individuals who had achieved exaltation:

> All . . . Gods are equal in power . . . in glory . . . each possesses a fulness of truth . . . of light, of intelligence. . . . When we speak of only one God . . . let it be distinctly remembered, that we have no reference to any particular person or substance, but to *truth* dwelling in a vast variety of substances.[40]

Young thought such unqualified polytheism was tantamount to atheism, but Pratt felt his conclusions were the only way to reconcile Joseph Smith's doctrine of the plurality of gods with the Bible's entrenched monotheism.[41]

Other differences between the men were also important. In his sermons Pratt was everywhere systematic, academic, and logically persuasive within the framework of his assumptions. His citations of biblical texts were direct, frequent, relatively exact, and often done from memory. They were most often marshaled not to urge his hearers to more "Christian" lives but to demonstrate the fulfillment of prophecy or the scriptural legitimacy of LDS concepts. With his scien-

39. Watson, ed., *A Chronological Compilation,* vol. 3 (March 30, 1856) and 1:iii; Bergera, "Pratt–Young Controversies," pp. 11, 13, 20, 52; England, *Pratt,* chap. 9, especially pp. 190–91; Arrington, *Brigham Young,* pp. 207–9, 407.

40. *The Seer* 1:24.

41. Pratt to Young, November 4, 1853, quoted in England, *Pratt,* p. 190; Scott G. Kenney, ed., *Wilford Woodruff's Journal,* 9 vols. (Midvale, UT: Signature Books, 1983), 4:287–89 (September 17, 1854).

tific mind, he often used the Bible, like many scholars outside his faith, as a compendium of facts requiring only careful scrutiny and classification. Following such a procedure, one needed simply to follow where scripture led. Other American scholars were sure that both scripture and nature verified Christian claims; Pratt knew that both witnessed to Mormonism.[42]

By contrast, Brigham Young, as president of the Church, rarely used the Bible to prove points of doctrine, as he had done when a missionary. After securely lodging his followers in the West, Young never physically left the Great Basin. He was aware that the nation eavesdropped, of course, but he spoke primarily and confidently to his own people. When making a point over the pulpit, he might vaguely observe that "the Bible says" thus and so, but his talks were often practical (exhorting followers to greater sacrifice, reflecting on the coming of the railroad, offering advice on women's fashions). Even when his sermons were theological, they rarely centered on a scriptural text to be elucidated. And on the relatively infrequent occasions when he did cite the Bible, Young used it incidentally, anecdotally, without reference to chapter and verse, as a means to illustrate some truth made on his own authority. Occasionally, when advancing a doctrine or practice, he might include the general assertion that nowhere did the Bible disagree with his views. The Bible supported Mormon theology, Young sincerely believed, but its fund of useful stories interested him most.[43]

Pratt's and Young's scriptural perspectives thus had both important similarities and important differences. This blend of Mormon diversity and cohesiveness—as well its evolution—is further clarified if one thinks carefully about how Pratt's and Young's biblical usage related to Joseph Smith's.

Change over Time

During his lifetime Smith dominated Mormon biblical style, and in fact tended to attract to his movement those who understood scrip-

42. Marsden, *Fundamentalism*, pp. 56ff.; Whittaker, "Pratt," p. 30.
43. Cf. the similar emphasis among black Christians: Henry Mitchell, *Black Preaching* (New York: Harper & Row, 1979), p. 113. In stressing Young's weaker sermonic attachment to the Bible vis-à-vis Pratt, I am summarizing tendencies within a great mass of varying and sometimes contradictory material. For a counterexample, see *JD*, 3:116.

Joseph Smith by unknown artist, c. 1840. (Courtesy Church Archives, The Church of Jesus Christ of Latter-day Saints.)

Joseph Smith by unknown artist, c. 1840. (Courtesy Church Archives, The Church of Jesus Christ of Latter-day Saints.)

Brigham Young in 1847, around the time of the departure of the first pioneer company for the Salt Lake Valley. (Courtesy Church Archives, The Church of Jesus Christ of Latter-day Saints.)

Brigham Young, c. 1860. (Courtesy Church Archives, The Church of Jesus
Christ of Latter-day Saints.)

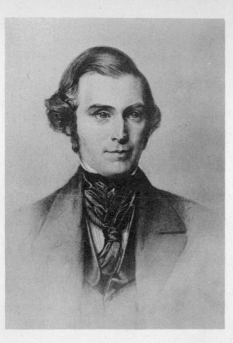

Orson Pratt, 1850. (Courtesy Utah State Historical Society Archives.)

Orson Pratt, c. 1880. (Courtesy Church Archives, The Church of Jesus Christ of Latter-day Saints.)

B. H. Roberts disguised as a tramp to retrieve the bodies of murdered Mormon missionaries from still-hostile territory, Nashville, Tennessee, 1884. (Courtesy Church Archives, The Church of Jesus Christ of Latter-day Saints.)

B. H. Roberts, c. 1922. (Courtesy Church Archives, The Church of Jesus Christ of Latter-day Saints.)

Joseph Fielding Smith, c. 1905. (Courtesy Church Archives, The Church of Jesus Christ of Latter-day Saints.)

Joseph Fielding Smith receiving a newly-published volume of his collected writings, *Doctrines of Salvation* (1954), from son-in-law Bruce R. McConkie, who compiled the book. (Courtesy Church Archives, The Church of Jesus Christ of Latter-day Saints.)

William Henry Chamberlin, c. 1897. (Courtesy David C. Chamberlin.)

William Henry Chamberlin. (From the 1921 edition of "The Crimson Annual" of Brigham Young College, courtesy Utah State University Special Collections and Archives.)

President J. Reuben Clark in his office, 1947. (Courtesy Harold B. Lee Library, Brigham Young University.)

J. Reuben Clark as U.S. under secretary of state, 1928. (Courtesy Church Archives, The Church of Jesus Christ of Latter-day Saints.)

Elder Bruce R. McConkie. (Courtesy Church Archives, The Church of Jesus Christ of Latter-day Saints.)

Lowell L. Bennion in Paris with wife Merle, 1931. (Courtesy Merle Bennion.)

Lowell L. Bennion on his boys' ranch for urban youth, Teton Valley, Idaho, c. 1962. (Courtesy Merle Bennion.)

ture somewhat as he did. The biblicist perspective, the selectively literalist mentality, the anticreedal and antihierarchical bias, the yearning for New Testament purity in theology and polity, the millenarian expectations, and the quest for religious authority amid the conflicting biblical interpretations spawned in young, restless, democratic America—all were characteristic of the "primitive gospel" milieu in which Mormonism initially thrived.[44] Those who could accept the notions of an open canon and a new prophet in response to these urges often found themselves attracted to Mormon claims.

Orson Pratt and Brigham Young embraced such ideas. They shared many assumptions with Smith about the nature of scripture before ever coming under his influence, and after joining Mormonism they naturally followed him further. Young and Pratt, for example, came to stress, as Smith did, the severe limits of human language and conceptions, a view with profound implications for Bible-believers. In the prophetic Mormon context this specifically meant not only an open canon but the malleability of already canonized texts.[45]

Young and Pratt also emulated Smith in underscoring the transmission and translation difficulties in the Bible's long history. Both men followed Smith in the belief that Christ's gospel had preceded his physical presence on earth; the same gospel (though with varying "ordinances and institutions") was preached by the ancient patriarchs, the apostles, and the Latter-day Saints.[46] Smith, Young, and Pratt all maintained a theoretical, if unevenly applied, enthusiasm for new knowledge from secular as well as scriptural sources. All enjoyed a sense of participation with biblical writers, including a belief that the Mormon people recapitulated biblical events, fulfilled biblical prophecy, and engaged in the prophetic process itself.

However, against the background of these shared perspectives, each of the three men also used the Bible in his own fashion. These variations were apparent in Smith's lifetime and more apparent after his death. Smith expressed his prophetic consciousness by receiving his own revelations (greatly influenced by the Bible), adding them to the written canon, and revising the biblical text itself to reflect his own (revealed) perspective. But a conflict inhered in his joint belief

44. Hill, "The Role of Christian Primitivism," pp. 6–36.
45. *JD*, 1:117; 2:314; 3:99–102; 9:311; 16:335; *TS* 6 (July 1, 1845): 953–54.
46. *JD*, 16:73; 12:247–54.

in the Bible and his own prophetic calling, for biblical writers did not always agree among themselves, let alone with his revelations. Smith identified with the role of the biblical writers so thoroughly that, coupled with his belief in progressive revelation, he felt his views were basically in accord with—but finally superior to—theirs, at least in the form in which they existed in the Old and New Testaments. He therefore appropriated the Bible: augmenting it, revising it, making it his own. His revelations, one might conclude, came not to "destroy" but to "fulfill" the traditional scriptures. His use of the Bible was profoundly shaped by his ambient culture but was ultimately unique. This ambiguous distinction sheds light on the persistent problem of why and how Mormonism was at once so American and yet so anomalous in America.

Brigham Young, fundamentally a Bible-believer, inherited this distinctive tradition from Smith. His sermons, often self-consciously "secular," were fully as authoritative as the Bible. For him, Mormon doctrine was Bible doctrine. The catch was that scripture, which had been written "by the spirit," had to be interpreted "by the spirit." Unless one understood Mormon theological insights, one did not really understand and believe the Bible. From one angle of vision, this is merely a case of blatant scriptural eisegesis. But as Young read the Bible, only "he who hath eyes to see" *could* see.

Unlike Smith, Young did not revise the printed biblical texts to conform to his notions,[47] nor did he often cite Smith's revisions. Instead, he resolved the tension between his biblical and extrabiblical beliefs by retaining a fundamental loyalty to the Bible while discounting parts of it as the words of mere men, and by heightening Smith's emphasis on the superior role of "living oracles."

Like his predecessor, Young had little patience for the notion of inerrant, unimprovable, verbally perfect scripture. It is impossible, he said, for puny humans to receive a revelation from heaven in all its perfection. God must speak to human capacity. Furthermore, "Should the Lord Almighty send an angel to re-write the Bible [or, for that matter, the Book of Mormon], it would in many places be very different from what it now is." Although his stance was like Smith's in that both declared there to be harmony in the doctrines of

---

47. I found one exception to this generality, and there may be others. See Watson, ed., *A Chronological Compilation,* vol. 4 (December 16, 1860).

ancient and modern prophets, Young felt less often than Smith the need to justify developing Mormon theology with the Bible.[48]

Orson Pratt was more academic in his approach but no less bold in asserting the need for divine wisdom beyond the contemporary Bible. He may have spoken and published more in logical defense of the necessity of living prophets, the limitations of the Bible, and the Mormon fulfillment of biblical prophecy than any other person in Latter-day Saint history. Yet for all his rational Mormon apologetics, Pratt was finally more bound to the Bible than either Smith or Young. Partly because of his proselytizing purposes, but partly, perhaps, for more personal reasons also, he felt the need to reconcile all Mormon claims with the Bible in a way that the other two men (Smith more than Young) ultimately did for public relations as much as for other reasons.

A People Apart

I have argued that the Latter-day Saints, as represented by Brigham Young and Orson Pratt, had much in common with many of their contemporaries in their approach to the Bible, including (despite the Book of Mormon) their basically biblical orientation, their selective literalism, and other traits shared by gospel primitivists. For the most part, they resembled other Americans in assuming the perspicuity and constancy of truth, and (especially in Pratt's case) in assuming that both the Bible and nature equally revealed God's truth. Although they were perhaps more frank about it, they joined other Americans in using the Bible to justify opinions held on nonbiblical grounds. They also reflected the national shift in emphasis from the Old Testament to the New that occurred during the course of the nineteenth century (Pratt preferring the Old; Young, the New).[49] They saw, like other Americans, the fulfillment of biblical prophecies in events of their own time and place—indeed, in themselves. Pratt in particular indulged in scriptural interpretation that paralleled the numerology of diverse adventist groups as he studiously

48. Ibid., 5:329; 2:314; 9:311.

49. At least Pratt cited the Old Testament far more often than he did the New, and Young explicitly observed that the New Testament "more pointedly" explicated "the doctrines of salvation" (*JD*, 1:237).

classified the implications of "plain scripture facts." He, like other Saints and other Americans, was intoxicated with the biblical theme of the millennium.[50]

Despite the traits they shared with other Americans, however, the Latter-day Saints were at least as different from others as they were similar in their approach to scripture. Historian Mark Noll has noted that the Bible for most Protestant Americans has represented two very different books. It was first a "compendium of instruction for faith and practice," but more often a typical narrative giving significance to the antitypical events and people of American history.[51] For the Latter-day Saints of the last half of the nineteenth century, the Bible served similar purposes, but with subtle yet fundamental shifts that set them apart. For Mormons, the Bible was not so much the controlling myth of the national experience but the record of prophecies specifically pointing to the Mormon "restoration." To the extent that biblical stories presented types to receive their echoes in modern experience, it was Mormonism, not America, that supplied the antitypes.

Both Young and Pratt assumed with other Americans that the Bible was a handbook of "faith and practice," but a more prominent use to which they put the Bible was in defense of the claim that it was consonant with Mormon doctrine—a sectarian use forced upon them by their missionary zeal and by an understandable sense of siege at the hands of religious antagonists. Privately, both men undoubtedly used scripture devotionally, much like other Christians. But in public Pratt's usage was more defensive than devotional, and Young used scripture less devotionally than as a pragmatic, supplementary guide to efficient and righteous living.

Before the 1870s, near the end of Young's and Pratt's lives, American Protestants were not divided over exact theories of biblical inspiration. This would change dramatically in the last quarter of the century, when a proper understanding of the relation of divine to human authorship in scripture would be used as a test of fellowship in a series of sensational heresy trials. But before that time, although

50. On this theme, see, among many scholarly possibilities, Ernest Lee Tuveson, *Redeemer Nation: The Idea of America's Millennial Role* (Chicago: University of Chicago Press, 1968). For Mormonism, see Grant Underwood, "Early Mormon Millenarianism: Another Look," *Church History* 54 (June 1985): 215–29.

51. "The United States," in *The Bible in America,* ed. Hatch and Noll, p. 43.

scholars were aware that German theologians were constructing theories allowing that the Bible was not necessarily inspired in matters of history and science, and although differences of opinion existed in America as well, the lines of battle were not yet sharply drawn. Most Protestant writers seem to have believed that the Bible was inspired in all its parts. God had not *dictated* scripture, but he had guided even the choice of its words, though each human writer expressed his own thought and personality. This was "plenary" inspiration. God had "superintended" the writing of the Bible. Just what this superintendence entailed, and whether or not different parts of scripture were inspired in different degrees, engendered lively discussion at mid-century. But in general the conversation occurred among those who agreed on the sure and final authority of scripture.[52]

Pratt and Young were of this generation and shared much of this belief. They remained unaware of (at least they did not comment on) the controversial new tools for biblical study that were filtering in from abroad. They believed God involved his superintending hand in the writing of the prophets. Yet, unlike the evangelicals, they believed this process was alive and well: the prophets spoke again; the canon was not closed. Furthermore, against the notion of "the Bible alone," Pratt and other Mormon missionaries emphasized not only the principle of "continuing revelation" but also their belief in apocryphal and pseudepigraphic works such as the *Book of Enoch* and the *Book of Jasher*. Sometimes such works were used to reinforce points of doctrine, but their content was generally less crucial than their very existence, which supported the idea that the Bible was not God's sole revelation.[53]

Another interesting difference between the Mormons and contemporaneous evangelicals is the fact that both groups appealed to the original biblical autographs, but with opposite motives. Protestant theologians such as Leonard Woods and Charles Elliot pointed to the original writings to preserve the notion of inerrancy in an increasingly besieged Bible. Said Elliot: "[If] any positive errors are found in the Scriptures, it must be proved that they existed in the original manuscripts. . . ." By contrast the Mormons, and no one more than Orson

---

52. Marsden in *The Bible in America,* ed. Hatch and Noll, pp. 88–90.

53. Pratt, *Divine Authenticity of the Book of Mormon* (Liverpool: R. James, 1850–1851); Welsh and Whittaker, "Mormonism's Open Canon," pp. 16–19.

Pratt, pointed to the original autographs precisely to underscore the fact that they did not exist; the thousands of variant readings in extant manuscripts demonstrated the errors and inadequacy of the Bible in its available form.[54] So deeply was Pratt imbued with his century's faith in the clarity of truth that he believed if modern society possessed perfect copies of the original scriptural texts, there would be no cause for so many denominations to exist.[55]

When difficulties arose between scripture and modern science, Christians tended to react in several distinct ways, and the lines between them should not be unduly blurred. Many were simply unaware of the difficulties and remained oblivious to science. Others, like Moses Stuart, insisted that science defer to scripture. Stuart even had the audacious integrity to demand that the Bible not be twisted to say something it did not really say simply to accommodate new scientific theory. Still others said the Bible should not be interpreted so rigidly, that its primary intent was not scientific and that its words, broadly understood, harmonized with modern scientific knowledge. Joseph Smith, by contrast, tended to confront such issues by reworking scripture itself, explicitly and implicitly suggesting the textual corruption of original texts, and asserting his prophetic right to amend the errors. It was another response entirely for Brigham Young to write off part of the Bible as fables, the sort of stories that adults told to children deemed unready for "the facts of life."

The Mormon identification with biblical peoples, events, and prophecies was experientially more all-encompassing than that of any other major group during the nineteenth century, and probably of the preceding and succeeding centuries as well. The Saints resembled the nation's Christianized slaves in rejecting America as Israel, but, unlike the slaves, they did not identify God's chosen people with "those who suffered unjustly among all peoples"[56] (though suffer they did).

54. Elliott, professor at the Presbyterian Theological Seminary of the Northwest, Chicago, is quoted by Marsden in *The Bible in America,* ed. Hatch and Noll, p. 98 n. 28. Pratt, *The Bible and Polygamy,* pp. 9–10, 26–27; *JD,* 7:26–27; 14:258(a), 257, 258(b) [pagination error in volume]; 16:218.

55. *JD,* 14:258(b). Pratt also revealed no awareness of the accruing progress in textual criticism, which culminated in the year of his death, in Westcott and Hort's *New Testament in the Original Greek* (New York: Harper and Brothers, 1881).

56. Albert Raboteau, *Slave Religion: The "Invisible Institution" in the Antebellum South* (New York: Oxford University Press, 1978), p. 251; Noll, "The Image of the United States," in *The Bible in America,* ed. Hatch and Noll, pp. 50–51.

Instead, they more closely resembled the whites from whom they fled by linking Israel with a newly gathered quasi nation, namely, themselves. Scriptural justification for American nationalism was transferred to Mormon Zionism; America was chosen—as the birthplace of Mormonism. While evangelical apologists published evidences of Christianity and showed the Bible to harmonize with science, Orson Pratt published evidences of Mormonism, also verified by contemporary science.[57]

Because of their belief in Joseph Smith, the Mormons were placed on a biblical course distinct from other Americans. The beginning point of that divergent course was the religious insufficiency of the Bible alone. Pratt used the same logic once marshaled by Smith and by Mercersburg Seminary's John W. Nevin in urging, against the main currents of Protestant America, the inadequacy of the Bible: As "a testimony that [the Bible is not sufficiently] plain, let me refer you to some five or six hundred different religious views, all founded on this same book."[58] Furthermore, even had the Saints accepted the nation's reigning notion of *sola scriptura,* the *scriptura* they had in mind was not restricted to the sixty-six books of the Bible. The Mormons not only possessed additional scriptures but expected to receive more at any time, channeled through the prophets in their midst. It was neither Protestant scripture nor Catholic tradition but the word of living prophets to which they gave their first allegiance.

Because they saw the process of revelation occur right before them, the status of the Bible was paradoxically both heightened and lowered for Latter-day Saints when compared with those outside their faith. On the one hand, they experienced a renewed sense of the involvement of God, of the actuality of prophecy and miracle. Biblical episodes did not seem "once upon a time" to them, for they experienced such miracles—relived such episodes—in their own lives. On the other hand, Mormon prophets insisted on their own limitations, which their followers could readily discern. Mormon revelation was not infallible; it was explicitly provisional, subject to refinement, given through ordinary human beings, and adapted to current capacities and circumstances. And if modern scriptures were thus

57. Marsden, in *The Bible in America,* ed. Hatch and Noll, p. 86; England, *Pratt,* chaps. 5, 8, 11.

58. For Pratt, *JD,* 14:257; for Nevin, see my introduction, p. 9; for Smith, *HC,* 1:4.

limited, how much more so the Bible, which had been given to different people under different conditions and was disfigured by the transmission and translation difficulties of two millennia.

These perspectives led the Saints to reverence and yet limit the Bible, setting them apart from other American Christians. Differing from the bulk of their evangelical peers, many Mormons limited the authority of the Bible by allowing for an extrabiblical canon, placing primacy on living prophets over written scripture, arguing the ̲rip-tural truth was but one source of truth among others (not simply meaning, like scholarly evangelicals, that nature alone was the other great source of truth, but meaning that all knowledge in every sphere was also part of the gospel), stressing the corruptions of the biblical text in its available form, and dismissing portions of the Bible as uninspired. As distinct from the dominant thousands whose rallying cry through most of the century had been "The Bible alone is good enough for me!" the Mormons restricted the Bible's authority, uniqueness, finality, sufficiency, and historicity.

Though the Holy Book remained crucial for the Mormons through the 1880s, the restrictions they put on its authority had significant consequences. Besides setting them apart as "Bible-believing Christians with a difference," these restrictions worked in concert with certain social factors to create a potential buffer against the coming onslaught of modern critical biblical studies.

4

The Mormon Response
to Higher Criticism

Between about 1880 and 1930 changes in America's intellectual climate precipitated what Sydney Ahlstrom has called "the most fundamental controversy to wrack the churches since the age of the Reformation." Central to that controversy was the nation's new awareness of an historical criticism that threatened traditional conceptions of scripture.[1]

Despite the centrality of the higher criticism, the extensive body of historical scholarship scrutinizing Mormonism has yet to explore thoroughly the LDS response to it. Basic Mormon perspectives may be symbolized through the reactions of three influential leaders from the first half of the twentieth century: B. H. Roberts, Joseph Fielding Smith, and William H. Chamberlin. Along with their theological heirs, these three suggest a spectrum of views current even today. The preponderant Mormon sentiment has been cool, antagonistic, or even oblivious to the new thinking, but attitudes of specific leaders have been as divergent as those of any denomination in the country, ranging from enthusiastic to scandalized. Officially, the Church pre-

---

1. Ahlstrom, *A Religious History*, 2:248. For broad treatments of the great conflict that arose among American Protestants because of these new conditions, see Hutchison, *The Modernist Impulse in American Protestantism*, and Marsden, *Fundamentalism and American Culture*. For lengthier consideration of the specifically biblical dimensions of the controversy in several traditions, consult Sperling and Levine, *History of Jewish Biblical Scholarship;* Fogarty, *American Catholic Biblical Scholarship;* and Noll, *Between Faith and Criticism.*

vented a rupture by greeting the higher criticism with a guarded "no comment."

Although the advent of biblical criticism has been acknowledged by those examining the transition of Mormonism to the modern era, the issue has remained overshadowed by the concurrent Darwinian controversy with which it was naturally linked.[2] The scholarly bias is understandable, for evolutionary theory did capture the popular imagination. Those who defended or attacked it reveal something important about an age in which perceptions of the relation of science and religion underwent inversion.

Yet focusing on the reaction to biological evolution without a similar regard for the issue of biblical criticism reverses the real importance of the two threats to Bible-believing Christianity. Evolution, after all, imperiled the Bible merely by implication, and principally the account of creation at that. Of course, one might (and many did) reason: If the historicity of Genesis chapters 1 and 2 are at risk, why not all of Genesis? Why not the complete Bible? If Adam was not a real person, what did one do with Paul's Adam–Christ typologies?

2. Apart from Sherlock's look ("Faith and History") at the contention surrounding Heber Snell's *Ancient Israel* (a book of the 1940s espousing modern scholarship), the Mormon response to modern biblical criticism has received no in-depth treatment. Hutchinson, in "LDS Approaches to the Holy Bible," has sketched a useful hermeneutical typology of some prominent LDS writers, but, as he notes, his approach is not historical. When biblical criticism does get mentioned in historical works, it is often limited to a 1911 controversy at BYU when several professors lost their positions because of their modernist teachings. Even in this instance, the issue tends to appear incidentally, and detailed study is reserved for the encounter with biological evolutionary theory. Gary Bergera and Ronald Priddis allot a few lines to biblical criticism in the 1911 affair in the course of a forty-page treatment of evolution in *Brigham Young University: A House of Faith* (SLC: Signature Books, 1985). Sherlock allows the issue proportionately more room in "Campus in Crisis," but again biblical criticism is overshadowed by evolutionary concerns and is restricted to Provo in 1911. Alexander, *Mormonism in Transition,* offers a fresh and insightful discussion of science and religion in early-twentieth-century Mormonism, but excepting matters relating to evolution and the creation, his discussion of biblical criticism is confined to two pages. Quinn does attend to the matter in his biography of J. Reuben Clark, but biographies and autobiographies of most prominent LDS leaders, including such promising figures as B. H. Roberts, James Talmage, John Widtsoe, and Joseph Fielding Smith, scarcely allude to higher criticism. The best general treatments of Mormonism, such as Arrington and Bitton's *The Mormon Experience* and Allen and Leonard's *The Story of the Latter-day Saints,* mention the issue briefly.

However, these were but implications of implications; from this quarter the challenge to Christian faith was doubly oblique. Many people seemed less upset by the potential evolutionary menace to their Bible than by the notion that their ancestors had been primates. Between the Civil War and World War II, countless pictorial spoofs on this theme appeared in the nation's press.[3] And even if one accepted some form of evolution, perhaps Genesis could yet be saved by construing a few passages metaphorically.

By contrast, historical criticism challenged the Bible directly and entirely. Not a single biblical book—indeed, as the twentieth century wore on, hardly a single word—escaped the new analysis. Equally sophisticated but not so easily popularized as Darwinism, the new approach to the Bible invited a much deeper and broader redefining of the nature of revelation, and thus of allegiance to Judaism and Christianity, than an acceptance of evolution did of itself. To borrow from Ahlstrom again, "Fossils and unimaginably remote developments in the plant or animal kingdoms were academic abstractions compared with the direct impact of historico-critical studies. . . ."[4] If more was actually said by Mormons about evolution than about biblical criticism, it was partly because so few had even a rudimentary grasp of the latter.

There is another reason that the issues should be separated. Certainly, it must be allowed that evolution and historical criticism derived from the same spirit. An intellectual revolution—a genuine Kuhnian paradigm shift—commenced during the last half of the nineteenth century. Change began to displace stationary fact as the key to "the nature of things." Permanence yielded to flux; the fixed to the flowing. But in tracing how religionists responded to these shifts, scholars have implied that those who accepted evolution also accepted the new biblical criticism; because the spirit of change applied to both, those who

3. See examples in Noll et al., eds., *Eerdmans' Handbook*, p. 324; Marsden, *Fundamentalism*, p. 213. Similar sentiments appeared among Mormons: "Some scientists take an honest pride in the idea that they have descended from the ape: they consider it shows progress and development. . . . Even if it were true, we should feel disposed to say but little regarding such a pedigree" ([General Authority] George Reynolds, "Thoughts on Genesis," *CT* 3 [October 1881]: 16).

4. *A Religious History*, 2:234. Josef Altholz similarly assesses the relative danger of the twin threats to the churches in Europe in *The Churches in the Nineteenth Century* (Indianapolis: Bobbs-Merrill, 1967), p. 132.

106 *Mormons and the Bible*

rejected the one naturally rejected the other.[5] That this was not necessarily so is illustrated by the response of B. H. Roberts, thought by many to be the preeminent intellectual in Latter-day Saint history.[6]

When the Book of Mormon appeared in 1830, it described its purpose as, in part, a verification of the Bible and of Christ's divinity.[7] Yet although those attracted to the book were pleased that God had spoken again, they hardly needed conversion to the Bible. They were thoroughly a part of antebellum America's Bible-believing culture. But by 1888, when B. H. Roberts became one of approximately two dozen general authorities in the Mormon Church, American culture had *evolved*. By this time, new Protestant awareness of potential scriptural problems had already sponsored the first skirmishes in the great battle for the Bible that—on a smaller scale and with occasional truces and shifts in demilitarized zones—was still being waged a century later.[8]

Of course, new awareness on the part of U.S. Protestants did not mean that cognizance of biblical problems was itself new. Although his work did not influence Jewish scholars for generations, the seventeenth-century Dutch philosopher Spinoza outlined a method of biblical interpretation with the intent of deducing the authors and times of the various books, concluding, among other things, that Ezra

5. From virtually all treatments cited in note 2 that mention both issues, one gains the impression that those who bothered to have an opinion were either progressive (pro-evolution and pro-higher criticism) or conservative. Similarly, George Marsden writes more generally of American Protestants: "Some would make virtually no concessions to the new . . . analysis of the Bible. Often these were the same people who would have nothing to do with Darwinism." (Noll et al., eds., *Eerdmans' Handbook,* p. 325.) This is an accurate statement, but it would not lead one to notice that, as with several key Mormons, some accepted evolutionary principles while remaining hostile to biblical criticism.

6. Roberts's intellectual stature is estimated in Madsen, *Defender of the Faith,* and Sterling McMurrin's prefatory essay in Roberts, *Studies of the Book of Mormon,* edited by Brigham D. Madsen. In 1968 Leonard Arrington sent a questionnaire to prominent Mormon thinkers who held a Ph.D. or its equivalent, asking each to list the five most eminent intellectuals in Mormon history. Of the thirty-eight respondents, thirty-five put Roberts at the top of the list. Arrington, "The Intellectual Tradition," pp. 23–24.

7. Book of Mormon title page; 1 Nephi 13; D&C 20:8–11.

8. E.g., Lindsell, *The Battle for the Bible* (Grand Rapids: Zondervan, 1976); George M. Marsden, *Reforming Fundamentalism: Fuller Seminary and the New Evangelicalism* (Grand Rapids: Eerdmans, 1987), passim.

authored the Pentateuch.[9] As early as 1697 Pierre Bayle, whose *Dictionnaire historique et critique* served as a model for later skeptics, engaged in a study of biblical stories, finding them neither edifying nor divinely inspired. Under rationalistic auspices in mid-eighteenth-century Germany, Hermann Reimarus insisted the Bible be treated like any other historical document, and Johann Semler and his followers replaced dogmatic exegesis with literary and historical analysis. Nineteenth-century scholarship, culminating in the work of Julius Wellhausen, interpreted the Old Testament as the history of the Israelites, whose conceptions developed gradually from a crude belief in a tribal deity to a more universal and ethical creed.

In New Testament studies, the famous Tübingen school arose in the 1830s. One result during the next several decades was the publication of a series of disturbing biographies of Jesus that ignored or rationalized the miraculous element in the Gospel accounts. In England by 1860, a group of Oxford graduates sought to acclimate their countrymen to the new Continental criticism by publishing *Essays and Reviews,* which quickly achieved synodical condemnation. Other difficulties followed, but by 1889, with the publication of the controversial (though actually moderate and reverant) *Lux Mundi* by Charles Gore and his colleagues, the Anglo-Catholics had caught up with their German contemporaries in thinking critically about scripture. The Bible was less crucial among Roman Catholics, yet scholars such as Alfred Loisy at Paris nonetheless prompted an official reaction by Pope Leo XIII, who in 1893 asserted a fundamentalist doctrine of biblical inerrancy, retarding modern studies among Catholic scholars for fifty years.[10]

Despite these battles, Europe's deep roots lent a sense of history as gradual, natural development and made relatively easy the acceptance of Darwinism and higher criticism.[11] In comparatively history-less America, where no monarch but the Bible reigned, the going was tougher. But even here such issues were not really new by B. H.

9. S. David Sperling, "Judaism and Modern Biblical Research," in *Biblical Studies: Meeting Ground of Jews and Christians,* ed. L. Boadt, H. Croner, and L. Klenicki, pp. 21–22.

10. "For all the books which the Church receives as sacred and canonical are written wholly and entirely, with all their parts, at the dictation of the Holy Spirit" (*Providentissimus Deus*). For biblical criticism in Europe, see Altholz, *The Churches in the Nineteenth Century,* pp. 10, 106, 126f., 130, 132–36, 159f., 162, 164, 167–68, 177.

11. Marsden, *Fundamentalism,* p. 226.

Roberts's time. Some awareness of new methods of biblical study had existed, primarily among Unitarians, from the early decades of the nineteenth century. Congregationalist Horace Bushnell had argued in 1849 that the language of creeds is intrinsically poetical, not literal— and it was a relatively small step for admirers after him to apply the thesis to scripture. A few American Catholics, although not advanced in such thinking, were nonetheless listening with fascination to the overseas theories of J. G. Eichorn, who suggested Moses had used preexisting sources in his writing.

A generation after Bushnell, Presbyterian David Swing preached in Chicago that the "inspiration of the Scriptures" signified a "divine assistance given to man," not a celestial warranty that human writers had inerrantly penned the mind of God. In fact the Bible, Swing said, contains many wrong and terrible things, like the vengeful 109th Psalm. God, not scripture, was perfect. The airing of such views resulted in a heresy trial but, at least in the Midwest, there was considerable tolerance even among doctrinally oriented Presbyterians: the Chicago Presbytery vindicated Swing by a vote of 48 to 13.[12]

Yet the issues of biblical criticism grew ever more troubling to the nation's believing Christians. By the late 1870s, according to Washington Gladden, those sensitive to the noises and silences of the theological forest could hear a rush in the tops of the trees. In several denominations during the last quarter of the century, other heresy trials followed Swing's. These often targeted a seminary professor, and the most spectacular case was that of Charles Briggs of Union Theological Seminary, who explicitly attacked the doctrine of inerrancy as framed by Princeton theologians A. A. Hodge and B. B. Warfield. Briggs was suspended from the Presbyterian ministry, with the further result that both he and his seminary took leave of Presbyterianism. His case, along with the writings of Lyman Abbott and Washington Gladden, did much to popularize the new methods of biblical study.[13]

12. For the Unitarian-dominated criticism before the Civil War, see Brown, *The Rise of Biblical Criticism*. Bushnell, "Preliminary Dissertation on the Nature of Language," in *God in Christ* (Hartford: Brown & Parsons, 1849), pp. 9–97. Fogarty, *American Catholic Biblical Scholarship*, p. 14 (for Catholic adjustments in scriptural perspectives resulting from advances in science before the Civil War, see p. 25). On the Swing affair, see Hutchison, *Modernist Impulse*, pp. 48–75.

13. Leading Mormons were well aware of the Briggs case, the effects of which also spilled over directly into Catholic controversies (Fogarty, *American Catholic Biblical Scholarship*, pp. 130–70).

The stormy but constant descent of the Bible's status, at least among the most visible parts of the public culture, continued until the rise of neo-orthodoxy in the 1930s.[14] For modernists, the Bible became one great religious document among others; Christianity was but one of the major religio-ethical traditions. To these modernists, what authority the Bible retained, it retained *as judged by philosophic, scientific, and experiential standards external to it*. Intellectually led by Princeton Seminary, conservatives during these decades responded to the threat by transforming the loose assumptions of plenary inspiration, which had prevailed through the mid-nineteenth century, into a rigid insistence on biblical inerrancy, which in turn became a new shibboleth of doctrinal orthodoxy.[15]

Among the Mormons: Early Responses That Weren't

The Latter-day Saints had within their tradition the resources to respond both positively and negatively to the new scholarship. On the one hand was a legacy of biblical literalism, reinforced beyond that of most Protestants by modern scripture that described, for instance, a literal Satan in conversation with Moses, and prophets who moved real mountains.[16] Mormon theology posited a gospel delivered once and for all to Adam and other ancient figures, followed by a series of apostasies and restorations. This thinking was foreign to the new notions of progressive theological evolution. Even more important,

14. The rise to prominence of fundamentalism and neoevangelicalism in recent decades has forced awareness that widespread conservative esteem for the Bible survived in America all along; it merely went temporarily out of public view after the seeming defeats of the 1920s.

15. For examples of controversies in several denominations, see Hutchison, *The Modernist Impulse*, p. 77. For Briggs, see Mark S. Massa, *Charles Augustus Briggs and the Crisis of Historical Criticism* (Minneapolis: Augsburg Fortress Publishers, 1990); Carl E. Hatch, *The Charles A. Briggs Heresy Trial: Prologue to Twentieth-Century Liberal Protestantism* (New York: Exposition Press, 1969); C. A. Briggs, *The Defence of Professor Briggs Before the Presbytery of New York* (New York: Scribner's, 1893). Ahlstrom, *A Religious History,* 2:244, 247.

16. *PGP,* Moses 1:12–24; 7:13. William Russell, in tracing the reaction of the Reorganized LDS Church in the late nineteenth century to the issues of higher criticism, notes only this side of the tradition. "The RLDS Church and Biblical Criticism: The Early Response," *John Whitmer Historical Association Journal* 7 (1987): 64.

miracles and prophecies of future events were live realities for the Saints; a scholarship prepared to dismiss those realities could naturally be regarded as hostile. Furthermore, Mormonism had been a radical part of the antebellum movement to reduce the role of a learned clergy, which was perceived to have come between the common folk and the direct word of God in scripture. The Saints were not anxious to replace a professional clergy, which they had earlier banished, with bookish academics.

On the other hand, Mormonism had originally been launched by proclaiming the Bible's limitations. Joseph Smith had discovered God through prayer when he found the Bible inadequate to resolve the claims of denominational rivals. Insisting on the reality of his revelations, he nevertheless stressed the weakness of human language as a vehicle for the mind of God. Far from assuming inerrancy, Smith experimented liberally with scripture. He made both the Bible and his own revelations adaptable and subject to refinement, given by God to humans in their weakness, "after the manner of their language" and conceptions. In fact, half a century before theories about the multiple authorship and redaction of individual biblical books were widely known in America even among scholars, Joseph Smith offered the world a forthright and dramatic instance of the "documentary hypothesis" at work: the Book of Mormon portrayed the fifth-century prophet-historian Mormon freely abridging, editing, and appropriating the records of many earlier writers in his account of the rise and fall of the ancient Nephite civilization.

Brigham Young went even further than Smith, repeatedly asserting his biblical allegiance but also emphasizing the circumstantial and progressive nature of revelation, dismissing parts of the Bible as fables, and noting that in writing of the creation Moses had adapted the traditions he had inherited from the fathers. The Mormons' anti-intellectual tendencies, conceptions of static "eternal" truth, and disdain for a learned, professional clergy were potentially offset by their beliefs in provisional, continuing, and imperfectly received revelation, their theology of learning and of the nature of intelligence, their insistence that their faith embraced science and included all truth from whatever source, and other deeply embedded values.[17]

17. On the LDS theology of education and intelligence see D&C 88:40, 77–80, 117–18; 90:15; 93:29, 30, 36; 130:18; 131:6; 2 Nephi 9:29.

With these two potentialities in mind, it should be made clear that the Saints did not respond much at all during the early years of the biblical controversy that increasingly engulfed the nation's scholars. Not only did the Mormon community deliberately lack trained theologians likely to be attuned to the new currents but during the several decades preceding Utah's achievement of statehood (1896) the Mormons, under duress of antipolygamy legislation, were preoccupied with their very survival as a corporate entity.

Even after the turn of the century the Mormons' interest in the new criticism was sporadic, often indirect, and expressed only occasionally in conference talks or short articles in Church magazines. "Higher criticism" was a familiar term, but for the most part the nods toward the new learning were negative and showed scant awareness of the real issues. General Authority George Reynold's assessment of the documentary hypothesis is representative:

> Some writers have maintained that throughout Genesis . . . there are traces of two original documents at least, some claim more. These two documents are characterized by giving different names to God. In the one he is called Elohim and in the other Jehovah. It appears never to have entered into the thoughts of these writers that possibly two different heavenly personages were intended.

Other LDS writers argued that because Joseph Smith's new scriptures depicted the creation as being shown in vision to Moses, "modern revelation has [therefore] decided the disputed question of the authorship of the Book of Genesis." Because, based on records predating the Exile, the Book of Mormon included passages from the so-called deutero-Isaiah, therefore the Book of Isaiah, as we know it, was written entirely by a single prophet prior to 600 B.C.E. Jesus alluded to the story of Jonah (Matt. 12:39–40); therefore Jonah was a historical person. On the few occasions that Mormon writers did show competence with the issues involved, they challenged the new criticism's tendency to assume that miracles could not occur, and they championed, like others in America, a Baconian system of logic and science as opposed to what they saw as a speculative abuse of facts.[18]

18. Francis Bacon's inductive scientific method meant, for many Americans of the time, little more than a rigorously careful, objective observation of "the facts" (whether the subject be theology or geology), followed by careful classification of these facts. "Speculative hypotheses" were seen as "unscientific" by these Americans

Obvious errors in the texts, such as popular etymologies for certain biblical names, were explained as corruptions of the original writings by intruding copyists.[19]

B. H. Roberts

Among LDS general authorities, B. H. Roberts was for many years virtually alone in engaging scriptural criticism with serious intellectual rigor. Roberts functions in Mormon history as the Latter-day Saint approximation of American Judaism's Isaac Wise or American Protestantism's Horace Bushnell. Neither all of Roberts's perspectives nor all of his scholarly methods are celebrated today, but many of them are. When combined with his honesty, his breadth, his brilliance, his voluminous writings, his willingness to stand his ground on what he considered issues of intellectual integrity, his influential status in the Mormon hierarchy, and especially his efforts to render LDS theology consonant with contemporary secular thought or at least respectable in the face of that thought, his attitudes secure his station as the father of modern Mormon liberalism.

Born in Warrington, England in 1857, Roberts was the son of impoverished Mormon converts. As a young child, he often listened to his mother read from the Bible. He crossed the ocean when he was nine years old and walked across the Great Plains to the Territory of Utah. Working on farms and in mines, he had little opportunity for schooling in his youth, though he did manage intermittent attendance

(Marsden, *Fundamentalism,* pp. 7, 15, 55–62, 111–12, 214–15). For more detailed treatments of the American interpretation of Bacon and the related Scottish Common Sense philosophy, see Sydney Ahlstrom, "The Scottish Philosophy and American Theology," *Church History* 24 (September 1955): 257–72; Bozeman, *Protestants in an Age of Science* (1977); and Hovenkamp, *Science and Religion in America, 1800–1860* (1978).

19. One of the more thoughtful respondents to publish in a Mormon periodical was non-Mormon J. E. Homans (writing under the pen name Robert Webb), "What Is the Higher Criticism?" and "Criticism of the 'Higher Critics,' " *IE* 19 (May 1916): 620–26, and (June 1916): 706–13. More typical responses were George Reynolds, "Thoughts on Genesis," *CT* 3 (October 1881): 16–17; A. A. Ramseyer, "Who Wrote the Pentateuch?" *IE* 9 (April 1908): 437–42; Joseph F. Smith, "Jonah and the Bible," *JI* (July 1911): 400–1; and J. M. Sjodahl, "Some Questions Considered," *IE* 32 (February 1929): 287–90.

at a private "pioneer school," where a single teacher encouraged seventy to eighty "scholars" of diverse ages.

Papers and magazines were too expensive to own, but young Roberts did belatedly learn the alphabet and struggled "painfully" for three years with "the mysterious art of reading" in the family Bible. The Holy Book also taught him how to write, and he later reflected that, quite apart from its religious content, "no other literature is so intellectually stimulating to the child, nor can he anywhere else find such a model of sturdy, sinewy English." Roberts eventually educated himself by wide reading, served a series of proselytizing missions in the southern states and Great Britain, was elected to Congress, and became a prolific author. Among his more than thirty books are nine historical tomes, eight theological works, three collections of sermons and commentaries, two biographies, and one novel.[20]

Despite his enormous native abilities, Roberts was not a biblical scholar of the first order. He possessed no formal biblical or philosophical training, and he read neither Hebrew nor Greek. His writings do demonstrate, however, a broad familiarity with both Testaments and with Bible commentaries. Indeed, he was highly dependent on Bible dictionaries and commentaries, and was given to extensive quotations from secondary sources that benefited his LDS audience yet also revealed his own inadequacies in dealing directly with the issues raised by modern biblical criticism.[21] Notwithstanding these limitations, he was, among Church officials, the best biblical scholar Mormonism produced in its first century. He possessed a formidable mind, a voracious appetite for learning, and a deep and rare candor to leaven his profound religious commitments.

Roberts believed that revealed truths must be reconciled with facts

20. This total does not include numerous tracts and pamphlets, three hundred periodical essays, and more than one thousand sermons. A highly selective bibliography is found in Madsen, *Defender of the Faith,* pp. 441–43. For specifics of his schooling and early exposure to the Bible, see ibid., pp. 56–57; Malan, *B. H. Roberts,* p. 85.

21. His survey of the Bible in *The Seventy's Course in Theology* is representative. This survey consists largely of quotations of various, usually conservative, Protestant scholars. Quotations in Roberts's own writings and notations in his personal books suggest his main sources for understanding biblical criticism included liberals or radicals such as David Strauss, Ernest Renan, Charles Briggs, Lyman Abbott, S. R. Driver, J. G. Fish, and R. J. Campbell. Conservative scholars from whom he commonly drew material included J. R. Dummelow, George Rawlinson, Charles Elliot, and Alfred Edersheim.

demonstrated by science and other means, and he battled those—and there were some—who thought otherwise:

> To give reasonable credence to [scientific] research . . . is to link the church of God with the highest increase of human thought and effort. On that side lies development, on the other lies contraction . . . One [side] leads to narrow sectarianism, the other keeps the open spirit of a world movement with which our New Dispensation began.[22]

His belief in scripture led him to reconcile the claims of evolution and Genesis creatively, though unsatisfactorily. However, he did show a respect for rational thought and a willingness to grapple with current issues. He believed the evidence for the antiquity of the earth and its life-forms, including pre-Adamic humans, was overwhelming. He thought the earth was at least two billion years old, that fossil records of life and death reached back hundreds of millions of years, and he was prepared to accept any such figures that science could establish. He was especially fond of the idea of "cosmic evolution," and recommended the writings of Herbert Spencer, John Fiske, and George Howison.[23]

An acknowledgment of the claims of science did not imply for Roberts their priority over scripture. Rather, science and scripture both revealed truths that must be used to interpret each other. In theory, Roberts held that scripture, including the Book of Mormon, "must submit to every test"—to literary analysis, historical scrutiny, archeology, and all forms of higher criticism:

> [The] methods of higher criticism are legitimate; that is to say, it is right to consider the various books of the scriptures . . . as a body of literature, and to examine them internally, and go into the circumstances under which they were written, and the time at which they were written, and the purpose for which they were written.[24]

22. Roberts's monumental manuscript, "The Truth, the Way, the Life," which he considered his most important writing, was suppressed and remains unpublished in the LDS Church Archives. The quotation is from chap. 31, p. 29.

23. "The Truth, the Way, the Life," chaps. 24, 25, 30–32; handwritten notes inserted in personal Bible, #73 in B. H. Roberts Memorial Library, LDS Church Archives. Roberts's creative but inadequate reaction to Darwinism is drawn out in two essays by Sherlock: "A Turbulent Spectrum," pp. 41–46, and " 'We Can See No Advantage to a Continuation of the Discussion,' " passim.

24. "Higher Criticism and the Book of Mormon," *IE* 14 (June 1911): 667, 668.

However, if Roberts possessed a theoretical respect for the new techniques of biblical study, he was hostile to the conclusions drawn by many of its practitioners, particularly conclusions that undermined the historicity of the biblical narrative, portrayed Christ as merely mortal, and reduced scripture from "the word of God" to merely "what is purest and holiest in religious feeling." He was astonished, he said, "to see what heavy weights are hung upon very slender threads."

When applying tests external to the Bible to check its inspiration, Roberts did so in such a way as to confirm his faith. On moral rather than strictly historical grounds, some critics had challenged certain biblical episodes. But for Roberts, it did not

> matter how much the conduct of Deity, as represented in such books, may violate what we understand to be the relative claims of stern Justice and sweet Mercy, [because] our knowledge of the operation of those qualities, and their effect upon men in time and in eternity, and under varied conditions, is so uncertain and imperfect that we are liable to confound good with evil, and that which is indeed an infinite mercy [with] barbaric cruelty.[25]

On the other hand, he discovered the touch of the divine everywhere in the biblical books: "in their composition, in their diction as well as in the excellence of their matter. . . ."[26] Thus whatever seemed worthy in scripture Roberts attributed to inspiration, whatever seemed flawed he explained by the limits of human vision. In this he resembled the famous contemporaneous Protestant defenders of the Bible, A. A. Hodge and B. B. Warfield.

Roberts's theory of inspiration resembled that of Hodge and Warfield in other ways. Like them, he insisted there were prominent human elements in scripture: biblical writers drew from natural sources when writing and gave evidence of their own special limitations of knowledge and intellect. The scriptures, all three men agreed, were written upon definite historical occasions that naturally colored their production, yet "a divine spirit is present in the midst of those human elements giving forth light and truth and wisdom such as is to be found in no merely human production." Actual dictation from God did occur on rare occasions, but this was not the general rule,

25. *The Gospel*, p. 84.
26. Ibid., pp. 84–85.

and allowance must be made for degrees of inspiration. Apparent inconsistencies with internal biblical as well as external secular sources were of course to be expected of imperfect copies of ancient writings, where the original reading may have been lost and because, in any case, "the human forms of knowledge by which the critics test the accuracy of Scripture are themselves subject to error." On two crucial points, however, Roberts parted company with Hodge and Warfield. Unlike them, he allowed not only for human traits but also for human mistakes in scripture. Also unlike them, he was loath to draw lines defining "orthodox" belief.[27]

Roberts was particularly (and, for Mormons, typically) offended by the tendency of the higher critics to assume the unhistoricity of miracles and, having made that assumption, to interpret passages containing miraculous elements as mythical or superstitious. Renan's *Vie de Jesus* and Strauss's *Leben Jesu,* to cite prominent examples, had both equated the supernatural with the unreal.[28] To Roberts, this postulate was highly prejudicial, and he was bothered by it perhaps even more than were biblical apologists outside his faith.

This was because many Christians believed miracles had ceased with the apostolic age. The Mormons, though, still lived in sacred time, in an age of miracles, apostles, and revelations. For them, especially, a criticism assuming at the outset the impossibility of miracles would guarantee a fundamental misreading of the Testaments. Such a criticism would erroneously take as granted, for example, that documents that included detailed prophecies of later events could not have been written prior to those events.

But for Roberts, as for Mormon leaders before him, "What is

27. Hodge and Warfield specifically attacked the idea that "the sacred writers, having been divinely helped to certain knowledge, were left to the natural limitations and fallibility incidental to their human . . . character. . . ." Roberts, by contrast, had no difficulty with the idea that a prophet might receive a divine truth, then, perhaps with the aid of secretaries, proceed to frame a document, which might subsequently undergo revisions, to announce the truth. Quoting the Book of Mormon, he also argued that scriptural writers themselves acknowledged the possibility of error in their own writing and not merely in the copying or translation of it. For their theology of inspiration, see Hodge and Warfield, "Inspiration," *Presbyterian Review* 2 (1881): 225–38. For Roberts, *IE* 8 (1905): 358–70; *New Witnesses,* 2:116–19; *Defense of the Faith,* pp. 517–18; "Higher Criticism," p. 674; "The Truth, the Way, the Life," chap. 16, p. 5.

28. Quoted and attacked in *New Witnesses for God,* 1:24–25, 31–33, 35.

prophecy but history reversed?"[29] Had not Joseph Smith, for instance, prophesied in remarkable detail, thirty years before the fact, of the rebellion of South Carolina that would lead to the war between the states? Roberts was convinced of similarly fulfilled prophecies "within my own knowledge." He knew, and cited examples to his own satisfaction, that "the future can be exactly revealed to the mind of man." Roberts did not wish to use miracles to *prove* the truth of any particular religion, long a Christian practice. He simply objected to the critical assumption of their impossibility that doomed much of the Testaments to dismissal.[30]

Roberts was equally offended that the higher critics tended to drop the preconception that the Bible is God's word. Lyman Abbott, asserting what modern students now commonly deny, had insisted the new "literary method" of study "assumes nothing." It examined the Bible as it would any other body of literature, leaving "the questions whether . . . [and] in what sense . . . and to what extent it came from God, all to be determined by examination of the book itself."[31] To this Roberts objected.

When using the scriptures himself, Roberts had an approach that might be described as a "liberalized literalism." He perpetuated the Mormon dispensationalist worldview, and took the story of the Flood as presented in Genesis at face value. Job was for him a real man who had lived on the earth, though Roberts undogmatically acknowledged the problems of such a position. Moses wrote the Pentateuch, and Ezra and/or Nehemiah probably amended it to make it intelligible to post-Exilic Jews. Moses may well have had earlier sources from which he worked, but "this new knowledge [does not] require us to doubt the inspiration which rested upon him and that enabled him to weave into splendid, coherent form the fragmentary truth among the ancient Egyptian, Babylonian, and other peoples." The apostle John wrote the Apocalypse, though Solomon likely did not author Ecclesiastes,

29. Parley Pratt, *The Voice of Warning* (New York: W. Sanford, 1857), chaps. 1 and 2; Roberts, "Higher Criticism and the Book of Mormon," p. 666.

30. For Smith's Civil War prophecy, consult D&C 87 and 130:12–13. For Robert's own experiences, see "Higher Criticism," pp. 775–77; *New Witnesses,* 1:27–35. Roberts was also fond of George Rawlinson's defense of miracles, *Historical Evidences of the Truth of the Scripture Records* (New York: J. B. Alden, 1885).

31. Abbott, "The Bible as Literature," a course of lectures given in Plymouth Church, Brooklyn, 1896–1897, quoted in Roberts, *New Witnesses,* 2:4.

nor David all the Psalms. The Book of Hebrews was probably but not certainly written by Paul.[32]

Although he often referred to the Bible as "our principal volume of scripture," Roberts used the Book of Mormon and the Doctrine and Covenants as naturally and confidently as he did the Bible, describing them all as equal in authority. Neither the Bible nor the Mormon Church had a monopoly on religious truth, for all the great teachers, including Buddha, Confucius, Mohammed, the Protestant Reformers, and various eminent philosophers were subject to degrees of inspiration. Yet The Church of Jesus Christ of Latter-day Saints was "an exact *fac simile*" (*sic*) of the church he felt Jesus had founded two millennia earlier, and the Bible was saturated with prophecies of the Mormon "restoration."

Roberts was aware of and welcomed the nineteenth century's advances in textual criticism. Against those who conceived of the Bible as God's homogenized word, Roberts stressed its diversity, as well as its insufficiency to settle important religious questions. He tried to dissuade Mormons from using text-proofing methods of argument or study. Because of transmission, translation, and interpretive difficulties, "Latter-day Saints must take wide latitude in interpretation of the Bible." Like Catholics and against many Protestants, Roberts argued that it "is a mistake to suppose that written scripture ever made the Church of Christ. It was the Church of Christ always that made scripture."[33]

A number of orthodox Christian apologists attempted to dismiss the new forms of biblical studies as an "attack that has failed."[34] Roberts disagreed. To the extent the new criticism had not affected believers, he said, "its non-effect is the result of [believers] not coming in contact with it," either because of the German language in which the earlier conversation occurred, because the discussion was

32. "The Truth, the Way, the Life," chap. 16, p. 10; *The Seventy's Course in Theology,* pp. 33, 71, 72, 75, 82, 83; *The Gospel,* p. 45.

33. *The Gospel,* pp. 58, 72–73 (notes), 83, 88; "The Truth, the Way, the Life," chap. 29, pp. 1–2, chap. 20, p. 7; *Defense of the Faith,* pp. 512–13; folder #290 in B. H. Roberts Collection, and handwritten notes inserted in personal Bible, #73 in B. H. Roberts Memorial Library, LDS Church Archives; *New Witnesses,* vol. 1, chaps. 9, 16, 19, 20, 22, 24; *The Seventy's Course in Theology,* p. iii.

34. E.g., Rawlinson, *Historical Evidences.*

simply over their heads, or, as with Catholics, because the authority and policies of the Church isolated the people from its findings.

But by the turn of the twentieth century, Roberts observed, it was scarcely possible any longer to pretend the "attack" had "failed." Defenders of "destructive criticism" were almost as plentiful on Protestant seminary faculties as "conservative critics," and the numerical balance was shifting rapidly in favor of the former.[35] Moreover, "what must ever be an occasion for . . . humiliation . . . to orthodox Christendom is its inability to meet in any effectual way the assaults of this New Criticism." In Germany, Roberts noted with more than a trace of sarcasm, believers were reduced to complaining against Strauss for having written his *Life of Jesus* in the German language: "If he must write such a book, so full of unbelief . . . , he ought at least to have had the grace to have written it in Latin!" And when he was driven out of Presbyterianism, the American Charles Briggs was able to argue—accurately, Roberts thought—that he had been overcome by numbers, not by intelligence.[36]

What is most striking about Roberts's defense against this onslaught of critical thought is that after describing its nature, after lamenting its impact on modern Christian faith and conceding that orthodoxy had failed to meet its challenge, after acknowledging that it might have virtues but detailing only its faults, all the while regarding the new techniques not as tools to utilize but as tests to endure[37]—after all this, the only significant criticism of the critics Roberts offered was their failure to allow for the possibility of miracles. He did castigate in general terms their "specious reasoning," and he mourned the fact that "however beautiful the moral precepts of the merely human Jesus may be, they will have no perceptible influence on the lives of the multitude unless back of them stands divine authority, accompanied by a conviction of . . . immortality. . . ." But virtually nowhere did he attempt to dismantle the reasoning of the critics, apart from their assumptions

35. By the twentieth century, liberals controlled the vast majority of Protestant seminaries in the North (Marsden, in *Eerdmans' Handbook,* ed. Noll et al., p. 326). By the 1920s modernists occupied so many professorships, pulpits, publications, and mission boards that many opponents lamented bitterly that modernism had simply "taken over" (Hutchison, "Protestant Modernism," in *Eerdmans' Handbook,* ed. Noll et al., pp. 383–84).

36. *New Witnesses,* 1:36–40; 2:8–9.

37. "Higher Criticism," pp. 665–66; *New Witnesses,* 2:9, 11, 37.

concerning miracles.[38] Instead, he urged that the inability of the orthodox to meet the real threat without dodging it required the arrival of a
new prophet, a new witness for God and Christ, who would speak not
by the authority of scribes and pharisees—scholars—but by the authority of God.

Joseph Smith and the Book of Mormon, said Roberts, were just
such witnesses. More than any other LDS leader of his time, Roberts
was willing to confront serious questions about the authenticity of the
Book of Mormon.[39] But once having committed himself to its truth,
he did not believe higher criticism undermined the Book of Mormon
so much as the Book of Mormon disproved certain theories of the
critics, notably the multiple authorship of the Book of Isaiah.[40]

Roberts's thought was rarely that Joseph Smith's knowledge of the
Bible might have shaped the production of the Book of Mormon but,
rather, that the Book of Mormon (or others of Smith's revelations)
verified the Bible.[41] The stylistic and theological break that critics
thought they discovered between Isa. 39 and 40 was not so great if
one allowed for the plausibility of inspired prophecy. Roberts chal-

38. He does in one instance devote eight pages to summarizing and quoting the work
of nineteenth-century scholars tending to show that the cultures, geographical facts,
and certain historical events of the Hebrews and their neighbors were in general
accurately portrayed in the Old Testament. Sometimes, however, these are only of
marginal relevance to the issues of historical criticism. For instance, his citations of
parallel narratives among Babylonians, Sumerians, and others about Sabbaths and
floods and the Creation tell one nothing about the historicity or inspiration of such
things.

39. Roberts, *Studies of the Book of Mormon.*

40. "Higher Criticism," pp. 667ff. Evidence suggests Truman Madsen is correct in
countering those who have argued that Roberts, on the basis of candid questions he
asked in a manuscript (published posthumously as *Studies of the Book of Mormon*) no
longer believed in the Book of Mormon's historicity by the end of his life. Roberts's
last (unpublished) book ("The Truth, the Way, and the Life") and dozens of sermons
during his last years not only are laced with citations from the Book of Mormon but
speak in the mode of "final testimony" preceding his death (Truman G. Madsen,
"B. H. Roberts and the Book of Mormon," *BYUS* 19 [Summer 1979]: 427–45; "B. H.
Roberts After Fifty Years: Still Witnessing for the Book of Mormon," *Ensign,* [Decem-
ber 1983]: 10–19; Madsen, correspondence with author, November 6, 1989).

41. *The Gospel,* pp. 56–62, 79–82; "Higher Criticism," pp. 669–77, 781–86. The
main exception, where Roberts did allow that the Book of Mormon might have been
directly influenced by the Bible, was his acknowledgment that Joseph Smith may have
copied the KJV language rather than laboriously translating those passages that he
recognized as similar (*IE* 7 [1903–1904]: 179).

lenged one authority, who wrote: "[It is] unthinkable that [chapters 40ff. were] written by the first Isaiah, because it would be necessary to immerse him in the spirit of prophecy, out of the environment of his life and his labors." Yet Jesus himself (whose perceptions Roberts assumed were beyond question) had launched his messianic career by quoting from Isa. 61, declaring it to have predicted his own coming. Why reject Isaiah's gift of before-the-event prophecy if the Master himself accepted it? It would, Roberts said, be no more difficult for the first than for the second Isaiah to utter this prediction of Jesus.[42]

Roberts's reaction to higher criticism was, then, profoundly ambivalent. He was receptive to it in principle—far more receptive, for instance, than either Isaac Wise or Solomon Schechter, respectively the chief American architects of Reform and Conservative Judaism, who considered much of the work of the higher critics to be "higher anti-Semitism."[43] Yet he was hostile to the specific conclusions of the new criticism's major practitioners.

Roberts insisted that demonstrable facts of science have their say where they bear on religious matters, and allowed that the methods of historical biblical criticism had theoretical merit and had made real contributions, but nowhere did he spell out just what he thought those contributions were. He lamented what he felt was the tendency of the critics to undermine the faith of traditional believers. His defense against this threat consisted primarily of a counterattack against the critics' naturalistic presuppositions, buttressed by the verification given the Bible by the Book of Mormon. Although he acknowledged the traditional Mormon themes of a corrupt biblical text and the need for living prophets, he was, in the new American context where scriptural authority was in jeopardy, quite at pains to demonstrate the essential integrity of the extant biblical narratives and to minimize any corrections made in the Bible by Joseph Smith.[44]

It is important to notice that Roberts, who died in 1933, never had

42. Luke 4:16–23. Roberts, "Higher Criticism," pp. 670, 777–81.

43. Wise, "The World of My Books," trans. Albert H. Friedlander, in *Critical Studies in American Jewish History,* ed. Jacob R. Marcus, 4 vols. (New York: KTAV, 1971), 1:180; Sperling, "Judaism and Modern Biblical Research," p. 23; Sperling and Levine, *History of Jewish Biblical Scholarship,* chap. 2.

44. *The Gospel,* pp. 46–58. Note the contrast with earlier leaders, like Orson Pratt and Brigham Young, who assumed the Bible's basic truth and importance but, against "Bible-alone" Protestants, stressed its limitations.

as his primary purpose a full exploration of biblical criticism. He was drawn into the subject only to underline the traditional Mormon claim of the need to modern revelation. Given his heavy ecclesiastical responsibilities, his lack of linguistic preparation, and his deep religious commitments, his attitude was remarkably open. Yet it must be seen as significant that the man widely regarded as Mormonism's preeminent intellectual leader in the early twentieth century did not engage the new criticism more thoroughly.

Joseph Fielding Smith

If B. H. Roberts waxed both hot and cold toward historical criticism, the censure of both its methods and its conclusions by his chief LDS theological rival, Joseph Fielding Smith, approached the absolute. During the course of Smith's exceptionally long ministry, the central themes of his position did not vary. Unlike Roberts, he had no use for human knowledge that did not conform to "the revealed word of God" as interpreted by a severe though selective literalism. Although he did not accept as historical the Genesis account of the creation of Adam and Eve, for example, he nonetheless regarded higher critics precisely as he regarded evolutionists: "Why is it," he wrote in a 1954 distillation of his thought, "that thousands of intelligent-looking human beings are willing to accept these stupid teachings? Frankly it is because Satan has deceived them and they love darkness rather than light." Similar assessments were sometimes made by conservatives of various denominations, who on occasion accused the higher critics of insanity, of having had their brains poisoned by tobacco and alcohol, and of performing "the sinister work of evil men."[45]

Smith was the son of the sixth president of the Mormon Church, and was grandnephew to its founder, Joseph Smith. He was born in 1876, before Brigham Young died, and served as a missionary and in Church-wide leadership slots from 1899 to 1910. In 1910 he was made an apostle, in which role he served for more than six decades until becoming the Church's president a year before his death in 1972. His career as an influential leader thus spanned much of the twentieth

45. Smith, *Man: His Origin and Destiny,* p. 138. For his linkage of evolution and higher criticism, see p. 33 and passim. Cf. Marsden, *Fundamentalism,* pp. 220–21.

century, and he remains one of the several most prolific authors of doctrinal material in Mormon history.

As the son of an apostle who eventually became Church president, Smith was naturally immersed in scriptural study from his earliest years. By age ten or so, he was likely to disappear in the middle of a ball game, only to be later found in the hayloft reading the Bible or Book of Mormon.[46] Throughout his life he never surrendered that extraordinary allegiance to the written word. He eventually came almost to define piety by one's knowledge of, and attachment to, scripture.

Among many Mormons, Smith was seen as the leading Mormon scripturist.[47] When he stood behind a pulpit, he was there "in all solemnity to teach the word of God as it is found in the scriptures." If this seems an unremarkable observation to make of a conservative Christian leader, one must remember the subtle decline of scriptural status relative to the word of "living prophets" that occurred in Mormon ranks during much of the nineteenth century.[48] Brigham Young's amusement at the exaggerated veneration given the Bible, and his "I would not give the ashes of a rye straw for all [scriptural] books . . . without the living oracles," stood in marked contrast to Joseph Fielding Smith's theology of scripture. "It makes no difference what is written or what anyone has said," Smith held, "if what has been said is in conflict with what the Lord has revealed. . . . My words, and teachings of any other member of the Church, high or low, if they do not square with the revelations, we need not accept them."[49] Mormon speakers in earlier generations had not shared the Protestant tradition of necessarily structuring their sermons around a scriptural text. Brigham Young, for instance, often cited no scripture at all in his sermons. Nineteenth-century Saints had taken the authority of scripture for granted but, in the face of the new higher criticism, it was Joseph

46. McConkie, *True and Faithful,* p. 69.

47. Mormon parlance prefers its own neologism: "scriptorian." For Smith's stature in this regard, see McConkie, *True and Faithful,* pp. 44–45. When Heber J. Grant was president of the Church, he wrote to Smith, saying that Smith was the "best posted man on the scriptures [among] the General Authorities" (J. F. McConkie, "Joseph Fielding Smith," in *Presidents,* ed. Arrington, p. 329).

48. Chap. 3.

49. Quoted in J. F. McConkie, "Joseph Fielding Smith," in *Presidents,* ed. Arrington, p. 328.

Fielding Smith, perhaps more than any other, who was responsible for a new emphasis in twentieth-century Mormonism on conscious, emphatic scriptural dependence.

From the time he was eight until his midteens, Smith observed his father living, like many Mormon leaders, in hiding from federal authorities who sought to enforce antipolygamy legislation. Life on "the Mormon underground" created tremendous hardships for the affected families, and related difficulties included the public vilification of beloved parents. Smith's own father, a pious man, was frequently defamed by a rabid press. *Cosmopolitan* absurdly described him as "furtive, lurking, and sly . . . a cat who would attack only when one's back was turned" and who might reenact the massacre at Mountain Meadows at any moment. *McClure's* called him "a man of violent passions. One could easily imagine him torturing heretics or burning witches to advance the kingdom of God."[50] The pain of such libels during the younger Smith's early life—and the fact that he came of age precisely as the emotionally and intellectually dislocating issues behind the modernist movement achieved prominence[51]—may have contributed to his propensity in later years to see every instance of critical thought as an attack on his faith.

As even some liberals acknowledged, the term *higher criticism* was easy to construe pejoratively,[52] and was doubly distasteful to Smith. *Higher* seemed to imply snobbery, as though a mere scholar could teach what the Holy Spirit could not. As a contemporary evangelical put it, "Have we to await a communication from Tübingen or a telegram from Oxford before we can read the Bible?"[53] "Criticism," in turn, did not mean "informed judgment" to Smith but, rather, "finding fault with God's word." So hostile was he to

50. *Cosmopolitan* (March 1911): 444–46, 696–97; *McClure's* (January 1911): 259; quoted in McConkie, *True and Faithful,* p. 29.

51. The main components of Protestant modernism were brought together during Smith's earliest years in the 1880s, and came to national prominence about 1910, just as Smith was made a Mormon apostle (Hutchison, "Protestant Modernism," in *Eerdmans' Handbook,* p. 383). During the first two decades of his apostolic tenure, the modernist–fundamentalist controversy was nationally in full bloom.

52. Harry Emerson Fosdick, a champion of higher criticism, acknowledged that "were one to search the dictionary for two words suggestive of superciliousness, condescension, and destructiveness, one could hardly find any to surpass these" (*The Modern Use of the Bible* [New York: Association Press, 1926], p. 6).

53. Joseph Parker, *None Like It* (New York: Revell, 1893), p. 73.

the new methods that, like others in the country, Smith thought of them as a conspiracy, a determined effort "launched on the part of certain scholars to tear asunder and destroy the authenticity of the holy scriptures."[54]

To Smith, scripture was "unequivocal and sufficient" and required a literal interpretation.[55] His literalism could be sufficiently unrelenting that if one passage of the original form of Genesis was not historically accurate, he felt Christianity would fall. When Isaiah wrote that some in future days would "fly as the cloud" (60:8), he was not speaking poetically of the speed of returning exiles but, Smith believed, of contemporary times: the ancient prophet had seen modern airplanes in a vision. Similarly, Nahum "without question" viewed our present means of communication. The tower of Babel narratives were true as written. And when Gen. 11:9 said people were scattered upon "all the earth," it meant *all* the earth. The Book of Mormon, to say nothing of Aztec legends, referred to these episodes and guaranteed their verity. Fulfilled prophecies, such as the scattering and gathering of Israel, authenticated scriptural accounts.

Smith scoffed at those, particularly members of his church, whose preconceptions of a God of peace enabled them to dismiss the divine hand in stories of Joshua's brutal occupation of the Promised Land. The principal authorities he used to interpret biblical texts were other scriptural texts (as he interpreted them) and the Holy Ghost.[56]

Smith's literalist propensities did not mean he was incapable of recognizing figurative language, of course. Indeed, while defending the Bible's accuracy he could find metaphor where Bible critics thought images were intended literally ("four corners of the earth," "four winds of the earth," "the pillars of heaven," and so on). Critics

54. *Man: His Origin and Destiny,* p. 490; Marsden, *Fundamentalism,* pp. 190–91.

55. Richard Poll, unpublished "Notes on a Conversation with President Joseph Fielding Smith," December 29, 1954, quoted in Gary Bergera and Ronald Priddis, *Brigham Young University* (SLC: Signature Books, 1985), p. 156. I use "literal" in the sense discussed in chapter 1.

56. McConkie, *True and Faithful,* p. 92; Smith, *Man: His Origin and Destiny,* pp. 10–11, 23, 25, 399, 419–20, 471, 481, 483–87, 527–28, chaps. 21, 22; Smith, *Seek Ye Earnestly,* p. 366; Smith, *Signs of the Times,* pp. 89–91; cf. Edmund Lab. Cherbonnier, "The Logic of Biblical Anthropomorphism," *Harvard Theological Review* 55 (1962): 182–206, and "In Defense of Anthropomorphism," in *Reflections on Mormonism: Judaeo-Christian Parallels,* ed. Truman G. Madsen (Provo, UT: BYU Religious Studies Center, 1978), p. 160.

such as Andrew White, who treated such imagery as crude and erroneous, were, said Smith, profoundly ignorant of "the poetical nature of
the Hebrew mind."[57]

Elder Smith's most fundamental hermeneutical assumption was
that the Bible and other Mormon scriptures were essentially God's
speech in print. Smith not only rejected new critical theories that
challenged this view but also showed little awareness of earlier Mormon notions of revelation as provisional, subject to error and refinement, and filtered through the minds of human participants and what
a more famous Joseph Smith had called their "crooked, broken, scattered and imperfect language."[58] Always in the background for Joseph Fielding Smith was the implied threat of biblical criticism to
specifically Mormon scriptures. Scripture to him represented "actual
facts"; history and science were "theory." Therefore, science and
history were to be viewed through the lens of scripture, not the con-
verse. Puny human reason has no business judging the word of God.
Nor is it appropriate to stretch the meaning of scripture "in a vain
attempt to make it conform to [human] theories and teachings,"
which will change soon enough of their own accord.[59]

Because he held such positions, some have yielded to the temptation to dismiss Smith as "unintelligent," "intolerant," "a zealot," and
thus unworthy of notice. But his influence on modern Mormonism
has been far too pervasive to dismiss him so facilely, and in any case
he was not unintelligent nor, if one allows for his perspective, particularly intolerant. He was simply an ordinary man with extraordinary
influence, a man whose loyalty to God, as he understood God, was
virtually boundless. In his mind, that which threatened the literality
and verbal inspiration of revelation threatened Christianity as a
whole, Mormonism in particular, and hence the meaning of life for

57. White, *A History of the Warfare of Science with Theology in Christendom,* 2 vols.
(New York: Appleton, 1896), 1:90; Smith, *Man: His Origin and Destiny,* pp. 471–2.

58. Joseph Fielding Smith did allow that revelation may admit of additional development or may, for cause, be revoked. But, apparently unaware of the history of many of
Joseph Smith's revelations, he held that revelation "admits of no change . . . there will
be no conflict between the part first revealed, and the latter part revealed. . . ." *Man:
His Origin and Destiny,* p. 470.

59. "Official Report of the One-Hundred Thirty-Sixth Annual Conference of The
Church of Jesus Christ of Latter-day Saints," (SLC: The Church of Jesus Christ of
Latter-day Saints, April 1966), pp. 70–71; *Man: His Origin and Destiny,* pp. 5, 9–10,
17, 47–48. Cf. Marsden, *Fundamentalism,* p. 226.

him and for the hundreds of thousands, even millions, under his apostolic jurisdiction.

Smith did not lack a sense of history construed as an interest in things past. Indeed, he had served and written as Mormonism's official historian. And, as the Church's most vocal scripturist, he had a mind dominated by figures and events of the past. What he lacked— or rejected—was a modern historical consciousness: the conviction that "knowledge of divine things, like knowledge of ordinary things, must be found squarely within the historical process or not at all."[60] He believed that revelation, ancient and modern, completely transcended history.

In several instances, Smith raised entirely plausible objections against the Bible's critics. Ironically, several of his contentions were more specific and substantive than those of the better equipped B. H. Roberts. Like Roberts, Smith thought the critics presumptuous to reject miracles and direct revelation out of hand. His own prophet-father had, after all, received a dramatic revelation, now adopted as the 138th section of the Doctrine and Covenants. Additionally, Smith noted, some enthusiastic scholars had argued against even the bare historical existence of Jesus. Because of its religious importance, the claims of the Bible had sometimes been subjected to tests of authenticity so rigid that had they been equally applied to secular figures like Hammurabi or Socrates, these too would have faded into legend. Much evidence arguing for the ancientness of certain elements in various biblical narratives was sometimes ignored or unduly subordinated by scholars to fit then-current theories. The Tübingen School had misread internal evidence and dated such crucial documents as the gospel of John in the second half of the second century.

Furthermore, Smith insisted with some justification, these tenuous theories had on occasion been pronounced with the finality of proven facts, and opponents of such dogmatism branded as dogmatists. Misunderstandings of ancient words and worldviews had caused premature and sweeping condescension toward biblical perspectives. Critics had sometimes been guilty of a presentist conceit, too certain that contemporary views about "the nature of things" are in all ways more accurate than ancient ones; that because modern readers could dis-

---

60. Wacker, "The Demise of Biblical Civilization," in *The Bible in America,* ed. Hatch and Noll, p. 127.

cern among biblical peoples assumptions no longer current, modern folks are free of their own assumptions. Also, theologies of later Christians were sometimes read back into biblical perspectives and then demeaned. Critical speculation was indeed here and there "hung upon slender threads" so that, in the words of one critic whom Smith cited,

> it became customary to consider it as highly scientific to challenge everything biblical and to alter the text at one's heart's desire. . . . [The] mania of seeing everywhere a wrong text and detecting all kinds of interpolations, glosses and anachronisms, and likewise the zeal to heap emendations upon corrections resulted in creating a new specialty for speculative "experts" to exert themselves in the art of text alterations and source-hunting.[61]

Despite such tenable criticism of the new scholarship, Smith was ill-prepared to meet it on its own terms, and at many spots revealed he did not understand it sufficiently to judge it. He did reasonably understand the central issues at stake as the authorship, antiquity, and accuracy of the various biblical books, as well as the question of the development of the idea of God and other notions. He was also familiar with the details of the documentary hypothesis of Genesis.[62] But he read only English and was everywhere dependent on secondary information, from which he assessed all materials that supported a traditional view of revelation as worthy, and everything that questioned it as sinister.

Because of adjustments or errors on the part of some critics, Smith, in contrast to B. H. Roberts, triumphantly quoted conservative scholars who maintained that higher criticism as a whole had in the early twentieth century been proven false; its theories "are now as dead as the extinct dodo." Which of the four gospels had been written first

61. Smith, *CN,* April 15, 1939; *Man: His Origin and Destiny,* pp. 5, 16, 55, 79, 386, 418, 471–76, 481, 496–99, 505–6, 524, chap. 20; Smith, *Seek Ye Earnestly,* p. 367. Modern criticism has continued to develop with a sophistication of which Smith scarcely dreamt, but its critics have likewise—and not so defensively as Smith—achieved increasing sophistication. A good recent example is Martin Hengel, who has questioned the fundamental presupposition of form criticism (the circulation of individual units of Christian tradition prior to the writing of the New Testament documents) and the relative importance of redaction criticism. See *Acts and the History of Earliest Christianity* (Philadelphia: Fortress Press, 1980), pp. 25–26, 56–57, passim.

62. *Seek Ye Earnestly,* pp. 364ff.

was immaterial to him, and he thought the "ingenious" argument for the priority of Mark was "sheer speculation" rather than an important working hypothesis that led to many insights. He felt that literary critics probably could not discern among various unsigned writers in the *New York Times,* so why should one believe the clever guesses of those who thought they could separate the strands in Old Testament writings? All internal contradictions and historical mistakes in the Bible were to be blamed on intruding copyists and translators.[63]

For Smith, then, modern biblical criticism was a conglomerate of errors and an almost absolute evil. His rejection of it was not the irenic plea of Dwight L. Moody that it represented an impractical distraction ("What is the use of talking about two Isaiahs when most people don't know there's one?") but was, like evolution, a satanically inspired assault "on the record which we have cherished." Smith was not above marshaling the methods of history when he felt they supported his cause, but criticism that threatened faith was merely a series of "fancy imaginary stories." He called on scholars who had supported it to "repent of the evil" and return to the defense of the Bible. "Destructive critics" should be warned by the plight of the rich man who lifted up his eyes from hell, crying to Father Abraham: "Have mercy on me, and send Lazarus . . . [to] cool my tongue." But Abraham said, "Son, remember that thou in thy lifetime receivedst thy good things, and likewise Lazarus evil things: but now he is comforted, and thou art tormented."[64]

William H. Chamberlin

Because of their contrasting attitudes toward secular learning, Smith and B. H. Roberts are often regarded as theological opposites within Mormon ranks. But so far as their responses to higher criticism go, Roberts holds a middle position on a continuum where Smith represents the far right. Smith's real opposite is better portrayed by the educator William H. Chamberlin (1870–1921), the first Mormon teacher to make extended use of modern methods of Bible study.

63. Ibid., pp. 364–65; *Man: His Origin and Destiny,* pp. 491–92, 494, 521, 523.

64. Moody, quoted in *Eerdmans' Handbook,* p. 326. Smith, *Seek Ye Earnestly,* p. 367; Smith, *Signs of the Times,* pp. 90–91; *Man,* pp. 502, 506, 513–15, and, for the selective use of history, passim.

Unlike previously considered figures, Chamberlin never became a general official of the Church. His influence instead was through occasional publications and more particularly in the classroom, where he guided a whole generation of aspiring young intellectuals who went on to positions of religious and secular prominence during the middle third of the twentieth century. Although Chamberlin's importance is thus substantial, and his perspectives enjoyed the sympathy of several top-ranking Church officials and numerous educational leaders, his lack of hierarchical status and his briefer treatment here symbolize the proportionately lesser impact his views had on the general Mormon populace. Whereas most adult English-speaking Saints today could identify or at least recognize the names of Joseph Fielding Smith or B. H. Roberts, far fewer could do the same for W. H. Chamberlin.

Like most of his Utah contemporaries, Chamberlin's early education was modest. He did read widely as a youth, however, and he sometimes engaged the Bible "so protractedly as to elicit the protest or interference" of his parents. Eventually, the boy's uncommon talent, ambition, and tenacity earned him a fine education. After graduating in science with the first class from the University of Utah, he obtained a master of arts degree in philosophy at the University of California and studied ancient languages and biblical criticism at the University of Chicago. He eventually spent two additional years at Harvard, where he impressed, among others, Josiah Royce. Interspersed with this study he taught, at various times, science, mathematics, geology, astronomy, psychology, theology, and philosophy at LDS College in Salt Lake City, Brigham Young College in Logan, Brigham Young University in Provo, and the University of Utah.[65]

In his mature years, Chamberlin came to advocate, in a Mormon context, precisely those ideas now identified as essential "modernism": divine immanence, divinely inspired progressivism, and cultural adaptation.[66] Influenced in part by philosopher Borden Parker

65. The essential biographical information is in Ralph Chamberlin, *Life and Philosophy of William H. Chamberlin.* Poor health finally induced Chamberlin, in 1917, to suspend pursuit of a Ph.D. in philosophy at Harvard (W. H. Chamberlin to Dean of the Graduate School, Harvard University, May 30, 1917 [David C. Chamberlin collection]).

66. Protestant modernism, at least, has received its clearest definition in Hutchison, *Modernist Impulse,* p. 2.

Bowne's "personalism," the heart of Chamberlin's religious philosophy was his belief that God, or at least God's power, is "in the midst of all things." He was especially fond of Doctrine and Covenants sections 88 and 93, which speak of "the light which is in all things, which giveth life to all things, which is the law by which all things are governed, even the power of God who sitteth upon his throne, who is in the bosom of eternity, who is in the midst of all things." This immanent God is at work in and through the natural world, bringing to pass his eternal purposes—his ever-arriving kingdom—through necessarily transitory religious forms.[67]

According to Chamberlin, God, in his efforts to lift mortals, communicates with human beings by using human ideas; otherwise communication is impossible. "If," for example, "one is anxious to train others in a belief that God is the creator of the world, he will have to use the Hebrew or Greek idea of the world in one age, or the commonly accepted Copernican idea of the world in this age." All of these ideas are limited—false, in a sense—yet through them humans with different conceptions in different ages have grasped the vital idea that God is the creator. God's aim, like that of a teacher, must be to establish fundamental attitudes, not the absolute truth of what passes among human beings as "facts." We must cherish God's word, but difficulty inevitably surfaces among groups who do so because the forms of expressing revelation commonly outlast the system of thought in which they arise.[68]

In the context of such a philosophy, Chamberlin did not value the Bible as a unique, infallible repository of the data of reality, whose only difficulty lay in the corruptions of transmission. For him, scripture conveyed, in addition to its truths, numerous ideas and hopes no longer plausible. Modern science, for instance, naturally improved on interpretations of the physical world casually expressed by scriptural writers, and conceptions of Deity had demonstrably evolved through the ages. Even so, without these "false" notions of God and human life, better ones could not have taken form. Yet it remained for anyone seeking to know God's will, either immediately or through

67. Chamberlin, "The Theory of Evolution as an Aid to Faith in God and Belief in the Resurrection," *The White and Blue* (a BYU student publication), supplement, February 14, 1911; *Life and Philosophy,* pp. 80–81, 169–76, 178, 200, 289, passim; Borden Parker Bowne, *Personalism* (Boston: Houghton, Mifflin, 1908).

68. *Life and Philosophy,* pp. 179–80, 175–76.

the scriptures "in which men have written down their own impressions of His will," to discern the eternal grains of wheat from among the supporting leaves. The leaves, once so necessary to the growth of the wheat, eventually become chaff, and there is "danger that the wheat may be confused with the chaff and cast away with it." This was the peril of modern intellectual society, which threatened to throw out the Bible and revealed religion altogether. But a more enduring and common hazard was that others might also confuse the wheat and chaff—confuse religion with its outward forms—and insist that they and everyone around them swallow both.[69]

By contrast, genuine religion demands constantly fresh expression in terms that accord with the widest knowledge of the time, including science.[70] The Hebrew prophets were foremost in crying out against the overly formalized religion of their day, with its perennial substitution of forms, sacrifices, and observances in place of the saving power of the truly religious spirit. It is difficult to have effective, organized religion without dogmas, but even canonized dogmas are mere formulations for imparting life's proper attitudes. Their partial and symbolic character must always be recalled if one is to see clearly the difference between religion and one's interpretation of it. Religion exists not in some external authority or record, not in a "vestry of verbs and texts," but in the hearts of living people.

Scripture is to be prized primarily as the record of religious experience and growth. The Bible should be read from a historical rather than an "absolutist" perspective. God revealed his character and humankind's best interests particularly in his dealing with the Hebrew people, and this revelation culminated in Jesus, who correctly taught that "he came to reveal God's character and man's fullest life."[71] Most formal modern thought, Chamberlin believed, was dominated by the spirit of Greek intellectualism: to know and understand, to attain wisdom as the supreme good. Neglected by modern thinkers was the yearning aspiration of the Hebrew prophets: to know God and to be righteous.

Chamberlin remained reverent toward the forms and rites of religion. Properly understood, he said, they symbolize those principles

69. Ibid., pp. 180–81.
70. Ibid., pp. 137, 161–62.
71. Ibid., pp. 113–14, 180–81.

and ideals of living God seeks us to understand. But real faith and ultimate truth can never be confined to even canonized statements of them, "limited by the moulds of pre-conceived notions and conventional terms." In fact, the effort to do so is irreligious. It constitutes, as other modernists had put it, bibliolatry.[72]

Against those who insisted the Bible was, without qualification, God's eternal word, Chamberlin pointed to the passing cultural views traceable in the scriptural record. This did not mean, however, that the Bible was merely a vast projection of the various peoples who had contributed to it. Chamberlin did believe in a real God who actually revealed himself, among other ways, in vision to prophets. The tangible resurrection of Jesus and of all God's children was a reality; personal life existed after death; Moses and Elijah actually conversed with Jesus about his death on the mount of transfiguration.[73]

The wheat in Chamberlin's borrowed image of the wheat and chaff was real and not to be dismissed. But in general, he felt, the concern for the miraculous was unimportant for both science and religion. Chamberlin usually treated the Bible as an incomparable record of religious experience in which "mighty prophets have acted or have written their thoughts about God and human duties." "It is pitiful," he said, "not to have entered into the soul of Amos or Isaiah" or, above all, Jesus. Nevertheless, the Bible was also full of legend, myth, poetry, parable (like the Book of Jonah), and error for which God could not be held accountable. That the Bible in its different portions is of unequal value, that it records evil deeds and principles as well as good, and failures as well as successes, added to rather than detracted from its value in illuminating the history of religious growth. The methods jointly known as higher criticism were to be embraced wholeheartedly, for one must strive to grasp the varied concrete problems the prophets faced in order to understand the spiritual realities behind the changing forms of their expression.[74]

Although his mind was conditioned by formal philosophy, relieved

72. Ibid., pp. 65, 204.

73. "The Significance of the Resurrection," in *The White and Blue,* March 21, 1913, p. 295; "The Theory of Evolution as an Aid to Faith in God and Belief in the Resurrection," pp. 1–4.

74. Account of a Chamberlin address in *The White and Blue* October 25, 1910, p. 19; *Life and Philosophy,* pp. 121–22, 128, 171, 181, passim; Ericksen, "William H. Chamberlin," p. 281.

of a heavy literalism, and soaked in the spirit of history, change, and evolution that dominated the intellectual climate of his era, Chamberlin's thought was well within the tradition of Joseph Smith and Brigham Young. Smith and Young had professed an authority beyond ordinary learning, but all three men, in the context of a deep Mormon faith, stressed the limitations of human language, the provisional nature of revelation, and the need of living prophets continually to reconvey and reformulate God's will to people of constantly changing circumstances.

The students to whom Chamberlin taught these views seemed overwhelmingly to have welcomed them as an aid to their religious perspectives. Their parents were not so sure. Many complaints were lodged with ecclesiastical leaders against Chamberlin, his brother Ralph, and two additional colleagues of similar opinions at Brigham Young University. In 1911 Ralph Chamberlin and Joseph and Henry Peterson were formally charged by the Church Board of Education with, among other things, "following the 'higher criticism' of Lyman Abbott; treating the Bible as 'a collection of myths, folk lore, dramas, literary productions, history and some inspiration' "; rejecting the Flood, the confusion of tongues, and the temptation of Christ as objectively real phenomena; and teaching the theory of evolution as a demonstrated law. Refusing to alter their teachings, the three left the university under duress, prompting a storm of controversy in the Utah press and a published petition signed by five-sixths of the student body protesting the board's action. The board, however, was unmoved. University administrators increasingly denied William Chamberlin access to his popular classes, and he was effectively forced to resign a few years later.[75]

The Spectrum of the Mormon Response

By envisaging William H. Chamberlin, B. H. Roberts, and Joseph Fielding Smith as points on a spectrum, one can discern a Mormon response to the advent of historico-critical thinking that can be com-

75. William H. Chamberlin to Ralph Chamberlin, December 18, 1915, and March 12 and April 9, 1916 (David C. Chamberlin collection). For extended accounts of other dimensions of the affair, see note 2.

pared to other religious groups. Among the relatively few Saints attuned to the issues, the dominant reaction was negative, accompanied by a sense that the faith of the people was threatened—as, indeed, some traditional conceptions were—by the new thinking. This negative reaction was split between total condemnation of modern methods as "satanic" and a more ambivalent position that was almost half-acceptance, one that allowed higher criticism an important role. In addition, a smaller but disproportionatly influential minority applauded the new critical approaches as crucial tools in discerning the permanent from the transient in the religious impulse.

Several cautions are in order concerning this sketch. One is that the spectrum represents intellectual or hierarchical leaders. These leaders wielded great prestige, but it remains true that most Latter-day Saints between 1900 and 1950, who had at least heard of Darwinism, probably had little awareness about the biblical criticism that in reality asked of traditionalists a deeper conceptual adjustment.

Another consideration is the unexplored points on my imaginary spectrum. Mormons in varying numbers were probably found all along the spectrum earlier in the century, as they are today. For example, the influential Harvard- and Göttingen-educated apostle, John A. Widtsoc, positioned himself ambiguously between Chamberlin and Roberts. Widtsoe sometimes used the Bible so literalistically that he followed Joseph Smith in pinpointing the precise location of the Garden of Eden, but he also insisted that "all sound scholarship," higher criticism included, was welcomed by Latter-day Saints. In popularized form, Widtsoe everywhere promoted reason, learning, and science among Church members. Provided that one accepted the existence and direction of God, he advocated the use of whatever tools could be fashioned to ascertain truth: "The Church therefore is in full harmony with the avowed purpose of the higher critics." Criticism, he said, should be used constructively, not destructively. Scripture is given by God "through earthly instruments," and thus while its inner substance preserves eternal truth, its outer form may contain many errors. The apostle allowed that we do not always know the real authorship of various biblical books and that the inadequate knowledge of ancient times was naturally reflected in the telling of ancient stories. He pointed out that the Bible contains history, poetry, and allegory and that these are not always distinguishable. He insisted that although miracles, properly understood, should not embarrass modern critics as unthinkable, there is still no reason that biblical miracles should not be weighed by human intelligence, and that "the whole of Holy Writ . . . is susceptible of interpretation." He also offered an informed and balanced assessment of the evolutionary nature of life on earth.[76]

Proportionately more leaders may be located on the spectrum between Roberts and Joseph Fielding Smith. The most important example is Apostle James E. Talmage, author of what are perhaps the two most influential nonscriptural books in Mormon history. An internationally known scientist, Talmage overtly ignored but was implicitly unfriendly toward the main thrusts of modern criticism. He noted the opening chapters of Genesis were not intended as a geological or biological textbook, but boasted that Mormonism excelled in scriptural literalism. In a single paragraph he observed that it is "eminently proper that we should inquire into the genuineness of the records upon which our faith is so largely founded," but then proceeded to convey the impression that there is scarcely a question concerning them worth bothering about: tradition, history, literary analysis, and prayer all showed the records to be well grounded. He was aware of the Tübingen critics and others but cited them only when they supported his views.

With his quasi-official masterwork, *Jesus the Christ,* Elder Talmage played a major role in embedding Mormon popular conceptions in the "Victorian lives of Jesus tradition," a primary purpose of which was to make the world safe from modern biblical criticism. Depending on such sources as Frederic W. Farrar, Cunningham Geikie, Alfred Edersheim, and numerous sources antedating the advent of modern biblical studies, Talmage concluded that there were two cleansings of the temple, two miraculous meals of bread and fish, and no essential contradictions in the narratives of the trial and crucifixion of Jesus. Further echoing the Victorian tradition, Talmage saw Jesus as the world's greatest champion of the rights of women. Like Joseph Fielding Smith, he also reacted negatively to the progress of textual criticism. However, in contrast to (and direct conflict with) Smith, he acknowledged an ancient earth with its increasingly complex life-

76. Widtsoe, *In Search of Truth* (SLC: Deseret Book, 1930), pp. 67–93; *Gospel Interpretations* (SLC: Bookcraft, 1947), pp. 251–54; *Evidences and Reconciliations,* 2 vols. (SLC: Bookcraft, 1943), passim; *A Rational Theology* (SLC: Deseret Book, 1937), passim.

forms. He embraced evolution by distinguishing it from a godless process of natural selection, insisting on the special creation of mankind, though allowing that pre-Adamic humans may have existed. He thus resembled B. H. Roberts in being somewhat hostile to higher criticism while allowing a conservative form of evolution.[77]

A final thing to keep in mind is that despite the strong feelings involved, Mormon authorities managed to avoid any major rupture. The preponderant sentiment was a conservative one, but leaders acknowledged a wide range of legitimate opinion. In 1922 Charles W. Penrose and Anthony W. Ivins, writing for the First Presidency of the Church, responded to an inquiry about the literality of the Bible by echoing Joseph Smith: the Bible was the word of God as far as it was translated correctly. They also noted, however, that there were some problems with the Old Testament and that the closing chapter of Deuteronomy proved the Pentateuch to have passed through hands other than Moses'. They believed in the historicity of Jonah, but acknowledged they might be wrong. It "is of little significance as to whether Jonah [or Job] was a real individual or one chosen by the writer of the book" to convey a lesson. Although they personally were sympathetic to the fundamentalist position laid out by William Jennings Bryan in his Union Theological Seminary lectures, they were as unwilling to commit the Church to a particular position on higher criticism as they were to pronounce the final word on evolution. Officially to "answer yes or no" to the higher critics was "unwise and should not be undertaken by one representing the Church."[78]

When one compares the scope of the conflict as it occurred in other denominations, even the exit of William Chamberlin and his colleagues from BYU could have been worse. As Professors Arrington and Bitton point out, no books were banned, no excommunications

77. J. R. Talmage, *The Talmage Story*, p. 232 (for his stature internationally, see pp. 87, 98, 116, 117, 137, 144, 153, 208); James Talmage, *Articles of Faith*, pp. 236–37, 250–51, 500, and *Jesus the Christ*, pp. 475, 484 n. 5, and passim; "Official Report of the Ninety-ninth Annual Conference of The Church of Jesus Christ of Latter-day Saints" (SLC: The Church of Jesus Christ of Latter-day Saints, April 1929), pp. 44–49; Pals, *The Victorian "Lives" of Jesus;* Thorp, "James E. Talmage and the Tradition of the Victorian Lives of Jesus"; Sherlock, "Turbulent Spectrum," pp. 38–41; Sherlock, "We Can See No Advantage."

78. Alexander, *Mormonism in Transition*, p. 283; Joseph F. Smith, "Philosophy and the Church Schools," *JI* 46 (April 1911): 209.

occurred, and no schisms took place.[79] By contrast, between 1874 and
the peak of the BYU controversy in 1911, almost every major Protestant denomination experienced at least one publicized heresy trial
involving the issue of an inerrant Bible. Furthermore, in a sequel that
goes unmentioned in virtually all references to the Chamberlin-
Peterson affair, a change was later made in the administration of the
Church school system. One result was that four years following his
resignation at BYU, Chamberlin was again teaching within the system
as a professor of philosophy at Brigham Young College in Logan, and
was subsequently even invited to return to teach at BYU.[80] Indeed,
within a few years of Chamberlin's death, the superintendant of the
Church's education system, future apostle Adam S. Bennion, volun-
teered his office as a distribution center for a new book about Chamberlin's life and philosophy. Anxious not to be interpreted as attacking his
predecessor in office (who had helped dismiss Chamberlin), Bennion
nonetheless desired every Church schoolteacher to read the book.[81]

On the other hand, one should not minimize the repercussions
unduly. Chamberlin lived for only five years after his dismissal from
BYU. His forced departure hurt him financially and personally in
ways from which some family members feel he never recovered.[82]
Countless Latter-day Saints were led to infer that his views were not
legitimate in the context of Mormon faith and that conservative
views, because they were allowed to dominate the teaching of religion at Brigham Young University, represented "real Mormonism."
Apostle and future Church President David O. McKay, who had
officially recommended that Chamberlin be reappointed to teach for
the Church's schools, lamented this perception. Calling Chamberlin
"a superior man in intellect and in spirit," McKay wrote: "That a
lofty, sincere soul like W. H. Chamberlin should have been com-
pelled to struggle in our community and to have been misunderstood by those who should have known him best, seems to me to be

79. *The Mormon Experience,* p. 260.
80. Ill health prevented him from accepting. Chamberlin, *Life and Philosophy,* p.
275.
81. Frank K. Seegmiller, member of the presidency of Latter-day Saints High
School, to Ralph Chamberlin, June 5, 1925 (David C. Chamberlin collection).
82. W. H. Chamberlin to Ralph V. Chamberlin, April 9, 1916, June 11 and 29, 1917,
October 30, 1917; W. H. Chamberlin to John T. Woodbury, April 5, 1917 (David C.
Chamberlin collection); David C. Chamberlin to author, November 29, 1989.

nothing short of a tragedy."[83] For at least a full generation BYU paid a price in intellectual respectability and loss of talent. Decades after the purge, for example, Thomas Martin, dean of the College of Applied Sciences, remained keenly aware that the growth of the university's stature had been stunted by the loss of the Chamberlins and Petersons, and was still feeling the effects. Lowell L. Bennion, among Mormonism's two or three preeminent religious educators of the twentieth century, refused offers of employment from BYU because he did not feel he would have sufficient intellectual freedom to teach religion there.[84]

The Legacy of the Early Responses

The responses of Mormon leaders to modern biblical scholarship during the first half of the century were continued and developed by others up to the present. The influence of William Chamberlin may be traced, at the far left of the spectrum, through such figures as E. E. Ericksen, who, despite the obscurity of his Salt Lake City base, rose to the presidency of the American Philosophical Association, and who attributed "the direction of my life's work" to his studies with Chamberlin.[85] By way of Ericksen this influence continues through, for example, philosopher-historian Sterling McMurrin, U.S. commissioner of education under John F. Kennedy and one of the most profound minds ever to emerge from Mormon ranks.

McMurrin considers himself supportive of the Church, but as a "culture Mormon" rather than as one who believes (as he once said when alluding to the experience of Joseph Smith) that boys receive

83. McKay to Ralph Chamberlin, February 17, 1926 (David C. Chamberlin collection).

84. Sherlock, "Campus in Crisis"; Lowell L. Bennion, interviews with author, March 1988. See also Christensen and Cannon, "The Fundamentalist Emphasis at Brigham Young University: 1935–1973." Although the specter of the Chamberlin–Peterson affair has long since faded for Brigham Young University as a whole, it is not farfetched to argue that the episode's legacy affects the personnel constitution of one or more departments even at present.

85. Ericksen to Ralph Chamberlin, May 8, 1925 (David C. Chamberlin collection). See also Scott G. Kenny, *Memories and Reflections: The Autobiography of E. E. Ericksen* (SLC: Signature Books, 1986).

books from angels.[86] However, Chamberlin's influence was also direct on more traditional believers.[87] Prominent among them was Russel Swensen, who, expanding a tradition initiated by Chamberlin, accepted with several other promising young religious instructors an invitation to receive advanced training at Church expense at the University of Chicago Divinity School in the 1930s. This training bore fruit during a long teaching career at BYU. During the 1940s, Swensen authored a series of widely used Sunday school manuals employing modern scholarship, though he was not permitted to cite non-Mormon sources.[88]

Equally important was Heber C. Snell, who had been among the majority of BYU students in 1911 signing a petition protesting the treatment given the Petersons and Chamberlins. Like Swensen, Snell had followed Chamberlin to the University of Chicago Divinity School, where Shirley Jackson Case directed his dissertation on the historical background to the teachings of Jesus (1932). He returned to Utah and became an instructor in the Church's Institute of Religion in Logan.

In the 1940s Dr. Franklin L. West, then the Church's commissioner of education, asked Snell to write a textbook on the Old Testament suitable for use by Church college students. When the manuscript was completed, however, Apostle Joseph Fielding Smith, offended by Snell's critically informed perspectives, led a successful campaign to prevent Church publication of the book.

86. "An Interview with Sterling McMurrin," *Dialogue* 17 (Spring 1984): 18–43; McMurrin, *Religion, Reason, and Truth: Historical Essays in the Philosophy of Religion* (SLC: University of Utah Press, 1982), preface.

87. Many BYU luminaries might be noted, including figures such as Carl F. Eyring, Wilford Poulson, Hugh M. Woodward, Thomas L. Martin, William J. Snow, B. F. Larson, and Vasco M. Tanner.

88. Swensen, "Mormons at the University of Chicago Divinity School"; personal interview with author, November 11, 1986. The public citing of only LDS sources had precedent. In sharp contrast to the philosophy of B. H. Roberts, the Church Board of Education in 1908 forbade its teachers to use as texts any books about the Bible written by non-Mormons, though they could consult them in preparing lectures. Swensen's Sunday school manuals include *Introduction to the New Testament* (SLC: LDS Department of Education, 1940); *The Synoptic Gospels*, (SLC: Deseret Sunday School Union, 1945); *The Gospel of John* (SLC: Deseret Sunday School Union, 1946); and *New Testament: Acts and Epistles* (SLC: Deseret Sunday School Union, 1947). Under the direction of Milton Bennion, this interest in serious scholarship in Mormon Sunday schools survived through the early 1950s.

In the company of Sterling McMurrin and Apostle Harold B. Lee, Snell later met with Elder Smith in hopes of vindicating his work. Elder Smith lamented he could find no "religion" in the narrative, and objected to its portraying Israelite conceptions of God as though they had changed over time. Drawn into the conversation by Smith, McMurrin insisted Snell's book was a genuine religious study, filled with references to God's revelation through the prophets, and that evidence of evolving Israelite conceptions simply came with serious knowledge of the Bible. He subsequently asked Smith more specifically what it was about the book that bothered him. Elder Smith's pointed retort: "Dr. Snell never once mentions the Book of Mormon."[89]

Suggestive of the diversity among Church leaders, Snell's book, eventually published as *Ancient Israel: Its Story and Meaning,* received plaudits from others. Among them were General Authority Levi Edgar Young and apostles John A. Widtsoe and Joseph F. Merrill, all of whom had doctoral training in various disciplines. Spearheaded by Joseph Fielding Smith, however, controversy continued to swirl about the book. Snell was fired from his position at the Institute of Religion and then, like William H. Chamberlin, rehired. At one point, Church President David O. McKay was forced to intervene to prevent efforts to excommunicate Snell from the Church.[90] That the contested borders of hermeneutical orthodoxy remain well patroled in some sectors of contemporary Mormonism is suggested by the 1988 firing of BYU Professor David P. Wright on the basis of his scriptural views.[91]

89. The papers of Joseph Fielding Smith, like those of other general authorities, are made unavailable to scholars. Snell's meeting with Elder Smith is recounted by witness Sterling McMurrin, audio cassette and personal correspondence with author, April 28 and August 5, 1989.

90. Sterling McMurrin, personal correspondence with the author, September 8, 1988. For other dimensions of the Snell affair, see Sherlock, "Faith and History"; Snell, "The Bible in the Church," *Dialogue* 2 (Spring 1967): 55–74.

91. Wright, formerly assistant professor in Asian and Near Eastern languages at BYU, received three specific reasons for his dismissal: (1) his view that the Book of Mormon is best explained as an inspired nineteenth-century work of scripture rather than a translation of a document from ancient America around 600 B.C.E.–400 C.E.; (2) his historical-critical view that the prophets of the Hebrew Bible generally spoke for their time and likely did not have in mind events far into the future, such as the era of Jesus or contemporary times; and (3) his approach to the Old Testament generally, an approach

The middle of the Mormon spectrum, represented in an earlier generation by B. H. Roberts, is symbolized more recently by Sidney Sperry (1895–1977), who entered Chicago's Divinity School four years after Chamberlin's death and was the first Saint to obtain a doctorate from such a school (1931). An Old Testament specialist, Sperry enjoyed a long career at BYU. He made real contributions to Mormon scriptural studies, helped incline many others toward more serious scholarship, and was largely responsible for such events as Edgar J. Goodspeed's summer classes at BYU in the 1930s. However, Sperry also insisted on the Mosaic authorship of the Pentateuch and the single authorship of the Book of Isaiah. He was often prepared either to submerge the conclusions of modern study in favor of the pronouncements of selected Church authorities or to use modern methods to arrive at the predetermined conclusions of those authorities; scholars should defer to prophets.[92] In this respect he was more

often skeptical of the historical accuracy of events described in it. Although Wright's view of the Book of Mormon was central to his being fired, he had made it a point not to teach these views in the classroom; his methods of biblical study, which he did teach, thus assume increased importance. Wright's letter of dismissal makes clear that apart from the foregoing matters he had been an exceptional scholar and teacher whose research, publications, teaching, administrative work, personality, morals, and conduct with other faculty and students had all been "exceptional." The case reflects the agonizing that occurs among some at BYU over how to incorporate Mormon faithfulness with intellectual freedom. It implies but fails fully to reflect the studied avoidance by a large portion of the BYU professoriate of crucial religious issues apt to stir controversy. Accounts of the Wright episode include "BYU Professor Loses Position Because of Divergent Beliefs" (*Daily Herald,* Provo, UT, August 7, 1988, p. 3); "BYU Has Lost the 'Wright' Stuff" (letter to editor, *Daily Herald,* August 15, 1988); "Personal Beliefs Cost Professor Job" (*Universe,* August 2, 1988); "Ex-BYU Professor Claims Beliefs Led to Dismissal" *Salt Lake Tribune,* July 30, 1988, pp. B-1, B-2); "BYU Professor Terminated for Book of Mormon Beliefs (*Sunstone* 12 [May 1988]: 43–44); "Scholar Dismissed" (*Student Review: BYU's Unofficial Magazine,* September 21, 1988); "Campus Memorandum," (Provost) Jae Ballif to David P. Wright, June 13, 1988, copy in author's possession; author's interviews with Wright, November 20, 1988, and November 19, 1989; author's conversations with various BYU teachers on numerous occasions.

92. Sperry, "Scholars and Prophets," *Dialogue* 2 (Spring 1967): 74–85; *The Voice of Israel's Prophets: A Latter-day Saint Interpretation of the Major and Minor Prophets of the Old Testament* (SLC: Deseret Book, 1952); with Merrill Y. Van Wagoner, *The Inspired Revision of the Bible* (Independence, MO: Zion's Printing and Publishing Co., 1947); *Old Testament Prophets* (SLC: Deseret Book, 1963); *Paul's Life and Letters* (SLC: Bookcraft, 1955); *The Spirit of the Old Testament* (SLC: LDS Department of Education, 1940); "The Text of Isaiah in the Book of Mormon" (master's thesis, University of Chicago, 1926).

conservative than B. H. Roberts, who, while reverencing the prophets, still urged the necessity of independent thought and openly acknowledged a diversity of opinion even among Church leaders.

Sperry may be thought of as the godfather of the dominant perspective of those who write about ancient scripture in the current Religion Department at Brigham Young University and in the Church education system more generally.[93] He understood Snell's position (and would have understood Chamberlin's) as heterodox and improper.[94] To assert that he was more conservative than Roberts and yet, like Roberts, occupied the center of the Mormon spectrum is not anomalous, because the center of the spectrum has shifted to the right since Roberts's generation.[95]

Until his death in 1972, Joseph Fielding Smith continued to champion the views of the extreme right of the spectrum. He received sometimes passionate support from apostles such as Mark E. Petersen, J. Reuben Clark, and Bruce R. McConkie, whose views have gained increasing prominence through Church manuals, magazines, and other media since mid-century.[96]

Mormons and Others

Because they seemed for so long to be apart from "the American religious mainstream"—an increasingly problematic metaphor—the Mormons have frequently been linked in the public mind, and even in some scholars' minds, with groups like the Jehovah's Witnesses. Often this linkage seems to have little other basis than the two groups' perceived obscurity or strangeness, their nonevangelical theology,

93. Representative of the sharply uneven literature currently offered by LDS religious educators is Kent P. Jackson and Robert L. Millett, ed., *The Gospels: Studies in Scripture* (SLC: Deseret Book, 1986) and companion volumes in the series. Twenty-five Church educators contributed essays to this book; all accept the notion that the individual Gospel accounts were authored respectively by the historical individuals, Matthew, Mark, Luke, and John, and all agree that the Gospels are theologically unified and historically accurate.

94. Swensen, "Mormons at the University of Chicago Divinity School," p. 38; Sperry, "Scholars and Prophets," pp. 74–85.

95. See also chap. 6.

96. Mark E. Peterson, *Moses: Man of Miracles* (SLC: Deseret Book, 1977), and several other books on Old Testament figures; Quinn, *J. Reuben Clark,* pp. 173–79; see also my chapter 5. Bruce R. McConkie is treated in more detail in chapter 6.

and their custom of door-to-door proselytizing. But so far as their use of the Bible goes, the linkage of the Saints and the Witnesses is superficial. It is true that a fundamentalist-like hermeneutic thrives in both movements, but this hermeneutic is essential in characterizing a Witness. In Mormonism the situation is vastly more complex and the fundamentalist hermeneutic is one prominent approach among others. Quite apart from the contrasting social makeup and the radically different theologies of the two movements, Jehovah's Witnesses, unlike Mormonism, has no significant wings amenable to modern methods of biblical study.[97]

More illuminating comparisons for the Latter-day Saints can be found elsewhere. Resistance to historical criticism that was proportionately similar to the resistance among Latter-day Saints occurred in evangelical denominations and was crucial in stimulating the growth of fundamentalism as an interdenominational movement. It was not until the 1920s and 1930s that traditional beliefs of many ordinary Americans reached a crisis or degenerated from a keen awareness of heaven and hell and the Holy Bible into what Robert and Helen Lynd have called an "unalert acceptance" of vaguely Christian notions.[98] Among scholars, however, and even among the laity in certain denominations, various conscious views on scripture appeared earlier. Among the Northern Baptists, for example, three positions were emerging as early as the 1870s: the majority still assumed the Bible's infallibility both in doctrine and historical detail; a few rejected inerrancy in favor of the subjective experiential verification of Christian truth; others assumed a mediating position.[99]

The Mormons, lacking professional theologians and preoccupied through the 1890s with seemingly more practical concerns, were naturally slower to sound the depths of the new currents. Controversies among even their intellectual and hierarchical leaders did not occur to

97. A survey of Witness literature makes this dramatically clear. See also Herbert Hewitt Stroup, *The Jehovah's Witnesses* (New York: Columbia University Press, 1945); Heather and Gary Botting, *The Orwellian World of Jehovah's Witnesses* (Toronto: University of Toronto Press, 1984).

98. Robert S. and Helen Merrell Lynd, *Middletown: A Study in Contemporary American Culture* (New York: Harcourt, Brace, 1929), pp. 315–31, 378–79, and *Middletown in Transition: A Study in Cultural Conflicts* (New York: Harcourt, Brace, 1937), p. 295.

99. Marsden, *Fundamentalism,* pp. 104–5.

any significant extent until the first decades of the twentieth century, when they took place among Americans generally. But early Mormon reactions, though a generation late in forming, were not so different from those of Northern Baptists. The difference is that among Northern Baptists an increasing appreciation developed as the twentieth century wore on. Among Mormons a similar pattern proceeded until midcentury, when a reaction set in. Contemporary LDS views more nearly resemble Southern than Northern Baptists.

Although Mormon attention to historical criticism was thus belated by some standards, it kept roughly apace of Jewish efforts, at least until recent decades (and allowing for the fact that Mormonism has no seminaries for professional theological education). Julian Morgenstern, the first American Jewish scholar with a primary interest in the Bible to practice higher criticism systematically, began his professional work at Hebrew Union College just as W. H. Chamberlin began his at BYU. Of course, Morgenstern's career flourished and Chamberlin's was aborted, which symbolizes the wider acceptance of modern methods among Jews than among Mormons. But Morgenstern met a great deal of resistance, and in some Jewish circles biblical criticism is even today considered a mark of heterodoxy. Orthodox Jewish seminaries do not teach biblical criticism at all, and Pentateuch criticism was avoided for most of the history of the Conservative Jewish Theological Seminary, which deferred to the disapproving ghost of its founder, Solomon Schecter. Not until 1981 did a biblical commentary wholly incorporating recent scholarship emerge from Jewish ranks.[100]

In other ways the response among American Catholics provides an interesting comparative context. Because neither Catholics nor Mormons pinned all their religious hopes on the Bible, a way existed for both groups to incorporate the new learning that was potentially less traumatizing than for many Protestants. But for Mormons and Catholics too, the path was often tortuous, rocky, or even the road not taken.

Pope Leo XIII's 1893 encyclical *Providentissimus Deus,* coupled

100. Sperling, "Judaism and Modern Biblical Research," p. 39; Sperling and Levine, *History of Jewish Biblical Scholarship,* chap. 2; Edwin S. Gaustad, ed., *A Documentary History of Religion in America* 2 vols. (Grand Rapids: Eerdmans, 1982–1983), 2:429; W. Gunther Plaut et al., *The Torah: A Modern Commentary* (New York: Union of American Hebrew Congregations, 1981).

with *Lamentabili,* a 1907 decree of the Holy Office, and Pius X's *Pascendi Dominici Gregis,* issued that same year, had jointly quashed the use of historical methods in Catholic biblical studies during the first half of the twentieth century. Some approving Catholic professors even boasted that after decades of college teaching, their students still had no idea that such a thing as "the biblical question" existed.[101] More serious scholars discussed the issues privately or in classes but were careful not to publish their research—silence was the way of professional survival.[102] An atmosphere of fear pervaded the 1930s, aborting and preventing the conception of progressive scholarship.

In 1938, however, the Catholic Biblical Association was founded, with the *Catholic Biblical Quarterly* emerging the following year. Pius XII issued *Divino Afflante Spiritu* in 1943, which is properly hailed as a landmark encouragement of Catholic biblical scholarship. The encouragement had its ambiguities, though, in that scholars were urged to use the historical method in accord "with the traditional teaching regarding the inerrancy of Sacred Scripture."[103] Responsible scholarship grew dramatically in the following decades, but progressive Catholic biblical scholars were still on the defensive on the eve of Vatican II and even through its first session. Indeed, a significant reaction against modern methods of study exists in American Catholicism today, and mirrors in muted tones the verbal battles fought at the beginning of the twentieth century.[104] A great proportion of the Catholic laity remains oblivious to such concerns.

So, too, among the Mormons. Amid the widespread inattention of ordinary members, scholars utilizing higher critical methods have received the applause, hostility, or silence of various Church leaders during the twentieth century. In some ways, progressive alternatives to the dominant conservatism enjoy less support today than they did earlier. Among LDS religious educators, historico-critical methods are discreetly appropriated by a minority, attacked by another minority, but often simply ignored, either because teachers are innocent of

101. Fogarty, *American Catholic Biblical Scholarship,* pp. 99, 172–73.

102. Ibid., pp. 180, 196.

103. *Divino Afflante Spiritu,* 1943 (Washington: National Catholic Welfare Conference, n.d.), p. 22.

104. Fogarty, *American Catholic Biblical Scholarship,* pp. 252, 259, 280, 281–310, 344, 349–50.

them, contemptuous of them, or because they believe their public use might cost them their jobs.[105]

Despite opinions sometimes deeply held, however, the Saints have usually found room for diversity. And although their views were colored by their own peculiar history and theological agenda, their reaction to historical criticism in the first half of the twentieth century made their biblical usage appear to resemble, more than any time in the past, that of their religious peers across the land.

105. Author's observations of Mormon classes, and conversations with LDS teachers at Brigham Young University and throughout the Mormon Church education system. See also note 93. A handful of LDS biblical scholars have, without surrendering an explicitly Mormon perspective, accomplished work demanding attention outside Mormonism. One such scholar is the prolific Hugh Nibley, whose genius is unquestioned (once, upon hearing him speak at a professional gathering, Harvard's renowned New Testament scholar George MacRae half-jokingly covered his head with his hands and lamented, "It is obscene for a man to know that much") but whose methods remain controversial. Another example is Avraham Gileadi, who works on the cutting edge of new knowledge of Isaiah's poetic and historical content, revealing it as among the most complex literary artifacts in human history.

5

Why the King James Version?

The Latter-day Saint use of the Bible has, since antebellum times, combined a basically traditional perspective with liberal, radical, and even unique dimensions. The worldview reflected in and derived from this distinctive combination helps explain why the Saints, for all their commonalities with others, remain a people apart. However, one aspect of Mormon biblical usage has in recent decades grown markedly more conservative than that of most denominations. Unlike Jews, evangelicals, or "mainline" Protestants (and in part for peculiarly Mormon reasons), the Saints have neither forsaken nor experienced substantial conflict over a deepening commitment to the King James translation—a translation they inherited, ironically, from the Protestantism they purported to reject.

This commitment was cemented in 1979, when the Latter-day Saints published their own edition of the KJV through Cambridge University Press. The new Bible made no changes in the Authorized text but boasted a creative new annotation format, was thoroughly cross-referenced with other LDS scriptures, and came complete with "Mormonized" chapter headings, Bible dictionary, and six-hundred-page topical reference guide. The mammoth project took almost seven years and involved hundreds of Church educators, employees, and volunteers. This edition is now standard in Mormon ranks and will continue to shape popular conceptions for the foreseeable future. In planning the new Bible, the production committee gave no serious consideration to any but the King James Version.[1]

Further committing the rapidly growing Church to a seventeenth-century English text carried deeper implications than most Saints were aware of. An understanding of the process through which this step came to seem natural to officials by the late twentieth century sheds light on Mormon biblical perceptions.

To understand the decision, one must distinguish between the sincere explanations offered by leaders and teachers in recent decades, and the several historical factors that, between 1867 and 1979, transformed the KJV from the common into the official Mormon Bible. In addition to a love of the beauty and familiarity of KJV language, these factors include the 1867 publication of Joseph Smith's biblical revision, the nineteenth-century Protestant-Catholic conflict over Bible reading in public schools, the menace of higher criticism, the advent of new translations perceived as doctrinally dangerous, and a modern popular misunderstanding of the nature of Joseph Smith's revelations.

While examining these influences, I give special notice to J. Reuben Clark, long-term member of the Church's First Presidency. By 1956 President Clark had appropriated most Protestant arguments for the KJV, linked them to uniquely Mormon concerns, and in the process made subsequent LDS spokesmen dependent on his logic. Although some Saints felt Clark's influential reasoning was unpersuasive, his logic nevertheless hints at deeper, irreducibly religious motives behind the Mormon course.

When the Geneva Bible was published in 1560, it made no attempt to disguise its Protestant origins: its prefatory dedication to Queen Elizabeth expressed the optimistic hope that Her Majesty would see all papists put to the sword in timely fashion. The marginal notes

1. In October 1972 Church President Harold B. Lee established an initial committee for the project. When the committee began its work, it received no detailed list of plans except a stipulation that it was to use the unaltered text of the King James Bible (Robert J. Matthews, "The New Publication of the Standard Works—1979, 1981," *BYU Studies* 22 [Fall 1982]: 388; also, author's telephone interview with committee member Ellis T. Rasmussen, January 28, 1988). The KJV is official, of course, for English only. Several dozen Bibles in foreign languages are approved for missionary and other uses (*Policies and Procedures Manual* #06-02-101 [Translation Department of the Church], October 1, 1981).

contributed greatly to the popularity of the version among the Protestant laity, but royalty, clergy, and Roman Catholics were disturbed by many of the notes' interpretations. The pope naturally objected to being identified with "the angel of the bottomless pit" (Rev. 9:11), and defenders of royal prerogative were equally upset by a note on Exod. 1:19 approving of the midwives' lying to Pharaoh. It was thus no great shock when England's new king, James I, commissioned a fresh translation in 1604.

When the result first issued from the press seven years later, not all readers were favorably impressed. Some thought its English barbarous. Others criticized the translators' scholarship. Outstanding churchmen, like the Hebraist Hugh Broughton, "had rather be rent in pieces by wild horses, than any such translation by my consent should be urged upon poor churches."[2]

The translators themselves were, of course, acutely aware of popular loyalty to the Geneva Bible, and foresaw criticism of their work. They pleaded their case in the 1611 preface, urging that their new translation was part of a necessarily ongoing enterprise to make God's word more accessible to each generation:

> We are so farre off from condemning any of their labours that traueled before vs in this kinde, either in this land or beyond sea . . . that we acknowledge them to have beene raised vp of God, . . . and that they deserue to be had of vs and of posteritie in everlasting remembrance. . . . Therefore blessed be they, and most honoured be their name, that breake the yce and give the onset vpon that which helpeth forward to the saving of soules. Now what can bee more auaileable thereto, than to deliuer Gods booke vnto Gods people in a tongue which they vnderstand? . . .
>
> So, if we building vpon their foundation that went before vs, and being holpen by their labours, doe endeavour to make that better which they left so good; no man, we are sure, hath cause to mislike vs; they, we perswade ourselues, if they were aliue, would thanke vs.
>
> For is the kingdome of God become words or syllables? Why should wee be in bondage to them if we may be free . . . ?

Fortunately for the revision—for this Bible was a revision of earlier versions—it was well received by the authorities, and thus autho-

---

2. Cited by F. F. Bruce, *The Books and the Parchments: Some Chapters on the Transmission of the Bible,* 3d ed. (Westwood, NJ: Revell, 1963), p. 229.

rized, though never formally, to be read in the churches. But for two generations this Authorized Bible waged a struggle to replace the Geneva translation in popular use. This struggle migrated with the Puritans to America, where the conceptions and arguments of the two factions in the famous antinomian controversy in Massachusetts (1637) were conditioned by the respective use of the two Bibles.[3]

Gradually, the Authorized Version came to be thought of as classically beautiful, and wielded a major influence on English literature and the language itself. So completely did its turns of phrase eventually capture the popular mind that by the eighteenth century many Protestants felt it blasphemous to change it or even to point out the inadequaces of its scholarship.[4]

In America, such sentiment was widespread but not unanimous. Around 1770 Benjamin Franklin said of the KJV and its era that "the language [of] that time is [now] so much changed and the style, being obsolete and thence less agreeable, is perhaps one reason why the reading of that excellent book is of late so much neglected."[5] Yet the efforts of Franklin and Noah Webster and others to mend the defects of the Authorized Version had little effect on most antebellum Americans. Religious citizens of Joseph Smith's generation, both Protestants and Jews,[6] were raised on the King James Version (as it came to be known in this country) as thoroughly as they were raised on food and water. How profoundly KJV language shaped Smith's everyday speech, the form of his revelations, and the bulk of his religious conceptions has been noted earlier.

Despite this influence, however, Joseph Smith was not bound to the KJV as an "official" Bible. To the contrary, he regarded the version he inherited as malleable and open to creative prophetic adaptation. He believed the Bible was the word of God, but only "as far as it is translated correctly." And, he insisted, the King James Version was

3. Harry Stout, "Word and Order in Colonial New England," in *The Bible in America,* ed. Hatch and Noll, p. 31.

4. David Daiches, *The King James Version of the Bible* (Chicago: University of Chicago Press, 1941).

5. Quoted in Harry M. Orlinsky, ed., *Notes on the New Translation of the Torah* (New York: Jewish Publication Society of America, 1969), p. 8.

6. Even when Isaac Leeser accomplished a translation for Jews (1853), it was so deliberately modeled on the KJV that modern Jewish authorities have referred to it as "the Judaized King James" (Sperling and Levine, *History of Jewish Biblical Scholarship,* chap. 2).

not translated or transmitted correctly in thousands of instances. The Prophet used the KJV as a baseline because it was generally available and known, but the thrust of his work was to break away from the confinement of set forms, to test new verbal and theological constructions while pursuing his religious vision. Through good honest study, he worked to understand Hebrew and, apparently, other tongues that would improve his scriptural perspective. While so doing, he experimented freely with Bibles in various languages, once observing that the German Bible (presumably Luther's) was the most correct of any.[7]

Neither did the KJV enjoy official status among the Saints as a whole. Like their leader, early Mormons took the familiar version for granted in many ways, but they routinely cited various translations of a given text, noting the King James rendition as but one among others.[8] Orson Pratt stressed the textual limitations behind *any* version. His allegiance was to the word of God as originally recorded— in Hebrew and Greek, as he believed. A translation from the original scriptural tongues was but an echo of God's word, and this specifically applied to the KJV.[9]

In fact, Mormon leaders such as Pratt, John Taylor, and George Albert Smith went out of their way to insist that the King James translators were not inspired.[10] Claiming no scholarly or prophetic basis for his view, Brigham Young casually guessed that, for all its errors, the Bible was probably translated "about as correctly as the scholars could get it." Yet what he sought was accuracy and truth, not loyalty to any traditional version: "If it be translated incorrectly, and there is a scholar on the earth who professes to be a Christian, and he can translate it any better than King James's translators did it, he is under obligation to do so. . . ."[11] For a generation after Joseph Smith's death, Mormons thought of the KJV as their common, not their official, Bible.

7. *HC*, 6:363–64.
8. E.g., *TS* 5:601 (August 1, 1844) and 6:791 (February 1, 1845).
9. *CT* 17 (1896): 162; *JD*, 7:26–27, 14:257a–260, 15:247–249, 16:218, 17:269.
10. *JD*, 1:25, 7:23ff., 12:264, 14:257–58, 17:269.
11. *JD*, 14:226–27.

Antecedents to "Official" Status

Following Smith's 1844 death, small pockets of Mormons residing throughout the Northeast and Midwest did not follow Brigham Young and the main body of Saints to the Rocky Mountains. Many of these simply stayed where they were, or gathered around various charismatic leaders who rejected the leadership of Young and the twelve apostles. These mostly ephemeral groups clustered in Wisconsin, Michigan, Pennsylvania, Illinois, and elsewhere. In the 1850s an enduring and more substantial body coalesced into "the Reorganization" movement, whose relations with the Mormon Church in Utah have evolved over the years from mutually hostile to cool to polite.[12]

The first discernible change in the status of the KJV among the Utah Mormons occurred in 1867–1868, when the newly formed Reorganized Church, which had access to Joseph Smith's original manuscripts, published a King James Bible incorporating the thousands of changes Smith had introduced. Some Utah Mormons, like Orson Pratt, were enthusiastic about Smith's "inspired revision."[13] But antagonism between the Utah Church and the smaller group in the Midwest that rejected his leadership led Brigham Young and most of his colleagues to suspect the new publication: Had their rivals altered Joseph Smith's original work? Furthermore, they reasoned, the Prophet had not been able to finish and publish his revision during his lifetime. Some now suggested this failure was providential.

When copies of the published work, *The Holy Scriptures,* began to proliferate in Utah, various leaders at the School of the Prophets in Provo voiced the Church's stand against the new revision: "the world does not want this [new Bible] . . . they are satisfied with the King James translation. . . ."; "The King James translation is good enough. . . . I feel to support the old Bible until we can get a better

12. For the essential story and sources for more detailed study, see Arrington and Bitton, *The Mormon Experience* pp. 88–93; Roger D. Launius, *Joseph Smith III: Pragmatic Prophet* (Urbana: University of Illinois Press, 1988), chap. 4; and Steven L. Shields, *Divergent Paths of the Restoration: A History of the Latter Day Saints* (Bountiful, UT: Restoration Research, 1982).

13. For early expressions of Pratt's enthusiasm, see *Pratt Journals,* August 4, 1833. For later expressions, see *JD,* 1:56, 15:262–65; Bergera, "Pratt-Young Controversies," pp. 39–40.

one."[14] This sentiment was not universal in Utah, and it was explicitly provisional ("until we can get a better one"), but it was reiterated in later years[15] and it marked the ironic beginning of a conscious stress on the King James Version.

An indirect influence increasing the status of the KJV among the Saints was the general Protestant antipathy to Catholic immigrants. Antipopery had long flourished in Protestant lands, of course, but the Catholic population in eighteenth-century (eastern) America was too small and too localized to incite broad conflict. By the 1820s, however, Protestants were viewing Catholics, who before mid-century would constitute the nation's largest denomination, as a genuine threat to an evangelical America.

Mutual suspicion abounded, and many Protestants discerned conspiracy everywhere: Catholics' first allegiance was not to democracy and to "the Bible alone" but to Roman "powers across the deep." Catholic "foreigners" simply did not belong—never mind that Maryland had been founded by Catholics and that Catholics had colonized American shores for one and one-half centuries before the Puritan migration. Large numbers of "papists" seemed to undermine American freedoms. Some evangelicals, like Lyman Beecher, believed Catholics were forbidden even to read the Bible "but by permission of the priesthood." Even then, they read an alien version; they did not read the "real Bible" of "real Christians."

Quite apart from Beecher's misconceptions, centuries of English-speaking Catholic leaders had indeed tried to protect their flocks from

14. Testimonies of G. G. Bywater and J. W. Fleming recorded in the "Minutes of the School of the Prophets," July 6, 1868, cited in Durham, "A History of Joseph Smith's Revision," pp. 245–75.

15. Apostle Charles Penrose's 1881 assertion was typical. The Church would use the Authorized Version, he said, "until the inspired . . . revision commenced by the Prophet Joseph Smith shall have been completed in a form acceptable to the Almighty . . . ." ("The Revised Scriptures," *DN,* April 22, 1881.)

This suspicion of the "Reorganite" production of Smith's biblical revision was still apparent in the Utah-based Church as recently as the early 1970s, after which it rapidly faded. See, for example, Mark E. Petersen, *As Translated Correctly* (SLC: Deseret Book, 1966), p. 30, and an unsigned editorial in *CN,* November 14, 1970, p. 16. The change was evidenced quite publicly when another *CN* editorial (November 16, 1974) expressed deep reservations about the "Inspired Version," but was followed (December 7) by a tactful correction that amounted to a retraction. In contrast to all of this, the Reorganized Church began in the nineteenth century its current practice of using Smith's Inspired Version as its primary Bible.

the King James Bible, misconstruing the decrees of the Council of Trent in the process.[16] Although lay Catholics did not often read the Bible, defense of the Douay translation became for them a defense of their Catholic identity. In the 1840s one New York priest outraged the nation's religious majority—and heightened its KJV sensibilities—by enforcing his convictions with excessive zeal: he collected and publicly burned the Bibles given his immigrant parishioners by one of the Protestant Bible societies. Even earlier, in the 1820s, the Catholic First Provincial Council had castigated the Protestant bias of public education—particularly the use of the King James Bible—and encouraged the founding of parochial schools. The issue did not fade for generations, and tensions often escalated to violence that was sometimes deadly.[17]

Thus, in restricted locales at first and across the land as the century wore on, the conscious use of the real, Christian, American, Protestant Bible—the King James Version—was increasingly important for many Americans. The KJV was still *almost* taken for granted, but to mention it specifically as one's own version often implied a declaration of one's Americanness and one's Christianity (which meant one bore no Catholic sympathies).

To some extent, the Mormons participated in this trend. Alienated from the culturally dominant Protestants in so many ways, the Saints might plausibly have identified with the embattled Catholics by defending alternative translations. But most Mormon converts had come from Protestant ranks that assumed the KJV. Moreover, the Saints themselves had inherited a significant strain of anti-Catholicism, and during the course of Mormon history some would identify the pope as the head of "the great and abominable church" mentioned in the Book of Mormon. An occasional Mormon leader even made these drifts explicit, remarking on the worth of the Authorized Version against Roman Catholics who objected to it.[18]

16. Fogarty, *American Catholic Biblical Scholarship,* pp. 3–5, 22–23, 217, 220, 238.

17. Ibid., pp. 12, 15; Ahlstrom, *A Religious History,* 1:666–81, especially 671, 675; Fogarty, "The Quest for a Catholic Vernacular Bible in America," in *The Bible in America,* ed. Hatch and Noll, pp. 163–65; Ray Allen Billington, *The Protestant Crusade: A Study of the Origins of American Nativism* (Chicago: Quadrangle Books, 1964), pp. 68–76; James Hennesey, *American Catholics* (New York: Oxford University Press, 1981), pp. 122–25.

18. George Q. Cannon, *JI* 10 (October 16, 1875): 246.

After the turn of the century, a more pressing influence—the newly perceived threat of modern biblical studies—helped entrench the Authorized Version. As noted in the previous chapter, Mormon responses to the higher criticism were actually quite diverse. Yet a good many leaders were decidedly hostile, seeing in the new approach to scripture a menace to Christian faith. Some became defensive, viewing any attempt to progress beyond the trusted King James Bible *through scholarship* as a related challenge to faith. Joseph Fielding Smith, for instance, was so bitter at the inroads made by historical criticism that he viewed textual criticism equally dimly.[19]

In addition to such causes, we must also acknowledge that Mormon loyalty to the KJV was—as it was for many Protestants—simply a natural attachment to the vehicle by which a people felt they had encountered the sacred. A similar phenomenon may be seen in the great struggle Roman Catholics had in producing an accepted vernacular Bible in America.[20] This love of the Bible "of one's youth" is easily traced in the resistance with which every major new translation, including the King James Version, has been greeted. This preservationist impulse will be explored more fully as we look at the later twentieth century, but it was doubtless a factor in earlier decades as well.

I must reiterate that this new emphasis on the Authorized Version in the late nineteenth and early twentieth centuries represented a real shift from Joseph Smith's era. But it is similarly important not to overstate the change. As many Saints had done since 1830, some Mormons continued simply to equate the Bible itself with its 1611 English translation; they had never known another. Indeed, although the KJV was spoken of with increasing self-consciousness as *the* Mormon Bible, considerable diversity continued to exist. B. H. Roberts and others were relatively open to ongoing studies that improved the Greek text from which better translations could be made.[21] A new generation of leaders continued to instruct that the KJV was not translated by inspiration, and noted here and there other versions without asserting KJV superiority.[22]

19. *Seek Ye Earnestly,* p. 364.

20. Fogarty, "The Quest for a Catholic Vernacular Bible in America," pp. 163–80, and Fogarty, *American Catholic Biblical Scholarship,* pp. 199–221.

21. *Seventy's Course in Theology,* p. 31.

22. Charles Penrose, *MS* 55 (August 21, 1893): 544; James Talmage, *Articles of Faith,* pp. 236–37; Frederic Clift, "The Bible," *IE* 7 (July 1904): 655, 663; *JI* 33 (October 15, 1898): 711.

Even when Church leaders did articulate reasons for recommending the King James over other translations, they rarely asserted that it was more accurate. They supported it primarily because they suspected the RLDS production of Joseph Smith's revision or because they believed the elegant familiar version had "taken too firm a hold of the popular heart" to forsake it.[23] Sometimes, in fact, they highly praised modern translations, offering only an appended tolerance for those who would continue to prefer the familiar version "because they have grown accustomed to its lofty phrases."[24]

Occasionally, a leader even argued extensively for the superiority of the major revisions of 1881 and 1901 (the British Revised Version and the American Standard Version). One writer noted that the KJV scholars did not have access to older manuscripts subsequently available and that even the Catholic version was more accurate in many instances than the KJV. He went on to ridicule the common "beautiful literature" argument—as though scholars should take it upon themselves to add "grace and dignity" to the original language of the uneducated fishermen of Galilee. Although loyalty to the Bible of one's ancestors was commendable, "those who accept the eighth article of the Church will seek for the best translation."[25]

Within this wide spectrum of attitudes, ordinary Saints during the first half of the twentieth century were not so much advocates or adversaries of the new translations that were beginning to multiply as they were indifferent to them. A few leaders increasingly noted that the KJV was the "best" version, but often gave no rationale for the assertion.[26] The Church produced various editions for its missionaries, children's organization, and educational system—all using the KJV.

23. Charles Penrose, "Revised Scriptures," *DN* 14 (April 22, 1881); "Editor's Table," *IE* 2 (1899): 621.

24. C. Frank Steele, *CN* (November 9, 1935): 6.

25. Frederic Clift, "The Bible: The King James Translation—a Compromise," *IE* 7 (July 1904): 654–64; "The Bible: English Revision, 1881–American Standard Revision, 1901," *IE* 7 (August 1904): 774–78. The Eighth Article of Faith begins, "We believe the Bible to be the word of God as far as it is translated correctly. . . ."

26. E.g., Joseph Fielding Smith, *Doctrines of Salvation,* 3:191; John Widtsoe, Gospel Interpretations, (SLC: Bookcraft, 1947), pp. 257–60. Elsewhere, Widtsoe did suggest that the language of the KJV was "unsurpassed," that it had an excellent "spiritual connotation," and, although he offered no basis for his guess, that it was probably superior in faithful adherence to the text available to its translators (*Evidences and Reconciliations,* 2 vols. [SLC: Bookcraft, 1943], 1:100–101).

In the days of Joseph Smith and Brigham Young, then, Mormon leaders had largely taken the KJV for granted. But they had also insisted on its limitations and had encouraged the exploration, through both scholarly and prophetic means, of new and better expressions of God's word. By contrast, leaders in the early twentieth century also took the KJV for granted but tended to resist scholarly improvements. They felt if God wanted them to have a new translation of the scriptures, he would let his prophet know. Nineteenth-century Mormons shared much with their contemporaries but reacted creatively against a confining orthodoxy; early twentieth-century Saints shared much with their non-Mormon peers but reacted conservatively against a changing, secular world. Of course, Church members continued to feel free—sometimes they were even encouraged— to compare various translations. But one wonders how many actually bothered.

J. Reuben Clark Jr.

The 1950s brought a significant change for LDS readers of serious literature. The Revised Standard Version appeared and met the stiff resistance of J. Reuben Clark, erudite and forceful member of the Church's First Presidency. In the wake of President Clark's still-influential response, a substantial number of Saints for the first time moved beyond assuming the preeminence of the KJV to believing they had prophetic and scholarly reasons for assuming it.

Brigham Young still had six years before him as an earthly prophet when J. Reuben Clark was born in the rural outpost of Grantsville, Utah in 1871. Clark's devout parents held daily family prayers and scripture readings, and from his very early years Reuben possessed an uncommon religious and academic intensity. His father's diary noted that the twelve-year-old "Reuben would rather miss his meals than to miss a day at school." This interest was borne out when, after successfully completing the eighth grade (the highest offered in Grantsville), Reuben eagerly went through the same grade two additional years. Eventually he was admitted to the University of Utah, classified as "preparatory special" because he lacked two years of high school work required of ordinary applicants.

From this intellectually modest beginning, Clark went on to an illustrious career in public service. After graduating from the university as valedictorian, he attended Columbia Law School, served as a principal editor of the *Columbia Law Review,* and graduated as one of the top students. Later, he became solicitor of the U.S. State Department, then U.S. under secretary of state, and finally ambassador to Mexico. Throughout his public career, Clark's brilliance, integrity, and thoroughness earned high praise from senators, justices of the Supreme Court, and U.S. presidents. Indeed, he regularly declined the urging of men like Harry Chandler, owner of the *Los Angeles Times,* to run for president himself. In 1933 Clark resigned as ambassador to Mexico in order to serve as one of two counselors to the president of the Mormon Church. He maintained this position in the First Presidency until his death in 1961, one of the longest periods of such service in LDS history.[27] One enduring legacy of President Clark's service resulted from his encounter with the scholarly revision of the English Bible.

The complete Revised Standard Version was launched in 1952 with a publicity campaign such as few or none of its predecessors had enjoyed. That, of course, did not protect it from adverse criticism. Some thought the new Bible was unnecessarily conservative and did not deviate sufficiently from the KJV.[28] A more vocal group thought it not only deviated excessively but was itself devious—scarcely Christian. The project had been sponsored by the liberal National Council of Churches, of itself enough to insure the mistrust of many evangelicals. Their fundamentalist cousins, in turn, made little attempt to disguise their hostility. The appearance of pamphlets like *The New Blasphemous Bible* and *The Bible of Antichrist* suggest the shrill outcry. In some areas of the country RSV Bibles were thrown into bonfires, and RSV translators deemed worthy of more enduring fires. Elsewhere, Senator Joseph McCarthy's Senate investigating committee formally charged members of the RSV translating committee with allowing Communist influences to subvert the Bible. Even among

27. The biographical essentials are available in Yarn, *Young Reuben;* Fox, *J. Reuben Clark: The Public Years;* Quinn, *J. Reuben Clark: The Church Years;* Yarn, ed., *J. Reuben Clark: Selected Papers.*

28. W. A. Irwin, *An Introduction to the Revised Standard Version of the Old Testament* (New York: Thomas Nelson & Sons, 1952), pp. 12–14.

more sober thinkers, the reaction was sufficiently strong to stimulate the eventual production of alternative new translations.[29]

The response among Mormons was more reserved, though some did use the occasion to affirm the stature of the KJV. An unsigned editorial in the October 1952 *Church News* asserted: "For the Latter-day Saints there can be but one version of the Bible"—the King James Version. One year later, Apostle Mark E. Petersen echoed that the Bible "officially used in the Church" was the KJV.[30] J. Reuben Clark was not the only Mormon who disliked the new Bible; he was merely the most resourceful.

Like Joseph Fielding Smith, President Clark was an outstanding Mormon opponent of modern biblical studies. He had, by his own description, rebelled for most of his life against "the pettifogging, doubt-raising attacks" of the higher critics. His biographer assesses him as "the primary spokesman of the Church against modern Biblical scholarship."[31] Yet his role in heightening the stature of the King James Bible among the Latter-day Saints was even more singular. His passionate objections to the Revisions of 1888 and 1901 launched him on a decades-long course of meticulous research in defense of the KJV. Over the years he expressed his views in personal correspondence, in private conversations, and in public sermons. Upon the appearance of the RSV (which, in the wake of its predecessors, he considered "more of the same, only worse"),[32] Clark spent several additional years preparing his research notes for publication. The end product was his monumental tome, *Why the King James Version*.[33]

Focusing exclusively on the New Testament, Clark argued his case

29. Bruce, *The English Bible,* pp. 194–209; Mark A. Noll, "Evangelicals and the Study of the Bible," in *Evangelicalism and Modern America,* ed. George Marsden (Grand Rapids, MI.: Eerdmans, 1984), pp. 110–11; Barr *Fundamentalism,* pp. 209–10.

30. *Your Faith and You* (SLC: Bookcraft, 1953), pp. 17–21. Elder Petersen was long responsible for the unsigned *CN* editorials and thus may have authored the one cited above.

31. Clark, *Why the King James Version,* pp. vi, 418, passim; Quinn, *J. Reuben Clark,* pp. 168–69, 173–79.

32. *Why,* p. 351.

33. The work was published in 1956 (422 pp. + index + bibliography). On the title page Clark justly described his work as "a series of study notes, neither treatises nor essays, dealing with certain elementary problems and specific scriptural passages, involved in considering the preferential English translations of the Greek New Testament text. . . ."

at great length, with a lawyer's skill and a churchman's zeal. His arguments were interwoven and reiterated throughout his work, but for purposes of analysis they may be separated into six categories. Most of these he shared with KJV apologists of various denominations; others were distinctive to the Latter-day Saints. Against the three Revisions, Clark believed the Authorized Version was (1) doctrinally more acceptable, (2) verified by the work of Joseph Smith, (3) based on a better Greek text, (4) literarily superior, (5) the version of LDS tradition, and (6) produced by faithful, prayerful churchmen who were amenable to the Holy Spirit rather than by a mixture of believing and unbelieving, or orthodox and heterodox, scholars. Clark cast other aspersions against modern versions but failed to develop them into arguments. For example, he accused the RSV scholars of "interpreting" rather than "translating," an accusation that was perhaps a misunderstanding, because all translation entails interpretation and because the KJV scholars as easily as the RSV scholars could have been accused of overtranslating. Similarly, Clark stressed that mortals ought not to mar God's word—a sentiment the RSV translators, as a group, shared.

Among the genuine arguments, the controlling one was Clark's belief that the Revisions were infected with a despicable, even conspiratorial, humanism. "As one notes . . . the havoc which [the Revisions] work upon vital portions of the Scriptures as contained in the Authorized Version, . . . one can but wonder if there be not behind this movement . . . a deliberate . . . intent to destroy the Christian faith. . . ." With a telling metaphor, Clark proclaimed the King James Bible the "citadel of Christianity."[34]

In particular, Clark feared that the Revised versions cast doubt on cherished phrases by offering alternative readings, supported by ancient texts, in the margin. Luke 23:34 of the Revisions, for instance, read essentially the same as the KJV, but the Revisions add a marginal note: "Some ancient authorities [that is, important manuscripts] omit *And Jesus said, Father, forgive them; for they know not what they do.*"[35] Clark was yet more offended that other treasured sayings were actually removed from the text and themselves given only marginal

34. *Why,* pp. 6–7, 27, 34, 121, 126, 356, passim.
35. Other examples troubling Clark were Matt. 17:21; Matt. 18:11; and the famous "long ending" of the Gospel of Mark (16:9–20).

status. He was understandably upset that the Revisions relegated to the margin the doxology ("For thine is the kingdom, and the power, and the glory. . . .") from the Lord's prayer in Matt. 6:13.[36] Equally distressing, familiar KJV words were translated by others: "charity." in 1 Corinthians 13 became "love"; "lunatic" in Matt. 17:14ff. became "epileptic."

But what disturbed the Mormon leader most deeply was what he viewed as the tendency to reduce the divine status of Jesus and the supernatural dimension of scripture in general. "Miracles" were now called "signs," "wonders," or "mighty works." Textual doubt over the phrase "the Son of God" was noted in Mark 1:1 of the Revisions. Marginal alternate readings were documented for Christ as "God over all" in Rom. 9:4–5. Like opponents of the Revisions nationally and internationally, Clark followed conservative Protestant scholars, above all, John W. Burgon and F.H.A. Scrivener, in citing example after example where modern translations scandalized traditional tastes.[37]

Clark's reasoning was unpersuasive to some Mormons, including many teachers in the Church's educational system.[38] "Traditional tastes," they felt, were precisely what obscured the original scriptural message. The *least* that could be said of the revisers' changes was that plausible scholarly reasons existed for making them. Moreover, some modern translations, including those Clark attacked, directly ascribe deity to Jesus in several passages where the King James Version does

36. Other prominent instances include Luke 2:14; 22:19–20; 22:43–44; 23:44. Clark seemed more concerned about the possibility of losing something from the scriptures than he was about canonizing words that may have been later additions.

37. See *Why,* index, where listings for Burgon and Scrivener are among the longest of any subjects treated. Christian defenders of the Authorized translation have often depended almost wholly on such scholars (Carson, *The King James Version Debate,* p. 43).

38. Conversations with various Church education personnel of Clark's era suggest that there existed among them considerable disagreement with Clark's views, as well as considerable support and a surprising degree of indifference or unawareness. The sentiments of those who gave Clark's book little credence are adequately represented here by George Boyd (interview with author, October 30, 1989), George Tanner (October 24, 1989), and Russel Swensen, (November 11, 1986), all of whom had received formal theological training and were prominent in the Church education system. It is to these and similar interviews I refer in the text when noting resistance to Clark's views among Mormon religion teachers.

not.[39] Some teachers thus thought it precarious to accuse such translations of systematic theological bias in ways exceeding the inevitable bias of any translation, including the KJV.

But President Clark marshaled prophetic and scholarly evidence to back up his doctrinal concerns. Intriguingly, he drew his prophetic support from a perception of Joseph Smith's revelations that seemed at variance with the Prophet's own. Specifically, said Clark, Smith's inspired revision of the Bible supported the King James Version in all essential matters. Whenever one compared Smith's "translation" with objectionable changes made in the RV/ASV/RSV, the Prophet's Bible more nearly resembled the KJV—thus demonstrating the errors of the modern Revisions.[40]

This line of thought was reinforced by Clark's understanding of revelation in general. He rejected, or never entertained, the view that Smith's revelations might have been conceptual in nature. Instead, Clark thought of them as almost verbally exact expressions recorded by the Prophet precisely as they fell from the lips of God. Clark believed that the Doctrine and Covenants, for example, preserved "the words of the Lord as He [actually] spoke them"[41] Similarly, he assumed Joseph Smith's changes in the KJV indicated the original form of the ancient texts.

Clark sired irony when he used Smith's "inspired translation," as published by the RLDS Church, to authenticate the KJV text. It had been, after all, Mormon suspicions about this publication that had sponsored the initial elevation of the KJV's stature among the Saints in the 1860s. But more than irony was involved here. Some Saints thought Clark was in danger of inverting historical reality.

President Clark's logic was built upon a definite, though perhaps not always conscious, theory of the nature of Joseph Smith's revelations: God spoke or inspired, Joseph recorded. The result was scripture—God's words, not merely God's word, in print. But other Mormons operated under different assumptions. These educators presumed Smith's biblical revision resembled the King James Version because that is the version he worked from and amended, not be-

39. See chapter appendix.
40. *Why,* pp. 3, 43, 318ff., 398ff., passim.
41. Lecture given at BYU, July 7, 1954, to seminary and institute teachers; printed in Durham, *Revelation and Scripture,* pp. 36–37.

cause God's native tongue was Late Middle or Early Modern English. For similar reasons, they felt, Smith's other revelations also retained a measure of the language of King James. However, the Prophet himself did not seem to consider all his revelations to be the exact words of God that he then recorded as if by dictation, for he frequently and unapologetically rearranged, reworded, conflated, and augmented them.[42]

To be sure, Clark's perspective was shared by many Saints. Because Joseph Smith was influenced by the inherited Bible translation of his time, and because he had couched his recorded revelations in the "first person" in behalf of Deity, the resulting documents left the impression that God was speaking directly to Joseph in a nineteenth-century dialect of Jacobean English. Hence many of the earliest Mormons, as immersed in biblical phraseology as their prophet, assumed this was God's manner of speech when addressing Americans. But a century later the language of the KJV was less taken for granted. Alternative translations in modern language, not merely revisions of the KJV, were rapidly appearing.[43] Allegiance to Elizabethan and Jacobean forms, to the extent it remained, became more conscious. It was in this context that, in celebrating the three hundredth anniversary of the KJV, a 1911 column in the Church-owned *Deseret Evening News* marveled that King James's "is the version given to the world by eminent scholarship in the very same language in which modern revelations are given."[44]

In Search of Scholarly Support

It was not on prophetic but on scholarly grounds, however, that President Clark made his most elaborate case for the Authorized text. He prefaced his academic argument with the disclaimer that he was not a

42. See especially Howard, *Restoration Scriptures*, but also chapter 2 of the present work; Cook, *The Revelations of the Prophet Joseph Smith;* Ehat and Cook, eds., *The Words of Joseph Smith.*

43. The translations of Goodspeed and Moffatt come quickly to mind, but see the exhaustive account in Margaret Hills, ed. *The English Bible in America: a Bibliography of Editions of the Bible and the New Testament Published in America, 1777–1957* (New York: American Bible Society, 1961).

44. April 21, 1911.

genuine biblical scholar, pointing out that he knew no biblical languages, had no formal training, and based his assessment entirely on secondary materials.

Despite his modesty, his use of these secondary sources was prodigious. If his major concern with the Revised Bibles was that they were laced with a modern humanism, his undergirding contention was that an *ancient* humanism—the heresy of Arianism[45]—tainted the Greek text upon which the Revisions rested. To legitimate the doctrinally more acceptable King James Bible, Clark championed the *Textus Receptus* (TR), the Byzantine-based Greek text from which the KJV had been translated. Those scholars who similarly supported the Byzantine text, Clark called "Sound" or "High Textualists"; those who did not, he labeled "Extreme Textualists."[46]

The details of modern textual criticism are complex and available elsewhere.[47] But to understand Clark's academic reasoning, a brief sketch of the development of the New Testament texts behind the KJV and the Revised versions is necessary.

Erasmus published the first Greek New Testament in 1516. His edition was based on six manuscripts, dating from the eleventh to the fifteenth centuries, and these in turn derived essentially from a single tradition that, anciently, had several rivals. Thus, by modern standards, his edition was inadequate. In fact, for small parts of the New Testament where he lacked any Greek manuscripts, Erasmus simply translated the Vulgate into what he conjectured the original

45. A fourth-century Christological position, eventually condemned, which held that Jesus' dignity as Son of God was bestowed on him by the Father on account of Christ's foreseen role and his abiding righteousness, as opposed to the "orthodox" position, which viewed Christ as uncreated, unchanging, God-by-nature. As used by J. Reuben Clark, Arianism meant that the humanity of Jesus was emphasized while his divinity was minimized or lost.

46. Or, rather, he followed other critics who had so labeled them. "Our Bible," in Yarn, ed., *J. Reuben Clark: Selected Papers*, passim; *Why*, pp. 7–8, passim.

47. E.g., Bruce M. Metzger, *The Text of the New Testament* (New York: Oxford University Press, 1969); Carson, "The Textual Question" in *The King James Version Debate;* Harold K. Moulton, *Papyrus, Parchment and Print: The Story of How the New Testament Text Has Reached Us* (London: United Society for Christian Literature, 1967); Raymond E. Brown, "Greek Text of the New Testament," in *The Jerome Biblical Commentary*, 2 vols. bound together (Englewood Cliffs, NJ: Prentice-Hall, 1968), pp. 580–85 in New Testament section.

might have been. One consequence is that there are no Greek manuscripts at all behind a dozen or so readings in the modern KJV.

Thirty years later Robert Estienne (Stephanus) produced Greek editions following Erasmus in the text but using several additional manuscripts and introducing a critical apparatus to show alternate readings in the margins. Theodore Beza enriched this tradition somewhat, publishing nine editions of the Greek New Testament between 1565 and 1604. Through two of these he influenced the King James translators. The resultant text subsequently became known as the *Textus Receptus,* a term some moderns have imbued with great dignity but that actually derives from a seventeenth-century advertising blurb. Thirteen years after the publication of the KJV, two brothers published a compact Greek New Testament, the text of which was essentially Beza's. Their blurb reads: *"Textum ergo habes, nunc ab omnibut receptum: in quo nihil immutatem aut corruptum damus"* (The text that you have is now received by all, in which we give nothing changed or perverted)—hence, *Textus Receptus.*

Beza and his predecessors had neglected several manuscripts of earlier date than those they used. More important, during the centuries after 1611, additional manuscripts—some more ancient by a millennium than those used by the King James scholars—became available. More important yet was the gradual recognition by scholars after 1725 that there existed manuscript *traditions* or "families," not merely numerous manuscripts, differing from the now traditional Greek text. This insight led to continual improvement of textual classifications and allowed "lower" criticism to proceed on a more scientific basis, a development that came to a head with the landmark work of Cambridge scholars B. F. Westcott and F.J.A. Hort, who in 1881–1882 published *The New Testament in the Original Greek.*

Hort and Westcott posited four major "families" of ancient texts. Of these, they said, the least corrupt, or "neutral" tradition, was the "Alexandrian." The "Syrian," represented by the whole Byzantine tradition, was the latest and most corrupt. This represented a direct challenge to the King James Bible. The theory was bitterly attacked but soon won the support of most scholars and underlies virtually all subsequent widely accepted work in New Testament criticism. As Raymond Brown notes, if the King James was a translation of the TR, the RV and the subsequent RSV were heavily influenced by principles akin to those of the Westcott-Hort Greek Testament.

Because of his belief that the Revised versions undermined cherished Christian conceptions, J. Reuben Clark turned the guns of his formidable mind against the Westcott-Hort text.[48] He followed Protestant critics who protested that the Westcott-Hort construction was overly dependent on the Alexandrian text-type, particularly the famous codices (manuscript volumes) Sinaiticus and Vaticanus. He further followed those who alleged that these codices were not only fourth-century (that is, late) manuscripts but represented a text-type that *originated* in the fourth century, under the influence of heretical conditions, which is why the early church rejected them.

Most textual specialists were unpersuaded by such theories. Subsequent discoveries have demonstrated, they believe, that the Alexandrian text-type goes back at least to the second century. Westcott and Hort seemed definitively to establish certain traditions as generally preferable to others, and it remains the scholarly consensus that the Alexandrian type has better credentials than any. The able textual studies of even archconservative Protestants like Benjamin B. Warfield and J. Gresham Machen argue that the Byzantine text-type is essentially a late one.[49]

But some of Clark's contentions were not so easily dismissed. Several aspects of the Westcott-Hort theory have, in the twentieth century, been modified. The textual traditions identified by the theory have been reclassified. And modern scholars recognize, unlike Westcott-Hort, that no text group has an essentially uncontaminated descent from the original autographs. Also, although the Byzantine cannot in general be preferred to the Alexandrian text, some of the Byzantine readings (as with all the major traditions) are genuinely ancient. Modern scholars acknowledge that Westcott and Hort had indeed, as Clark charged, been overly dependent on the Vaticanus and Sinaiticus codices. In these and other matters Clark deserved a

48. *Why,* pp. 67–118, 126, 364–65, passim. Opponents of the KJV note that the *Textus Receptus* and the Byzantine text-type are not synonymous. The TR is based on a mere handful of relatively late manuscripts, in comparison with the thousands in the Byzantine tradition. The closest manuscripts within the Byzantine or any other textual tradition average six to ten variants per chapter. Thus, these opponents contend, even a successful defense of the superiority of the Byzantine tradition (which most scholars reject) would not constitute a successful defense of the King James Bible, which is a translation of the TR. Carson, *Debate,* pp. 37, 67–68.

49. Carson, *Debate,* p. 43.

hearing. What he failed to allow for, his critics felt, is that modern critical editions of the New Testament are eclectic, established on a case-by-case basis, using the best available evidence. They are not slavishly dependent on the Alexandrian or any other tradition.[50]

But Clark went further in his criticism. Because modifications in the critical text were ongoing, occasionally reversing earlier conclusions, and because scholars admitted they were likely to continue indefinitely, Clark implied that readers therefore need not take changes that went beyond the TR too seriously. His view allowed little room for what his opponents insisted was the tentative nature of all progress in knowledge.

Of course, proponents of the RSV had never based their case solely on the existence of better manuscripts than those available to King James's scholars. As such proponents were quick to point out, the discovery of a wealth of papyri in the twentieth century had significantly deepened students' understanding of the New Testament language as a whole, and linguistic progress has been yet more dramatic in the case of the Old Testament.

Perhaps the most enduring argument marshaled for the King James Bible has been its unmatched literary elegance. As we have noted, this was not self-evident when the work first appeared in 1611, but within fifty years of its publication its virtues were increasingly acknowledged; feelings of reverence became ever more deeply attached to its beauty. By the nineteenth and early twentieth centuries, these feelings were so entrenched that, as a 1923 editorial in the *Chicago Tribune* asserted, altering the Authorized Version was like "chipping a cathedral." The excellence of the KJV was recognized not only by Protestants but also by Catholics, who used the Douay Version and who, according to the principal Catholic authority on the matter, remained defensive about the superiority of the KJV for centuries.[51]

During most of the nineteenth century Mormons said little about

50. Scholarly consensus, of course, does not mean unanimity. A small minority of competent Protestant and LDS scholars, such as Brigham Young University's Richard L. Anderson, feel the most widely used critical Greek texts pay only lip service to eclecticism, and remain overly dependent on Vaticanus and Sinaiticus (Anderson, personal conversations with the author).

51. E. J. Goodspeed in *As I Remember,* in Edwin S. Gaustad, ed., *A Documentary History of Religion in America,* 2 vols. (Grand Rapids: Eerdmans, 1982–1983), 2:382; Fogarty, *American Catholic Biblical Scholarship,* pp. 5, 23–24.

the Bible's literary value. Their oft-repeated refrain was that all texts and translations were corrupt, and accuracy was what they professed to care most about. However, against the backdrop of social and intellectual changes occurring at the end of the century, and especially with the appearance of major new revisions, the literary importance of the KJV was increasingly stressed.

For J. Reuben Clark, this was a theological, not merely an aesthetic, issue: "Could any language be too great, too elegant, too beautiful, too majestic, too divine-like to record the doings and sayings of Jesus . . . the Christ?" The language of God was ill-served when rendered "on the level of the ordinary press reporter's style of today."[52]

Clark's concern had practical consequences. Before publishing *Why the King James Version,* he sought permission from Church President David O. McKay, whom he served as counselor in the Church's First Presidency. The two men enjoyed mutual respect and a cordial friendship but were so fundamentally different in administrative style, political philosophy, and theological attitudes that Clark privately confided that other administrators who lined up behind one or the other of them were known to inner circles as "Clark men" or "McKay men."[53]

President McKay was not in the habit of enforcing his views of what his associates should and should not publish, but he resisted Clark's request for permission. "We ought to be a little careful," he said, "about criticizing the Revised Version" because in some places it was more accurate than the familiar text and it also got rid of confusing, outdated terms. Clark countered that McKay, who had literary training, would probably not wish to rewrite Shakespeare's plays for the same purpose. The irenic Church president did not contest the point and finally acquiesced to Clark's publication of the book.[54]

Clark's belief in the decisive importance of the linguistic superiority of the KJV was shared by countless Christians, certainly including many Latter-day Saints. Clearly, however, his was not the only Mormon position—the ultimate Mormon arbiter, the prophet and president of the Church, remained of a different opinion. Mormon leaders

52. *Why,* pp. 355, 377, passim.

53. For the overall relations between the conservative Clark and the liberal McKay, see Quinn, *J. Reuben Clark,* pp. 113–45.

54. Ibid., p. 177.

earlier in the century had already expressed reserve toward the tendency of learned scholars to inflate the humble dialects that characterized many of the original biblical writings into a "masterly English" that would tickle the fancy of modern readers. Twentieth-century scholarship made a similar point, discovering what the scholars of the RV and ASV, to say nothing of the KJV, did not know, namely, that the New Testament had been written in koine or common Greek. As one eminent authority put it, "an elaborate, elegant style is unsuited to" biblical translation, "and in proportion as it is rendered in a conscious literary style, it is misrepresented to the modern reader."[55]

Defenders of the RSV alleged other weaknesses in the literary argument for the KJV. President McKay pointed to the most salient: the KJV's archaic style and use of archaic terms that were sometimes charming but often difficult for modern readers to understand. Clark allowed the problem but insisted that the Authorized Version "can yet be understood in all essential parts by the careful, thoughtful reader." A little work with a reference book, he said, could overcome this small obstacle.

From President McKay's vantage, it may have been Clark's own diligence that led him to overestimate the ambitions of the ordinary reader. The difficulty of occasional Jacobean words and phrases might here and there be overcome by the few who would bother to consult reference material or when people were reading brief passages or material so familiar as the Sermon on the Mount, yet this would hardly suffice for those who wished to understand, say, the intricate and sustained arguments of the Epistle to the Romans. But McKay hardly needed to press the issue. Clark subverted his position by his own experience, acknowledging that he did not grasp much of Paul.[56]

Many of Mormonism's religious educators, those charged with making scripture comprehensible to the Church's young people, simply ignored Clark's assertions. Some frankly averred that President Clark's administrative authority, to which they gave allegiance, had nothing to do with his scholarly arguments in a field in which he had no training. "His book on this subject did not cause a riffle in the group I ran around with," George Tanner would later observe. Others allowed their students to choose, providing them with copies of

55. Quoted by Clark in *Why,* p. 355.
56. *Why,* p. 60; Quinn, *J. Reuben Clark,* p. 162.

both the KJV and the RSV, and observed that the majority chose the RSV.[57]

Beyond the literary argument, President Clark pointed to Mormon tradition, noting that the Authorized Version was the Bible that had successfully guided the Church from its beginning. He reinforced the point by insisting that "the great bulk of our people know and use only the Authorized Version, and do not have access either to the Revised Versions . . . or to other versions." "References in our Standard Church Works and our Church literature," he said, "are to the Authorized Version," and Bible commentaries and dictionaries are in good part "keyed" to it.

President Clark's reasoning privately startled more than a few Saints. Any logic in defense of the King James Bible that pointed to traditional Mormon usage had also to account for the refusal of nineteenth-century Mormon leaders to be confined by the KJV. To these critics, Clark's other points seemed empty; gaining access to various versions was scarcely an insurmountable problem, and was only compounded by his making the KJV appear more official to ordinary believers. Commentaries and dictionaries by the most competent scholars, they were sure, were not long destined to be "keyed" primarily to the KJV.[58]

Clark's final assault on the Revised translations derived from his doctrinal concerns. Despite, or perhaps because of, his Columbia education, it also revealed a deep distrust of intellectuals, which he candidly acknowledged.[59] Clark intimated the King James translators had been "amenable to the promptings of the Holy Spirit," and the Revised scholars had not. Said he: no "clear cut statement of the Revisers is noted that . . . they either sought or enjoyed the help of the Spirit of the Lord. . . . It would seem the whole Revision was approached in the same spirit they would employ in the translation of any classical work." Against this, Clark contrasted the Authorized translators' description of their work in their preface:

> And in what sort did these assemble? In the trust of their own knowledge, or of their sharpness of wit, or deepness of judgment, as it were

57. Russel Swensen, George Tanner, and George Boyd, private interviews with author; Tanner, personal correspondence with author, October 31, 1989.
58. Ibid.
59. Quinn, *J. Reuben Clark*, pp. 173–79.

in an arm of flesh? At no hand. They trusted in him that hath the key of David . . . ; they prayed to the Lord, the Father of our Lord, to the effect that St. *Augustine* did; *O let thy Scriptures be my pure delight; let me not be deceived in them, neither let me deceive by them.* In this confidence, and with this devotion, did they assemble together.[60]

Clark's posture on this point, like others we have considered, was borrowed from earlier Protestant scholars. In a Mormon context, however, it possessed an air of novelty, because in implying the KJV translators had been inspired, it directly opposed the almost unanimous voice of previous Mormon leaders who had commented on the matter. Proponents of the Revisions were further disconcerted by Clark's characterization because the revisers had in fact invoked the hand of God over their work. In an essay sufficiently pious to have embarrassed the modern translators of any work but Holy Scripture, the British Revision concluded its preface thus:

> We now conclude, humbly commending our labours to Almighty God, and praying that his favour and blessing may be vouchsafed to that which has been done in his name. We recognised from the first the responsibility of the undertaking; and through our manifold experience of its abounding difficulties we have felt more and more, as we went onward, that such a work can never be accomplished by organised efforts of scholarship and criticism, unless assisted by Divine help.

> Thus, in the review of the work which we have been permitted to complete, our closing words must be words of mingled thanksgiving, humility, and prayer. Of thanksgiving, for the many blessings vouchsafed to us throughout . . . our corporate labours; of humility, for our failings and imperfections in the fulfillment of our task; and of prayer to Almighty God, that the Gospel of our Lord and Saviour Jesus Christ may be more clearly and more freshly shown forth to all who shall be readers of this Book.

The preface to editions of the later RSV went on to say:

> The Bible is more than a historical document to be preserved. And it is more than a classic of English literature to be cherished and admired. It is a record of God's dealing with men, of God's revelation of Himself and His will. It records the life and work of Him in whom the word of God became flesh and dwelt among men. [The] Word must not be

60. *Why*, pp. xxvii, 4–5, 274–86, 355–56, 418–19, passim. Italics in original.

disguised in phrases that are no longer clear, or hidden under words
that have changed or lost their meaning. . . .

J. Reuben Clark found such professions weak, reserved for the end of
the respective prefaces of which they were a part, and more remarkable for what they did not say than for what they did. Their authors,
he seemed to feel, damned themselves with faint praise of God.

Clark's assertion that the revisers were more restrained in their
overt piety than their KJV predecessors was incontestable. The
seventeenth-century writers had written effusively, at great length, in
their eloquent preface. But Clark's opponents thought he allowed
insufficiently for the difference between modern tastes and those of
an age of rhetorical flourish. He appeared to take the worshipful KJV
preface at face value, as though it could readily be transferred to the
twentieth century with little change. That such a wholesale transfer
would have been extreme, they said, could be seen by a glance at
what modern standards would judge as the obsequious 1611 dedication to the increasingly unpopular and autocratic King James.[61]

So distressing was James's behavior to the Puritans that his reign
became but a preface to that of Charles I, whose more drastic actions
prompted the great Puritan exodus to New England, then civil war,
and finally his own execution. Despite such tensions, the age of literary extravagance induced the Puritans, well represented among the
Authorized translators, to support the flattering "Epistle Dedicatory"
to King James: "Great and manifold were the blessings, most dread
Sovereign, which Almighty God, the Father of all mercies, bestowed
upon us the people of England, when first he sent Your Majesty's
Royal Person to rule and reign over us." The appearance of His
Majesty was "as of the *Sun* in his strength, instantly [dispelling]
mists . . . accompanied with peace and tranquillity at home and
abroad." His "very name is precious" and his subjects looked to him
"as that sanctified Person, who, under God, is the immediate Author
of their true happiness." This affection was upheld by "infinite arguments." His humble servants hoped, "Your most Sacred Majesty,"
that their translation would "receive approbation and patronage from
so learned and judicious a Prince as Your Highness is. . . ." Similar
effusion was not absent from the Authorized "Translators to the

61. For James's increasing difficulties with his subjects, see Ahlstrom, *A Religious
History,* 1:134–35.

Reader," and some critics thought Clark was expecting too much if he thought its grandiloquence should be duplicated by modern scholars.

Repercussions

J. Reuben Clark's justifications of the King James Bible, then, did not represent all Mormon sentiments. Indeed, although he held his views passionately, Clark certified they were purely personal: the initial words of *Why the King James Version* were: "For this book I alone am responsible. It is not a Church publication."[62]

Yet as a member of the Church's First Presidency, President Clark held an exceedingly prominent position in Mormondom. In fact, during much of the 1950s, when his book was published, he was the most productive, vigorous, and visible figure in this body, while his colleagues David O. McKay and Stephen L. Richards suffered repeated illnesses and hospitalizations.[63] Despite President Clark's own disavowal, his book was inevitably taken by some Mormons as representing God's opinion on biblical translations, particularly because Clark was echoed by other vocal officials, and the contrasting views of President McKay and his supporters were never published.

In addition, Clark was unusually erudite. Though it remains unclear how many Saints actually read his difficult book that rested on so many of their shelves, they were well aware of its general conclusion. Because of the forcefulness with which its author expressed himself, making it seem that to abandon the King James translation in favor of another was to abandon one's faith, and because no one of general Church influence publicly rose to present an alternative view, Clark's book galvanized conservative impulses among the Saints and gradually acquired a quasi-official aura. Virtually all subsequent apologies for the Authorized Bible depended primarily on Clark or used similar arguments less ably than he.[64]

62. *Why,* p. v.

63. Quinn, *J. Reuben Clark,* p. 129.

64. Petersen, *As Translated Correctly,* pp. 16, 24–25, 44, 52; Petersen, "It Was a Miracle!" *Ensign* 7 (November 1977): 11–13; Bruce R. McConkie, "King James Version of the Bible" in *Mormon Doctrine,* pp. 421–23; McConkie, *Doctrinal New Testament Commentary* 1:59–63; McConkie, "The Bible, a Sealed Book," in *A Symposium of the New Testament,* supplement (SLC: Church of Jesus Christ of Latter-day Saints, 1984);

Since he wrote, Mormon leaders have very occasionally offered reasons for continued KJV usage that Clark did not detail. Joseph Fielding Smith, for example, suggested Mormons retained the Authorized Version because it was accepted by most Protestants, providing "common ground for proselyting purposes."[65] Perhaps this is what Clark was implying when, in a subset of the tradition argument, he stressed that the RV and ASV had not displaced the King James Version in popularity.[66] He was sure it would be the same with the RSV.

There was precedent for this claim because the KJV had for so long retained an entrenched loyalty. Even as recently as 1979, when the Mormons produced their new edition of the Authorized Bible, 34.8 percent of American homes used the KJV as their primary Bible. That is an impressive figure but, obviously, it no longer represents the majority of Christians, and it continues to shrink as newer translations gain an ever larger share of the market.[67]

Franklin S. Gonzalez, "I Have a Question," *Ensign* 17 (June 1987): 23–25; *The Life and Teachings of Jesus and His Apostles,* Institute of Religion manual for Religion 211, 212 (SLC: Church of Jesus Christ of Latter-day Saints, 1978 [see also its Old Testament counterpart for Religion 301]). An unsigned editorial in *CN,* October 4, 1952, p. 16, was either written by Clark or was entirely dependent on him; so also "Why the King James Version," *CN* June 2, 1956, p. 16. See also unsigned *CN* editorials, November 14, 1970, p. 16, and September 9, 1972, p. 16, possibly penned by Mark E. Petersen. Sidney Sperry, "The Three Hundred and Fiftieth Anniversary of the King James Version of the Bible" (*IE* 64 [July 1961]: 498–99, 546–50), was more balanced than Clark in pointing out the limitations of the KJV, but his arguments in its behalf largely follow Clark.

65. Smith, *Answers to Gospel Questions,* ed. Bruce R. McConkie, 2:207.

66. "Our Bible," in Yarn, ed., *J. Reuben Clark: Selected Papers,* pp. 78–79, 92.

67. Walter A. Elwell, "The King James Even Better?" *Christianity Today,* November 2, 1979, p. 48. RSV sales averaged one million copies a year during its first decade, and, according to Donald Kraus, Senior Bible Editor at Oxford University Press, had risen to a total of approximately fifty million copies in print by 1990. The RSV has been adapted for use by Catholics, who also produced the superbly annotated Jerusalem Bible (1966) and, as their main version, the New American Bible (1970). By 1981 American sales of the paraphrased Living Bible stood at twenty-five million; the New American Standard Bible (a conservative revision of the Authorized Version) at fourteen million; both the Good News Bible (Today's English Version) and the New English Bible at twelve million each; and the New International Version at three million. The NIV has since captured a broad audience, as has, for more scholarly use, the Anchor Bible. The Revised English Bible also seems destined for lasting success. The New King James Bible, a significant revision of the KJV, was issued in 1979, just as the new LDS edition came out. For relatively recent figures, see Richard N. Ostling, "Rivals to the King James Throne," *Time,* April 20, 1981, pp. 62–63.

Among members of evangelical professional organizations, the King James Bible

In recent years, conservative LDS religious educators have here and there extended Clark's logic, particularly his uniquely Mormon argument that Joseph Smith's modern revelations verify the accuracy of the KJV. One teacher compares many passages where he feels modern translations obscure "doctrines of the Restoration," whereas the KJV language "triggers" them. For instance, the "dispensation of the fulness of times" (Eph. 1:10) has a very specific Restorationist meaning for most Latter-day Saints.[68] Therefore, translating the Greek phrase behind it as "when the time is right" or "when the time fully comes," as some scholars do, mars a proof-text for Mormon doctrine and abandons "unique terminology seemingly preferred by God."[69] Other Mormons insist this approach fosters illusions by forcing theology to depend on incidental KJV phraseology rather than on the genuine intent of the original authors or on some other basis.[70]

retains surprisingly little loyalty even for family use. A recent survey revealed that only 22.1 percent of members of the Wesleyan Theological Society used the KJV for family use. This figure dropped to 8.4 percent for scholarly Bible study. For members of the Evangelical Theological Society, the figures were even lower: 18 percent for family use, 2.1 percent for study. For members of the Institute for Biblical Research, the figures were minuscule: 2 percent and 0 percent. The versions dominantly used by members of these organizations are the New International Version, the Revised Standard Version, and the New American Standard Version (Noll, *Between Faith and Criticism,* p. 206).

68. "Dispensation of the Fulness of Times" in popular Mormon thought means the era ushered in by God through Joseph Smith, wherein all of the lost or corrupted teachings and priesthoods of ancient times have been restored in preparation of the Lord's Second Coming.

69. Franklin Gonzalez, "The King James Bible," (unpublished handout, Religion 211, LDS Institute of Religion [adjacent to the University of Utah], n.d.). The notion that the language is "seemingly preferred by God" derives from the fact that KJV language echoes throughout the D&C and Book of Mormon—an idea treated more fully in chapters 1 and 2 of the present work. Other examples Gonzalez cites wherein LDS notions are cemented to the particular phraseology of the KJV include the idea of a preexistent "first estate" (KJV Jude 6; *PGP,* Abraham 3:26, 28) rather than a "proper domain" (New King James Version); the "veil" of the temple (KJV Mark 15:38; D&C 110:1) rather than the "curtain" (RSV); and "We have . . . a more sure word of prophecy" (KJV 2 Peter 1:19; D&C 131:5) rather than "confirms for us the message of the prophets" (New English Bible).

70. Private conversations with contemporary Mormon educators; George Tanner, personal correspondence with author, October 31, 1989. Although the idea of successive divine dispensations is as old as the Old Testament, the modern form of "premillennial dispensationalism" is usually tied by scholars to John Nelson Darby of the Plymouth Brethren (Ahlstrom, *A Religious History,* 2:277–79), though my own impression is that the idea was too diffuse in Darby's time to be traced so neatly to him as its "effective originator."

Another Mormon writer uses Joseph Smith's modern revelations to verify the accuracy of the KJV from a slightly different angle. He notes that the Prophet translated the Book of Mormon and recorded his own revelations in the idiom of the KJV. The writer goes on to argue that Smith's successor prophets have continued to record revelations in the same idiom. He cites as "obvious illustrations" D&C 135, 136, and 138 by John Taylor, Brigham Young, and Joseph F. Smith respectively. Because of this continued use of KJV idiom, the clear "intent is that [all scripture] be woven together as one book."[71]

Latter-day Saints with other views have seen this line of thought as a retreat to mere expediency. It gives little weight, they contend, to the probability that Joseph Smith cast his revelations in KJV idiom because, raised on the KJV, he (unconsciously?) equated it with religious terminology. Indeed, as we have noted in this study, Smith did the same thing with early accounts of his first vision, yet greatly lessened the tendency in later narrations (particularly the now canonized one) as his confidence in his prophetic calling grew. And Brigham Young, who thought his sermons "as good scripture as . . . this Bible," did not preach in KJV idiom. Furthermore, of the three "obvious illustrations" cited to show the necessary continuance of King James English, only D&C 136 is clearly in KJV style. Section 138 uses transitional language, retaining heavy vestiges of Jacobean language because it purports to be an inspired commentary and expansion of certain KJV passages. But it itself is not unambiguously in KJV form. Section 135 is manifestly *not* in Jacobean idiom; it retains only slight traces of the KJV because of its subject matter.

Despite this diversity of opinion in Mormon ranks, Church authorities in 1979 published an "official" LDS edition of the KJV, heavily cross-referenced with other Mormon scriptures. The mammoth project was initiated earlier in the decade by Church President Harold B. Lee, long a protégé of J. Reuben Clark. Widely promoted by Church leaders and diverse Mormon organizations, this Bible has insured the dominance of the King James Version for the indefinite future. With this publication, the metamorphosis of the King James Bible from the common to the official version among English-speaking Mormons was complete.[72]

71. Joseph Fielding McConkie, "Modern Revelation," in "*To Be Learned Is Good If* . . .", ed. Robert Millet (SLC: Bookcraft, 1987), p. 126.

72. See note 1 and, for Lee's relationship with Clark, Quinn, *J. Reuben Clark,* pp. 58, 88, passim. The KJV's official stature in contemporary Mormonism should not be

Mormon scriptural usage has for a century and a half been marked by an "in-house" diversity and by a distinctive blend of traditional and nontraditional perspectives. Though scholars have not always been attuned to its significance, this peculiar recipe has contributed to the widely acknowledged difficulty in defining the Saints, who in some ways have been cultural insiders in America, and in other ways have been outsiders.[73] But with respect to their choice of a biblical translation, the Saints are more easily classified. As they approach the twenty-first century, they have settled on an early-seventeenth-century translation as their official Bible. Unlike many other Christians, any controversy over the issue has been decidedly muted. At least on this matter—though partly for their own distinctive reasons—the Saints have traveled a well-worn path, showing themselves to be more conservative even than most of their evangelical peers.

Yet if arguments marshaled for the King James Bible are contested by the standards of modern scholarship, Mormonism's KJV loyalties are understandable on religious grounds. This can best be seen in the context of global religious perspectives.

The insistence on some one linguistic style for its sacred texts by any religious body is motivated in part by the concern to find or preserve prose as satisfying to the worshipper as to the scholar (or sometimes even over and against the scholar). Language has for ages been viewed as embodying elements of the sacred; it follows that a yearning for the "highest" language will often accompany what believers feel are receptions of divine communications. At least at the unconscious level, the quest is often as much for a sense of the numinous, a sense of holiness and mystery and divinity and dignity, as for the mere content of a given passage.

Mohammed's seventh-century recitations, for instance, fell on ears

misread as the LDS equivalent of a Tridentine censorship of other versions, which has never existed in Mormon history. Individual teachers and leaders continue to make use of various versions, and it is quite possible that Mormon growth in non-English-speaking countries will foster a change in status for the KJV. In 1980, for example (and despite Joseph Smith's praise of what was probably Luther's German translation of the Bible), the Mormon Church adopted the Uniform Translation as its official Bible for German-speaking Saints. Unlike the KJV, the Uniform Translation is in contemporary idiom and makes use of recent scholarship.

73. See my Preface, pp.vii–ix.

finely tuned to the shape and nuances of speech. The sheer rhetorical excellence of the Qur'an was from the beginning taken by Muslims as proof of its divine origins.[74] Hence the Muslim insistence on Arabic alone as the true word of God in the Qur'anic recitations; translations do not qualify. Similarly, the ancient Vedanga commentaries on Hinduism's Vedas set Sanskrit apart as the only medium of revelation, "the breath of the Supreme." The language is *sam-skrita,* "refined," "perfectly structured"; the Supreme Being himself arranged the letters of the alphabet. The sounds of spoken Sanskrit are primal, possessing not an arbitrary but an essential and objective attachment to their referents.[75] Indeed, here in the West before the eighteenth century, people often thought of language as natural—directly related— to the objects and concepts to which it alluded. The belief derived in part from the Genesis account, which portrays Adam as naming the animals in the garden, using an Adamic language in which the name is perfectly adequate to the thing named; the name partakes of the nature of the thing.[76]

Even in twentieth-century America, a preoccupation with preserving the ideal scriptural tongue can be traced, and not alone among Mormons or conservative Protestants. Influential and learned twentieth-century Catholics have argued that updating the language of translation to contemporary standards threatens inspiration itself.[77] Among American Jews, reverence for the KJV was clear in Isaac Leeser's nineteenth-century biblical translation, and remained strong through the mid-twentieth century. As the Jewish scholar Max Margolis, editor in chief of the influential 1917 English translation of the Hebrew Bible, thought, "All attempts at modernizing the [KJV Bible] must necessarily fail. Once and for all time the revisers of 1611 fixed the model for all future undertakings." (The 1917 revision was

74. Frederick M. Denny, "Islam: Qur'an and Hadith," in *The Holy Book,* ed. Denny and Taylor, pp. 88–89.

75. Robert C. Lester, "Hinduism: Veda and Sacred Texts," in *The Holy Book,* ed. Denny and Taylor, pp. 133–34. I am also indebted to Hindu expert Douglas R. Brooks, Department of Religion and Classics, University of Rochester, for helpful explanations.

76. Michel Foucault, *The Order of Things* (New York: Vintage, 1973).

77. Fogarty, *American Catholic Biblical Scholarship,* p. 208.

motivated primarily by concern to remove non-Jewish and anti-Jewish expressions.)[78]

Thus, although the logic of J. Reuben Clark and his followers does not convince all Latter-day Saints, the urge to *canonize* a particular rendition of the *canon* does connect the Mormons with a religious impulse seen in many places, in many times, and among many peoples. However, the work of J. Reuben Clark lays bare a modern Mormon dilemma—one that separates Mormons from other scriptural loyalists. If the Saints forsake the King James Bible in favor of more accurate and more readable translations, will not the language of their Book of Mormon and the Doctrine and Covenants, patterned after the KJV, appear increasingly anachronistic? Will any modern prophet feel called to adapt the work of Joseph Smith to the needs of an English-speaking populace in the twenty-first century, or is Smith's English, like Mohammad's Arabic, permanently sacrosanct?

Appendix

J. Reuben Clark gave the bulk of his attention to the revisions that culminated in the RSV, and he of course did not have access to translations appearing after his death. However, because he argued that the KJV is singularly loyal to the notion of the divine stature of Jesus, and because spokesmen after him have depended on his logic, it seems apt to include several modern versions published after Clark in the comparison below. The chart notes eight places in the New Testament where the Greek can possibly (either by the right choice of textual witnesses or by the appropriate grammatical interpretation) be construed to specifically call Jesus "God." The comparison is adapted from Victor Perry, "Problem Passages of the New Testament in Some Modern Translations: Does the New Testament Call Jesus God?" *Expository Times* 87 (1975–1976): 214–15. An "X" means the version in question does directly ascribe deity to Jesus; an "O" means it does not. NEB = New English Bible; NIV = New International

78. Max Margolis, *The Story of Bible Translations* (Philadelphia: Jewish Publication Society of America, 1917), pp. 104–5; Leonard Greenspoon, *Max Margolis: A Scholar's Scholar* (Atlanta: Scholar's Press, 1987), p. 65; Sperling, in *History of Jewish Biblical Scholarship*, ed. Sperling and Levine, chap. 2.

Version; NWT = New World Translation (Jehovah's Witnesses); mg. = marginal reading.

	John 1:1	John 1:18	Acts 20:28	Rom. 9:5	2 Thess. 1:12	Titus 2:13	Heb. 1:8	2 Pet. 1:1
KJV	X	O	X	X	O	O	X	O
RV	X	O	X	X	O	X	X	X
RV mg.		X	O	O		O		O
RSV	X	O	O	O	O	X	X	X
RSV mg.		X	O	X		O	O	O
NEB	X	O	O	O	O	X	X	X
NEB mg.		X	O	X		O	O	
Moffatt	O	O	O	O	O	O	O	X
Goodspeed	O	O	X	O	O	X	O	X
NIV	X	X	X	X	O	X	X	X
NIV mg.		O	O	O	X			
NWT	O	O	O	O	O	O	O	O

Whether Jesus was divine and, if so, in what sense, are issues that have been debated for nearly two millennia. But the results of the comparison above discourage the conclusion that the KJV is the champion defender of the divinity of Jesus while the Revisions systematically obliterate it. Only the Jehovah's Witnesses' NWT omits all references to Jesus' deity. Even Moffatt and Goodspeed, whose liberal propensities have been well publicized by opponents, manage one and three references respectively. The KJV accepts only four of the eight possibilities, the same number as the RSV and NEB. The RV, which so bothered Clark, accepts six such references, two more than the KJV. The evangelical NIV, translated not from the *Textus Receptus* but from an eclectic Greek text, has the highest incidence of passages suggesting a divine Jesus.

6

The Bible in Contemporary Mormonism

Like Episcopalians, Baptists, or virtually any major denomination, Mormons have within their ranks what might be called "liberals" and "conservatives."[1] As with Reformed and Orthodox Jews, however, Mormonism's expressions of liberalism and conservatism occur in a distinctive context. They are not properly understood simply by equating them with analogous positions among other religious groups.

The propensities of the two types of Mormons are clearly manifest in their views of revelation and scripture. One could, in fact, define the types by their attitudes on these matters. Archetypal expressions of conservative and liberal understandings of the Bible in recent Mormon history are found in the thinking of two figures, the late apostle Bruce R. McConkie, and the octogenarian educator and humanitarian Lowell L. Bennion. Significantly, McConkie wasn't—and Bennion isn't—a trained biblical scholar. These men reveal two major thrusts in contemporary Mormon thought, showing how Mormons differ from other Christians in the theological content of their biblical views while resembling them in their attitudes. The chapter concludes with a look at the new LDS edition of the Bible and its tendency to support Elder

---

1. Such terms are naturally relative. Protestant modernists of the 1920s saw fundamentalists as conservative, but in the same era the group eventually known as the Lutheran Church–Missouri Synod flayed fundamentalists as incipient liberals (see Smith, Handy, and Loetscher, eds., *American Christianity: An Historical Interpretation with Representative Documents,* 2 vols. (New York: Scribner's, 1960), 2:349–54).

McConkie's outlook, a tendency that has helped reorient late-twenti-eth-century Mormonism.

Historian Richard Poll has suggested imaginative symbols for liberal and conservative Mormons: "Liahona Saints" and "Iron Rod Saints," terms fittingly borrowed from the Book of Mormon. The Iron Rod was the Word of God. Despite the uncertainties and temptations of the world, those who held to it could follow the narrow path to the Tree of Life (that is, the love of God and, by implication, heaven). The Liahona was a compass used by emigrants from Israel to guide them on their journey. The compass, however, could not fully mark the path; the clarity of its directions varied with the circumstances of the user.

Iron Rod Saints tend to discover answers to all their important religious questions in three authorities: scripture, pronouncements of Church officials, and the Holy Spirit. Clear and certain revelation is the Iron Rod that will lead to exaltation in the heavenly kingdom. Although Liahona Saints also allow for inspiration, they may frequently be skeptical of the answers Iron Rod Saints think they find in their sources, and skeptical even of the kinds of questions they ask. For "Liahonas," no human instrument can communicate God's word so fully and clearly that it can be universally understood and appropriated. For Iron Rodders, Liahonas depend too much on human learning—"the philosophies of men."

Mormons far to the left of Liahonas may surrender their conscious Latter-day Saint commitments, becoming only "culture Mormons" or forsaking Mormonism altogether. Those far to the right of Iron Rod Saints may leave the fold to form or join fundamentalist sects or other groups. The attempt here is to analyze only the mainstream of believing Mormons.[2]

Poll's Iron Rod and Liahona images are often used loosely by those familiar with them. It is therefore worth noting that their creator, without elaboration, specified that the essential difference between the two types of Mormons was rooted "in their approach to the concept 'the Word of God.' " The contrast between these approaches

2. Poll, "What the Church Means to People Like Me," in *Faith and History: Reflections of a Mormon Historian* (SLC: Signature Books, 1989), pp. 1–13.

becomes clear by examining the biblical perspectives of Bruce McConkie and Lowell Bennion.

This is not to say Bennion and McConkie are typical of ordinary Latter-day Saints, many of whom would justly resist imprisonment in a scholar's pigeonhole. Moreover, few Mormons would or could state their attitudes with McConkie's rigor or Bennion's depth. Poll's Iron Rod and Liahona are merely symbols of "ideal types," useful only in a Weberian sense. More complex models for analyzing Mormon social and intellectual patterns could and have been proposed.[3] Nonetheless, the tendencies behind these symbols are real and basic, and they suggest something important about the state of contemporary Mormonism. Bennion and McConkie closely embody these ideal types, and thus represent valuable windows into Mormon understandings of the Bible. Their strong and clearly stated views make explicit the often inchoate orientations of many others.

One astute observer of Mormonism has noticed that

> even though it is a revealed religion, Mormonism is all but creedless. . . . While certain doctrines are enunciated in the standard works and some doctrinal issues have been addressed in formal pronouncements by the First Presidency, there is nothing in Mormonism comparable to the Westminster Confession of Faith or the Augsburg Confession. Few of the truly distinctive doctrines of Mormonism are discussed in "official" sources. It is mainly by "unofficial" means–Sunday School lessons, [high school and college] religion classes, sacrament meeting talks and books by Church officials and others who ultimately speak only for themselves—that the theology is passed from one generation to the next. Indeed it would seem that a significant part of Mormon theology exists primarily in the minds of the members.

This writer also argued that "the absence of a formal creed means that each generation must produce a new set of gospel expositors to restate and reinterpret doctrines."[4] Although these assertions are overstated (because, despite Joseph Smith's antipathy toward creeds,

---

3. E.g., Jeffrey C. Jacob, "Explorations in Mormon Social Character: Beyond the Liahona and Iron Rod," *Dialogue* 22 (Summer 1989): 44:74; Hutchinson, "LDS Approaches to the Holy Bible."

4. Peter Crawley, "Parley P. Pratt: Father of Mormon Pamphleteering," *Dialogue* 15 (Autumn 1982): 20–21. Cf. Mark P. Leone, *Roots of Modern Mormonism* (Cambridge: Harvard University Press, 1979), pp. 171–72.

certain documents have achieved almost a de facto creedal status in modern Mormonism[5]), their general insight is still worth noting.

Mormonism's official doctrinal interpreters are its series of Church presidents, but the most lasting theological expressions, with the prominent exception of Joseph Smith, have frequently come from other Church leaders who have authored "great synthetical books." Such works have appeared in every generation, produced by such figures as Parley and Orson Pratt, B. H. Roberts, James Talmage, and John Widtsoe.[6]

However, with the passing of these leaders, punctuated by the death of Widtsoe in 1952, only two LDS general authorities remained who possessed a public passion for theology. These were Joseph Fielding Smith and Bruce R. McConkie, neither of whom shared Widtsoe's liberal inclinations. David O. McKay, Hugh B. Brown, and other liberals continued to preside, but for the most recent generation of Latter-day Saints, Smith and McConkie have been the most conspicuous theologians, the only ones to produce the kinds of comprehensive syntheses of Mormon doctrine to which ordinary Saints commonly turn for authoritative answers to theological questions. This signifies a shift in the Church's orientation: liberal Mormonism is less visible among the leadership; conservative Mormonism has become partially institutionalized through certain influential books and what since the 1960s have become the committee-produced, "correlated" lesson manuals often dependent on them. This literature in turn shapes popular perceptions of Mormon orthodoxy, including the perceptions of many eventually chosen as general authorities. The lynchpin in this circular process—both a cause and a result of it—is Mormonism's scriptural hermeneutic.

Bruce R. McConkie

From the perspective of the sort of Bible student who might publish in *The Journal of Biblical Literature,* Apostle Bruce McConkie was not really a scholar but, rather, a preacher and an extraordinarily

5. The "Articles of Faith" or some of the questions asked by Mormon bishops of LDS temple patrons are examples. I am indebted to Thomas G. Alexander for the observation (correspondence with author).

6. Crawley, "Pratt" p. 21; Alexander, "The Reconstruction of Mormon Doctrine: From Joseph Smith to Progressive Theology"; chap. 14 in *Mormonism in Transition.*

diligent expositor of doctrine. His central motive was to instruct and inspire his people. In one important sense, then, it would be improper to assess him by critically informed standards. From this vantage, lengthy attention to his hermeneutic is not productive, and he himself would have spurned the criteria of judgment. But remembering that our task is not to focus on Elder McConkie personally but through him to probe the contemporary Mormon use of the Bible, McConkie's scriptural approach becomes a crucial topic. Evidence of his influence is pervasive.

Some years ago a prominent LDS religious educator estimated that if one were to "ask any ten Mormons on the street who is the Church's leading scholar today . . . most—if not all—will say it's Bruce R. McConkie."[7] With McConkie's death in 1985, the slightly exaggerated statement would have to be altered, but only modestly. McConkie's singular influence seems largely attributable to his doctrinal sources (principally Joseph Smith), his position as an apostle, his authoritarian tone, his clear and forceful expressions and extensions of what many Saints already assumed, the fact that his research often outflanked those with contrasting views, and the sheer volume and format of his publications, which serve as handy reference works.

Many Saints realize Elder McConkie's views are not official pronouncements of the Church; still, it is unlikely that any modern Mormon leader has been quoted more frequently during the second half of the twentieth century. This seems clear on doctrinal matters and especially clear on issues of New Testament interpretation. The more than two thousand pages in McConkie's three-volume *Doctrinal New Testament Commentary* constitute the most widely read biblical commentary by a Mormon author. An example reflecting the prestige of this literature is the New Testament manual recommended for college students in the Church's far-flung educational system. Among past or present Church authorities, the manual cites McConkie nearly three times as frequently as his nearest rival, Joseph Smith.[8] And this man-

7. Cited by Buerger, "Speaking with Authority," p. 8.

8. *The Life and Teachings of Jesus and His Apostles* (SLC: Church of Jesus Christ of Latter-day Saints, 1978–1979). Of those Mormon leaders most frequently referred to, McConkie is cited 251 times; Joseph Smith, 87 times; James Talmage, 79; Joseph Fielding Smith, 54; Spencer W. Kimball and Harold B. Lee, 47 each; and David O. McKay, 26 times.

ual preceded publication of McConkie's massive six-volume Messiah series.

Scriptural interpretation is central to Elder McConkie's eleven books, all of which intend to define Mormon theology. None is light material for average readers, yet all enjoy enormous sales. Among works written by the Church's general authorities, McConkie's encyclopedia of LDS theology, *Mormon Doctrine,* is among the ten best sellers in Mormon history.[9] Cumulatively, his books total nearly seven thousand pages. The apostle may have been accurate when, reacting against Protestant fundamentalists who had questioned whether Mormons were Christians, he said, "It just may be that I have preached more sermons, taught more doctrine, and written more words about the Lord Jesus Christ than any man now living."[10]

One can quickly grasp McConkie's essential perspective on the Bible by attending to five dimensions of his approach: his disdain for higher criticism, his criteria for proper interpretation, his concern for "correct doctrine," his selective commitment to literalism and inerrancy, and the limitations he put on biblical authority without imposing them on revelation generally.

Born in 1915 in Ann Arbor, Michigan, McConkie served as a missionary in the eastern states. Subsequently, he married Amelia Smith, daughter of Apostle Joseph Fielding Smith. By 1939 he had obtained bachelor of arts and bachelor of laws degrees from the University of Utah, from which he later received a doctorate in law. He went on to employment as an assistant Salt Lake City attorney and city prosecutor, as a U.S. Army intelligence officer, and as a newspaper editorialist. In 1946, at the precocious age of thirty-one, he began a four-decade tenure as a general authority of the Mormon Church. For fifteen years before his death, he served as the most outspoken of the Church's twelve apostles. Not all Saints shared his views, but his resourcefulness, devotion, integrity, courage, and earnestness were widely recognized.[11]

9. According to Buerger, "Speaking with Authority," p. 9.

10. "Our Relationship with the Lord," BYU Fireside and Devotional Speeches (Provo, UT: University Publications, 1981–1982), pp. 97–103.

11. McConkie's personal papers are unavailable to scholars. Biographical data are available in Sheri L. Dew, "Bruce R. McConkie: A Family Portrait," *This People* 6 (December 1986): 48–54, 57–58, 61–63; (no listed author) "Elder Bruce R. McConkie: Preacher of Righteousness," *Ensign* 15 (June 1985): 15–21; (no listed author) "Elder

As a youth, McConkie's devotion to scriptural study was prodigious and portentous. While still a teenager, and on his own initiative, he exhaustively explored the Book of Mormon: line by line, he meticulously examined and cross-referenced the entire five-hundred-page text with the Bible and other LDS scriptures. He then painstakingly rewrote each of its sixty-eight hundred verses in his own words, finishing with a stack of papers over a foot high.[12] Later, as president of a Mormon mission in Australia, he was known to gather the young missionaries together and spend as long as seven hours explicating a single verse.[13] As with his father-in-law, Joseph Fielding Smith, the scriptures to McConkie were "everything." He relied essentially on his own understanding of them, he said, as mediated by the Holy Spirit. He was dramatically independent and, with few exceptions, he seldom researched what other Church leaders had said about a given passage.[14]

If Elder McConkie did not give excessive weight to the scriptural views of other Mormons, he thought rather less of the opinions of modern scholars. Under the entry for "Higher Criticism" in his *Mormon Doctrine,* the first cross-reference heading reads, "See Apostasy." Like his lawyer–general authority colleague, J. Reuben Clark, McConkie believed that "the uninspired Biblical scholars of the world—men without faith, without revelation, without the gift of the Holy Ghost, without a knowledge of the plan of salvation; men who do not accept Christ as the literal Son of God—have studiously dissected the Bible so as, in effect, to destroy its divine authenticity."

McConkie began his Messiah series by discarding "almost everything that wordly men" have written about Christ. The unfortunate theories of these scholars were, he felt, based "on speculative evolu-

Bruce R. McConkie: Biographical Sketch," (unpublished vita, n.d.; copy in Church Historical Archives).

12. *Ensign* 15 (June 1985): 18.

13. Robert McDougall, "Bruce R. McConkie Touched Many Lives," *Provo Herald* (April 21, 1985), p. 3.

14. E.g., "Last week I quoted Parley P. Pratt for the first time in my life. I did it because I could square what he said with the scriptures and because he said it better than I could have" (Dew, "Bruce R. McConkie," p. 53). In his first book, *Mormon Doctrine,* McConkie did borrow substantially from Joseph Smith, Joseph Fielding Smith, Joseph F. Smith, and, to a lesser degree, James E. Talmage. However, in his subsequent *DNTC* volumes and the Messiah trilogy, the principal nonscriptural authority McConkie cited was himself (Buerger, "Speaking with Authority," pp. 10–11.)

tion, on speculative archeological deductions, and on pure imagination." "Occasionally some of these views are even found in the true [that is, Mormon] Church and creep into lessons and class discussions. In the final analysis they are doctrines of the devil. . . ."[15] The principal non-LDS biblical authorities McConkie cited in his *Doctrinal New Testament Commentary* and his Messiah series were the same Victorian writers James Talmage had relied on in his 1915 Mormon classic, *Jesus the Christ.*[16]

McConkie created his own system for rating the importance of various aspects of Bible study. On his scale of 1 to 10 (10 being the highest rating), he ranked scholarly commentaries and dictionaries as 1 or 2 when they bore on historical and geographical matters. On theological issues, they dropped off the scale to -10, -100, or -1000. The use of the King James Bible was important (rating 5 or 6), but comparing other versions rated 1 because "in general they simply set forth the religious predilections of their translator." "Some, for instance, have Christ born of a young woman rather than a virgin."

Unlike Joseph Smith, McConkie found little worth in learning biblical languages. Knowledge of Hebrew and Greek, which he did not acquire, merited 1 or 1.2 on his scale, though if used improperly, "its value sinks off the scale to a minus five or a minus ten, depending upon the attitude and spiritual outlook of the user."[17] If worldly scholars "get anything right, it is an accident." In short, he said—framing a graphic metaphor—revelation in scripture is like a stream of living water flowing from the Eternal Fountain. When drinking from this stream, one ought not "drink below the horses" of intellectual or sectarian commentary.[18]

As opposed to "scholars of the world," McConkie posed his own requisites for successful scripture study. The most fundamental of these were (1) diligent private searching of the scriptures, (2) submission to the living "prophets and inspired interpreters," and (3) living worthily to receive the spiritual "gift of scriptural understanding and

15. *Mormon Doctrine,* pp. 353–55.

16. Alfred Edersheim, F. W. Farrar, Cunningham Geikie, Robert Jamieson, et al. In addition to these, McConkie borrowed from J. R. Dummelow's *One Volume Bible Commentary* (New York: Macmillan, 1908).

17. "The Bible, a Sealed Book" (1984), pp. 3–5.

18. Ibid., p. 6.

interpretation."[19] By following this course, individuals could interpret the Bible by revelation—so long as their interpretations and perspectives were in harmony with those of Church leaders.[20] Officially, "leaders" meant, first, the prophet and president of the Church, and second, apostles and lesser lights. This necessarily included Elder McConkie himself, an apostle and the Church's most visible doctrinal commentator. As he wrote in 1980 to an LDS intellectual, "It is my province to teach to the Church what the doctrine is. It is your province to echo what I say or to remain silent."[21]

Despite the wide respect they commanded popularly, McConkie's views and forcefulness dismayed some Mormon leaders. Members of the Church's First Presidency, for example, wrote in 1960 that McConkie's *Mormon Doctrine* "had been a source of concern to the Brethren ever since it was published" and "is full of errors and misstatements." They urged, though they did not long enforce their judgment, that the book should "not be republished even in a corrected form," for to do so "would be embarrassing to [McConkie] and lessen his influence with the members of the Church."[22]

These Church leaders were generally charitable and publicly discreet about their private differences. Over time, however, this policy had one apparently unintended result. Their public discretion coupled with McConkie's public daring helped broaden his influence. Although his approach sometimes seemed strong medicine even to Mormons who quoted him frequently, it came increasingly over the years to be perceived as the orthodox path. He was viewed by many as "willing to call a spade a spade," and as a militant Mormon champion of vital Christian religion in an American wasteland of theological error, nit-picking philology, and emasculated religious tolerance-become-neutrality. The arid terrain of secular scholarship might inform here and there about technical trivia but was even more likely to obscure spiritual understanding. As an effective synthesizer and a dauntless, self-reliant spokesman against what he saw

19. *DNTC,* 1:56–58.

20. "Ten Keys to Understanding Isaiah," pp. 80–83; "Understanding the Book of Revelation," pp. 86–89; *DNTC,* 1:6, 2:5, 3:5; "The Bible, a Sealed Book," pp. 5–6.

21. Quoted in Buerger, "Speaking with Authority," p. 12.

22. David O. McKay Office Journal, January 7, 8, 27, and 28, 1960; Marion G. Romney to David O. McKay, January 28, 1959; cited in Buerger, "Speaking with Authority," p. 9.

as an entrenched academic establishment and the soul-risking flaws of rival denominations, McConkie's interpretation of Mormonism seemed, to some, to be Mormonism itself.

This version of Mormonism was gravely concerned with "correct doctrine." To obtain celestial exaltation, one had to believe the right tenets, for only those who obeyed God's commandments could be saved, and, naturally, they could not obey the commandments unless they understood them and their proper theological context. Of course, virtually all Mormons shared an interest in fundamental teachings like the reality of God, the purposes of human existence, and the exploration of life-styles and societies consonant with those purposes. McConkie, however, went further and was more specific, holding that correct views on such issues as evolution, or whether erring humans "get another chance" after failing the tests of this life, were crucial to one's salvation. Given that belief, and because he cared so deeply about souls, he courageously and tirelessly went to great lengths to limit the contagion of perceived heresies.[23]

Thus, for example, he urged teachers in the Church's educational system to teach doctrine, not mere ethics. "If we teach the great and eternal doctrines of salvation, we succeed, and the ethical principles will thereby take care of themselves."[24] McConkie's implied understanding of John 17:3 ("And this is life eternal, that they might know thee, the only true God . . .") was that, in order to gain eternal life, one must believe certain things about the members of the Godhead (Trinity) and the relations among them. As the apostle observed in one sermon, "I shall set forth what we must believe relative to the Father and the Son in order to gain eternal life." In doing so, he said, "I shall express the views of the Brethren, of the prophets and apostles of old, and of all those who understand the scriptures and are in tune with the Holy Spirit."[25]

When Richard and Reinhold Niebuhr and other neo-orthodox theologians of the mid-twentieth century disparaged Protestant liberals as

23. E.g., "The Seven Deadly Heresies" (1980).

24. "The Bible, a Sealed Book," pp. 6–7.

25. "BYU 1981–82, Fireside and Devotional Speeches" (Provo, UT: University Publications, 1982). Another example: "Unless and until men believe the doctrines of the restoration, they can never—never, never, never—worlds without end, prepare themselves to abide the day of our Lord's return. . . ." (McConkie, "The Doctrinal Restoration," in *The Joseph Smith Translation*, ed. Nyman and Millet, p. 8).

slaves to passing cultural trends, some liberals questioned whether
their accusers were aware of their own cultural boundedness.[26] In a
Mormon context, Bruce McConkie attacked scholars generally as
dupes of intellectual fashion, while he himself held fast to the eternal,
unchanging gospel. He was conscious of no cultural entanglements,
"having no private views to expound, no personal doctrines to set
forth, no ideas that originate with me alone." He sincerely desired
only "to present those things which will cause men of good will everywhere to believe in Him by whom salvation comes."[27]

The Mormon apostle emphasized revelation and scripture, but he
is easily distinguished from other Christian biblicists by the limitations he put on biblical authority. One could overstate these limitations, for McConkie thought the Bible important—a "book of
books," providentially preserved, and of "transcendent worth." The
gospels, for example, were the place to go to "fall in love with the
Lord," and "there is more knowledge in the four gospels, more revealed truth relative to the nature and kind of being that God . . . is,
than in all the rest of holy writ combined." For McConkie, Paul's
epistles are "treasure houses of doctrine and wise counsel"; the Book
of Revelation "sheds forth a blaze of light and understanding"; Exodus and Deuteronomy are of "surpassing worth"; and "it just may be
that . . . salvation . . . does in fact depend upon our ability to understand the writings of Isaiah. . . ." For all its faults, the Bible "has
been the most stabilizing force on earth since the day it came into
being."[28]

Elsewhere, however, McConkie restricted the Bible's importance.
For all its transcendent worth, it was, for him, a truncated and miscellaneous compilation. Canonicity had been accomplished unevenly by
uninspired men ("Can it be that the books in our present Bible are
there more by historical accident than by divine design?"). Portions
and even entire books had been lost or deliberately suppressed—to
the utter confusion of the human race until the Mormon Restoration.
Other passages had been retained but altered at the hands of unen-
lightened or calculating scribes. A bewildering multiplicity of transla-

26. Hutchison, *Modernist Impulse,* pp. 288–98, 304.

27. *The Promised Messiah,* p. xvii.

28. *Ensign* 5 (April 1975): 70; "The Bible, a Sealed Book," p. 3; *DNTC,* 3:430; "Ten
Keys to Understanding Isaiah," p. 78; "The Doctrinal Restoration," in *The Joseph
Smith Translation,* ed. Nyman and Millett, p. 12.

tions confounded honest seekers of truth. The meaning of texts had been wrested by intellectuals and ministers "whose delight it is to twist and pervert its doctrines and to spiritualize away the plain meanings of all its important parts."

The books of the Bible were not of equal worth for McConkie, and he was no less bold than Martin Luther in dismissing some of them.[29] 2 and 3 John were "of no special moment." Leviticus had "no special application to us." Proverbs, Ecclesiastes, and Lamentations were "interesting books." Job was "for people who like the book of Job," and the Song of Solomon was "biblical trash." Because of McConkie's emphasis on doctrinal correctness, he was even prepared to say, "If it came right down to it, those of us who live in the dispensation of the fulness of times could be saved if there were no Bible at all, because the gospel truths and powers have all been given anew to us by direct revelation."

McConkie's overall estimate of the Bible was that it was of enormous value and inspired of God; yet it was, in its corrupted available form, only a shadow of the clearer, unmarred revelations Joseph Smith wrote and spoke. Said McConkie:

> There are no people on earth who hold the Bible in such high esteem as [Mormons] do. We believe it, we read and ponder its sayings, we rejoice in the truths it teaches, and we seek to conform our lives to the divine standard it proclaims. But we do not believe . . . the Bible contains all things necessary for salvation. . . .
>
> [Our present Bible] contains a bucket, a small pail, a few draughts, no more than a small stream at most, out of the great ocean of revealed truth that has come to men in ages more spiritually enlightened than ours.[30]

No one reading such sentiments would confuse the Mormon apostle with a traditional Protestant.

Elder McConkie mocked "verbal revelation," the notion that "some version or other of the Bible is the exact word spoken by Deity."[31] But this did not really mean he disbelieved in verbal revela-

---

29. The German Reformer relegated Hebrews, James, Jude, and Revelation to an appendix in his New Testament.

30. 1 Nephi 13:24–29; "The Doctrinal Restoration," in *The Joseph Smith Translation,* ed. Nyman and Millett, pp. 8–15; "The Bible, a Sealed Book," pp. 2–3; *Mormon Doctrine,* pp. 82–83, 111, 453–55.

31. *Mormon Doctrine,* p. 82.

tion as such. What it meant was that the Bible as it now exists is not verbally inspired; it has been corrupted. In its original form, though, the Bible had been "perfect scripture"—"the will and mind of the Lord." It was thus not the limitations of revelation as filtered through human beings that prevented biblical inerrancy; it was simply that when scholars rather than prophets became the "keepers of the Book," the text quickly degenerated with both accidental and intentional errors of translation and transmission. Thus the Bible, but not revelation, was flawed.

Protestant fundamentalists had also, of course, long pointed to the "original autographs" to protect their view of inerrancy, but McConkie's position was not quite theirs. His view, in fact, had almost as much in common with Islamic or Jewish traditionalism as with Christian Fundamentalism. He reserved for the Doctrine and Covenants and the Book of Mormon essentially the same attitude that portions of the Talmud maintained toward the Pentateuch: "He who says . . . 'The whole Torah is from God with the exception of this or that verse, which not God but Moses spoke from his own mouth'—that soul shall be rooted up."[32]

Hence McConkie did not share an overall view of the Bible with his Protestant fundamentalist cousins, nor did he share the particular content of their theology. What joint ground he held with them was more basic, and common to fundamentalists of many world religions. What he shared was their assurance, their view of the nature of revelation, and their readiness to battle those who would dilute the faith.

Lowell L. Bennion

One person who did not share McConkie's perspective was his religion teacher at college. In 1934 Lowell Bennion, newly returned with a doctorate from France, was appointed as the first instructor of the Church's Institute of Religion adjacent to the University of Utah. McConkie, who would graduate in 1937, was among his first students.

Excepting Bennion and William Chamberlin, the figures examined

---

32. Tractate Sanhedrin of the Babylonian Talmud, Sanhedrin 99a; cited in Grant, *A Short History of the Interpretation of the Bible,* pp. 7–8.

in this study were general authorities of the Mormon Church. Chamberlin was selected as an exception in part because his academic prominence coupled with his lack of hierarchical stature symbolizes the real but comparatively modest influence of his views among the Mormon people. Bennion's case is somewhat different. Despite his absence from the official hierarchy, he has come to enjoy a nearly unique status in twentieth-century Mormonism.

Bennion's challenges to an affluent society and his pioneering charitable work with diverse underprivileged groups of any or no religious persuasion have been broad and influential, increasingly acknowledged nationally.[33] Indeed, he occupies roughly the same position in Mormon history that Dorothy Day holds in American Catholicism. The social dimension of his work outflanks our focus here but is nevertheless intricately linked with his scriptural hermeneutic, rescuing it from any accusation of "mere abstractions." Bennion has been called, with some plausibility, "the conscience of modern Mormonism."

Such a description, however, does not account for Bennion's intellectual contributions. The translation of his doctoral thesis, *Max Weber's Methodology,* was the first book-length treatment of Weber in the English language.[34] By the 1960s, Bennion was already regarded by LDS scholars as among the seven most eminent intellectuals in Mormon history.[35] Yet it was in the subsequent decades that he accomplished his most important writing. His bibliography includes some thirty books and study manuals, and more than one hundred essays.[36] It reveals competent work on philosophy, religious and social and personal ethics, sociology, scripture, history, practical living, education, world religions, politics, and a whole range of specifically Mormon topics. When the publicity surrounding his social action and the fact of his rarely paralleled leverage with four decades of college

---

33. Bennion's creative social work has long been noted in Utah, other intermountain states, and Mormonism generally. Attention given him nationally is symbolized, most recently, by his selection as "one of the ten most caring people in America" by the Caring Institute, an organization through which governors and other American leaders periodically nominate the "most caring" humanitarian in their states or regions.

34. Paris: Les Presses Modernes, 1933.

35. Arrington, "The Intellectual Tradition," p. 22.

36. A nearly exhaustive bibliography is found in England, ed., *The Best of Lowell Bennion,* pp. 287–95.

students are combined with the impact of his writing,[37] it is doubtful that more than a handful of modern figures have wielded greater enduring influence on major sectors of Mormondom. Among those, none, excepting perhaps Bruce McConkie, has articulated a hermeneutic so clear and thorough.

Bennion was born in Salt Lake City in 1908 to a committed Mormon family. His father, who had studied philosophy at Columbia and Berkeley and taught at the University of Utah, was his dominant early intellectual influence. As an eighteen-year-old missionary in New Zealand, his father had "practically memorized" the New Testament. He regularly discussed the Psalms, Proverbs, and New Testament with his children. In religious matters, his father emphasized the ethical over the dogmatic, searching for universals more than the particularities of Mormonism.[38] Bennion appropriated those views and never forsook them, finding support for his predilections through the study of sociology, philosophy, religion, and economics at the universities of Utah, Washington, Arizona, Erlangen, Vienna, and Strasbourg.

When in 1933 Bennion returned to Salt Lake City from his studies abroad, he expected eventually either to run for the Senate or to become a professor. Jobs were scarce at universities during the Depression, however, and the following year, with some ambivalence, he accepted the invitation of John A. Widtsoe, Church commissioner of education, to found an LDS Institute of Religion near the University of Utah.[39] Expecting to stay approximately five years in the post, Bennion remained for twenty-six years until he was relieved of his duties for reasons that remain unclear.[40] He spent the next ten years

37. For example, Bennion may be Mormonism's most prolific author of religious study manuals. Those he authored were in common official use, for diverse age groups, from the 1930s through the 1960s.

38. Bennion, Oral History, Church Archives, pp. 26, 48; "Saint for All Seasons," *Sunstone* 10 (February 1985): 7; *Understanding the Scriptures,* p. 81.

39. For the nature of the institutes, which now enroll approximately seventy thousand college students annually, see Thomas O'Dea, *The Mormons* (Chicago: University of Chicago Press, 1964), pp. 183, 227–29, and Leonard J. Arrington, "The Founding of the L.D.S. Institutes of Religion," *Dialogue* 2 (Summer 1967): 137–47.

40. He spent two additional years initiating a similar Institute of Religion program at the University of Arizona. Astonishingly, Bennion was never informed of the reasons for his dismissal, though circumstantial evidence links it with the disapproval of Apostle Joseph Fielding Smith and others to his liberal positions on such issues as revelation

as a professor and associate dean of students at the University of Utah, where he taught the sociology of religion, replacing the eminent Catholic scholar, Thomas O'Dea. In 1970 he "retired" by expanding his already developed social and charitable agenda into full-time concerns.

Like Bruce McConkie, Bennion knows no biblical languages and has produced no works that would dent the world of professional biblical specialists. His treatments of scripture are, above all, practical. They are written with a directness that transcends complexity and with the clear intent that people of a wide range of educational backgrounds can profitably engage them.

McConkie and Bennion are not perfect opposites in their scriptural usage. Their Mormon allegiance by itself is almost sufficient to set them apart from others.[41] Within the confines of devoted Mormonism, however, the two men do approximate direct opposition. As Bennion, invited to reflect on his former student, put it, "I appreciated Bruce McConkie, [but] I don't think I taught him anything. I think he already had his mind made up. . . ."[42] McConkie is not on record about the matter but conceivably would have agreed. Given this oppositeness, Bennion's approach may be succinctly presented by contrasting it with McConkie's.

Like most modern Christians, McConkie paid more attention to the New Testament than to the Old. Bennion has been less typical. Excepting the Gospels, which, of course, deal directly with Jesus and

and the then-current Mormon policy excluding blacks from holding the priesthood. Despite his generally irenic style, Bennion in his earlier years had the capacity to be combative. His liberal perspectives, expressed in debates and other public forums *con molto passione*—at least on rare occasions—won him the enduring enmity of certain conservative teachers at Brigham Young University and one or two administrators of the Church's educational system who eventually went on to ecclesiastical positions of great influence. These were apparently pleased to see him dismissed from his position ("Saint for All Seasons," pp. 10–11; correspondence with author by ear- and eyewitnesses to these debates and the controversy they evoked. My correspondents wish to remain unnamed.)

41. McConkie, however, stressed the limitations of the Bible in order to show the superiority of Mormonism. Bennion has found inspiration in specifically Mormon scriptures but also in the Upanishads, in the Bhagavad-Gita, in Lao-tse, and elsewhere (Oral History, Church Archives, pp. 3, 105). Bennion's biographer calls him "a bit of a Buddhist" (Mary Bradford, letter to author, January 15, 1988; her as-yet-untitled biography is forthcoming).

42. Oral History, Church Archives, p. 199.

are central to Bennion's thought, he has attended particularly to the "ethical monotheism" developed in Deuteronomy and extended by such prophets as Hosea, Amos, Micah, Jeremiah, and Isaiah. This concern for the ethical prophets points to the controlling difference between the scriptural philosophies of McConkie and Bennion. The contrast may be seen by recalling Richard Mouw's "taxonomy" of biblical usage among twentieth-century American Protestants, mentioned earlier. Mouw's typology noted four primary tendencies among Bible-believing Protestants: doctrinalism (intellectual submission to correct beliefs), pietism (devotional emphasis), moralism (the Bible as a source book for personal ethics), and culturalism (the Bible as stimulus for cultural transformation).[43] So far as this classification goes, McConkie and Bennion have both used scripture devotionally, for meditation and worship. Apart from this common ground, however, they are drastically separated. McConkie, as we have seen, was deeply concerned about dogma; one's salvation depended in part on proper theological belief. Bennion has been preoccupied with what Mouw calls "moralism" and "culturalism."[44]

The difficulty with the term *moralism* is that it may be misconstrued as a reduction of religion to ethics. But Mouw did not so intend the term, and Bennion himself is careful not to equate religion and ethics. There are, he wrote, many dimensions to the religious life:

> One aspect is intellectual: a knowledge of theology, scripture, and religious history is valuable. [Another encompasses] ritual, church activity, and attending services, [actions that] bind an individual to his or

43. See my Preface, p. xiii, and Mouw, "The Bible in Twentieth-Century Protestantism: A Preliminary Taxonomy," in *The Bible in America*, ed. Hatch and Noll, pp. 139–62. Like all typologies, Mouw's tends toward reductionism. He notes that in actual practice most Protestants are hybrids of two or more types. He also notes the existence of subcategories, such as "errantist doctrinalism" and "inerrantist doctrinalism," and points out that his four categories are not exhaustive (e.g., they do not account for literary or historical approaches) but represent the dominant thrusts of modern Protestant usage.

44. Bennion's definition of a religious (Mormon) liberal denotes a person with an ethical emphasis, who is concerned with people more than with doctrine, who is prepared to adapt the theology and structure of a church to serve human values, and who is open-minded and free to think rather than feeling obligated a priori to accept the pronouncements of either scripture or human authority figures ("Saint for All Seasons," p. 12; Bennion, "Being a 'Liberal,' " in *Do Justly and Love Mercy*.

her cobelievers. . . . Service and personal worship of God through prayer are also essential to the religious life.

However, for Bennion, no expression of religious values is acceptable to God without an overriding concern for justice and mercy. "There can be no true spirituality without genuine social morality." Theoretical doctrine has its place, but of itself "it saves no one."[45]

Of course, Elder McConkie also advocated justice and mercy, but, perhaps influenced by his legal background, his orientation to scripture was profoundly juristic. By contrast, Bennion stresses that the scriptures are not static legal documents. Like liberals of many religions, he insists indeed that the Bible is not predominantly theological at all, let alone legalistically doctrinal: "*Theology* is abstract and intellectual, an organized statement of beliefs, of definitions about God and his relationship to man. *Religion* is living, actual worship of and service to God."[46] To be sure, the scriptures contain theological statements. The definition of faith in Hebrews 11:1 or many of Paul's assertions are examples. Fundamentally, however, scripture, for Bennion, is not theological but "the most authentic record we have of religion." And if the Bible's theological dimensions are secondary to its religious aspects, the importance of scientific or many historical claims made in its behalf are essentially incidental.[47]

McConkie's doctrinalism was often expressed through his fascination with predictive prophecy, with millennial events and the Book of Revelation. He came by these interests naturally because millennial anticipations weighed on countless Americans when Mormonism first

45. *I Believe,* p. vii; *Unknown Testament,* pp. 47, 49–59.

46. *Understanding the Scriptures,* p. 20 (emphasis added); "Reflections on the Restoration," *Dialogue* 18 (Fall 1985): 165. For a liberal Jewish comparison, see Abraham J. Karp, *The Jewish Way of Life and Thought* (New York: KTAV, 1981), p. 193.

47. Bennion, *Understanding the Scriptures,* p. 7. Although McConkie's view of revelation demanded that he define evolutionists, for example, as heretics, Bennion concluded early on in his career that "the two greatest contributions of religion, for me, are faith—faith in God, faith in Christ, faith in the meaning and purposes of life—and a clarification of life's values. . . . So instead of trying to get my description of reality out of the scriptures, as far as the nature of creation and the age of the earth go . . . I decided those things have nothing to do with religion" (Oral History, Church Archives, pp. 80–81, 193). See also "The Religious Intent of the Book of Mormon," in *The Book of Mormon: A Guide to Christian Living,* pp. 1–7; *Understanding the Scriptures,* pp. 16–20; *Teachings of the New Testament,* pp. 6–8.

appeared in the 1830s, and have remained, in diluted form, important for many *Latter-day* Saints to the present. Other Mormons spend little time on such matters, and Bennion's writings show no concern with them.[48] Applying scriptural admonitions to the here and now has been a full-time job for him, and he believes "in not elaborating the unknown."[49] To McConkie, however, much of Bennion's "unknown" *is* known—through predictive prophecy.

Bennion's interest in the practical is not merely an aversion to using the Bible to predict the future, but serves as a basic hermeneutical standard. He is fond of borrowing architectural guidelines for interpretation. As a chair or a cathedral may be judged by three primary criteria ("Is it sound? Is it functional? Is it beautiful?"), so scripture may be judged. With criteria like "sound" and "functional," Bennion invites scripturists to ask whether their explications contribute in any way to bettering human life and whether they are reasonable. Sounding a bit like Peter Abelard in dialogue with St. Anselm, he writes, "Faith takes us beyond knowledge, but I don't see how any interpretation . . . can be enlightening if we don't understand it." He questions "interpretations that contradict common sense, good judgments, verified experience, and the counsel of wise and good men and women."[50] McConkie was more leery of human perspectives.

Bennion's greater estimate of human thought limits but does not obliterate for him the notion of suprahuman inspiration. He has noted, as firmly as any skeptic, that anyone can claim the authority of God for any proposition whatsoever by saying, "I know by the Spirit." Nonetheless, he makes the "prompting of the Holy Spirit"—a phenomenon he feels he has experienced—a fundamental standard for scriptural comprehension. But because both reason and perceived inspiration are fallible, they should serve as supportive checks on one another. Reminiscent of the eighteenth-century "supernatural rationalists," Bennion acknowledges that revelation may be above reason,

48. For example, his 374–page *Teachings of the New Testament* refers frequently to the Old Testament, to other Mormon scriptures, to such secular writers as Montague, Goethe, and Shakespeare, and to Chinese sages like Chuang-tze and Lao-tze. By contrast, he does not cite the Book of Revelation at all, excepting a two-sentence paragraph summarizing its nature.

49. Bennion Oral History, Church Archives, p. 190.

50. *Understanding the Scriptures,* p. 38.

but if authentic and understood, the content (as distinct from the process) of revelation should not be irrational.[51]

As with any self-respecting exegetes, McConkie and Bennion note the importance of context: literary context, historical context, and the context of the Christian gospel.[52] Their differing conceptions and weighting of the terms, however, prompts contrasting approaches. McConkie, for instance, felt one did not know Isaiah unless one understood Mormon theology. Of ten "keys" he offered for interpreting Isaiah, seven concerned New Testament perspectives or those of Latter-day revelation, one enjoined diligent study, and only two dealt with the ancient context of the Old Testament prophet.[53] In general, Bennion repudiates such methods. Just as many Christians "Christianize" the Old Testament in a manner disturbing to Jewish scholars, so, Bennion held, Latter-day Saints frequently err by "Mormonizing" the Bible. "We have a right," he said,

> to enlarge our Christian understanding by reference to [the distinctively Mormon scriptures], but I believe we should recognize them for what they are—additional sources of knowledge—and not assume that they are part of the Old Testament as we have received it. Each scripture is unique. . . . Each should be studied and appreciated for what it is. Each should be respected for its own integrity.[54]

For him, using "the gospel context" to interpret scripture meant employing the fundamental (especially ethical) aspects of Christian and Mormon-Christian belief to distinguish in the texts the transient, human, or erroneous from the permanent, divine, and true.[55]

Does the Bible, then, contain error in Mormon eyes? Clearly, for McConkie and Bennion and Mormons throughout their history it does and, by definition, this partitions them from those in other faiths who espouse an inerrant Bible. But this similarity between McConkie and Bennion is comparatively superficial. To McConkie, the Bible

51. *Understanding the Scriptures,* pp. 2–3, 18, 23, 38, 39; *Unknown Testament,* pp. 5, 6; *I Believe,* pp. 7–8. For supernatural rationalism, see Conrad Wright, *The Beginnings of Unitarianism in America* (Boston: Starr King Press, 1955), pp. 3, 135, 136, 246–48.

52. McConkie, "The Bible, a Sealed Book," p. 4; Bennion, *Understanding the Scriptures,* pp. 26, 27–34; *Unknown Testament,* pp. 4–5.

53. "Ten Keys to Understanding Isaiah," *Ensign* 3 (October 1973): 78–83.

54. *Unknown Testament,* pp. 4–5; "A Response" (to Moench's "The Mormon Christianization of the Old Testament"), *Sunstone* 5 (November/December 1980): 40ff.

55. Oral History, Church Archives, p. 193.

contained error because of textual corruptions occurring during the long course of its transmission. The Bible was flawed, but revelation was not. To Bennion, no such thing as "perfect scripture" exists.

McConkie's favorite passage on the nature of scripture was Doctrine and Covenants 68:4: "Whatsoever [elders] shall speak when moved upon by the Holy Ghost shall be scripture, shall be the will of the Lord, . . . the mind of the Lord, . . . the word of the Lord, . . . [and] the voice of the Lord. . . ."[56] McConkie interpreted this passage literally, believing that one possessed of the Holy Spirit spoke precisely the words God would speak were He personally present under the same circumstances. Bennion acknowledges the passage but argues it must be understood in light of another passage, also from the Doctrine and Covenants, describing the character of scripture: "Behold, I am God and have spoken it; these commandments are of me, and were given unto my servants in their weakness, after the manner of their language, that they might come to understanding."[57]

Though Bennion believes biblical authors sometimes rose above their natural capability, it is also true, for him, that writers of Israel's history sometimes gave credit or blame to God for actions and decrees unworthy of Deity, as when 2 Kings implies that God's power was behind the deaths of the little children who had mocked Elisha's bald head.[58] McConkie limited the Bible by noting that some of its injunctions and prohibitions were restricted to local times and circumstances, by insisting on the impurities of the text, and by acknowledging that on occasion authors gave their own opinions on various doctrines.[59] Bennion agrees, but despite his habit of stating things affirmatively, he goes further: some of the writing of the Bible, even in its original form, was a consequence of human error, both morally and historically. A major hindrance for many devoted

56. *Mormon Doctrine*, pp. 83, 230, 535; *DNTC*, 1:55.
57. D&C 1:24; *Understanding the Scriptures,* pp. 22–23.
58. 2 Kings 2:23–24; see *Understanding the Scriptures,* pp. 24–25.
59. Generally, McConkie thought, these instances would be prefaced with an acknowledgment by the scriptural authors that they were temporarily speaking for themselves rather than God, as Paul did when writing on marriage in 1 Cor. 7. Very rarely in his thousands of pages of writing on scripture, McConkie even goes so far as to point out that certain writers, who did not specify that they spoke for themselves, were in error. See, e.g., *DNTC*, 3:380–81 for his comments on 1 John 2:18.

Christians is "the perception . . . that every line of the Bible except mistranslations is divine."[60]

I have suggested personal and social ethics play a crucial role in Bennion's use of the Bible. Like all Christians, he borrows many of his own ethical precepts from scripture. But he does not merely take ethical ideas from scripture; he also deliberately brings an ethical consciousness *to* scripture. That is—unlike McConkie's conscious intent—Bennion deliberately interprets the Bible with his own ethical vision, only part of which originated in scripture. For instance, because he understands God to be an intelligent, impartial, loving, just, merciful Parent, he refuses to accept "any interpretation . . . that portrays God as being partial, unforgiving, hateful, or revengeful."[61] Whereas Bruce McConkie would tend to explain such passages as the result of a marred text or the actions of a stern God taking harsh but necessary actions, Bennion would explain them as projections of human weaknesses onto God's character. "It is," he wrote, "more important to uphold the character and will of God than it is to support every line of scripture."[62]

By a "proper interpretation," Bennion has in mind not so much what the original author intended—he takes it for granted this should never be distorted—but whether the interpretation is "sound, functional, and beautiful" as applied to one's personal life and to society. If it is not, then the authority of its historicity or canonized status is irrelevant. Although Bennion shows no antagonism to the methods of higher criticism, neither have these methods dominated his thought.[63]

In brief, then, Bennion gauges a scriptural interpretation as worthy of it (1) is consistent with gospel fundamentals as defined above, (2) is confirmed by the prompting of the Holy Spirit, (3) appeals to thoughtful ethical judgment, (4) has won wide agreement among

60. *Unknown Testament,* pp. 3, 5, 15–16, 37, 43, 67–68; *Understanding the Scriptures,* pp. 6, 11; Oral History, Church Archives pp. 87, 105. Bennion's characteristically affirmative way of dealing with biblical errors or irrelevancies is not so much to focus on them as to take them for granted. A sample: "Although written in another time and place, scriptures contain much that is valid for us today" (*Understanding the Scriptures,* p. 6).

61. *Understanding the Scriptures,* pp. 34, 36.

62. Ibid., p. 36.

63. Bennion's methods have much in common with some assumptions of higher critics, though his interest is rarely technical, and he denies that scripture may be adequately approached merely as any other book (*Understanding the Scriptures,* p. 3).

informed and rational persons of good will, (5) allows for the human as well as the divine in revelation, and (6) is primarily concerned with scripture's religious intent. He has continued to caution his fellow religionists that scripture among devoted people runs the risk of becoming an end in itself, as occurred in ancient Israel. His central admonition is that—as Jesus said of "the Law" and "the Prophets"—all proper scriptural interpretation must "hang" on the love of God and neighbor.[64]

If Richard Mouw is right (and keeping in mind the ambiguities and hybrids that cloud "real" as distinct from "ideal" attitudes), one way of looking at the Protestant fundamentalist–modernist controversy of the early decades of the twentieth century is as a battle between biblical doctrinalists and biblical moralists.[65] Both groups had strong elements of pietism in their orientations, and liberals sometimes showed a degree of culturalism. But so far as the differences betwen them erupted into conflict, Mouw's doctrinalist (fundamentalist) versus moralist (modernist) model seems useful.[66]

Such a model is fairly easily transposed to a Mormon context. Although his specific doctrine was Mormon, McConkie's approach to revelation was fundamentally that of Mouw's (Protestant) doctrinalist;[67] the scriptures to which Bennion referred on any given occasion could almost as easily have been the Book of Mormon as the Bible,

64. "Reflections on the Restoration," *Dialogue* 18 (Fall 1985): 165.
65. "The Bible in Twentieth-century Protestantism," in *The Bible in America*, ed. Hatch and Noll, pp. 154–55.
66. Equating "moralist" with liberal and "doctrinalist" with conservative is, of course, highly simplistic and represents a tendency only. These positions could be compared at great length with an array of hybrids delineated by Mouw: the doctrinalism–moralism frequently manifest among Missouri Synod Lutherans, for instance, or the strong culturalism in black Christianity of the nineteenth and twentieth centuries or the pietism–culturalism of "left-wing charismatics" (Mouw in *The Bible in America,* ed. Hatch and Noll, pp. 153–56).
67. Mouw observed (ibid., pp. 142–43) that doctrinalists often do battle on two fronts, attacking, on the one hand, those who do not value "correct doctrine" as crucial in the sense that they themselves do and, on the other hand, fighting doctrinalists whose interpretations contrast with their own. Such a description would clearly apply to McConkie, who regularly disparaged both liberal intellectuals on the one hand and "heretics" or "sectarians" on the other. For an example of a doctrinalist who left Mormonism in order to attack current Mormon doctrinalists, see Tanner, "The Bible and Mormon Doctrine."

but his attitude toward revelation in general has been essentially moralist–culturalist.

The New LDS Edition of the Scriptures

Mormonism, of course, could not fairly be portrayed as a bastion of modernist philosophy. Conservative perspectives, though with Mormon distinctions, have always been prominent among the Saints. Nevertheless, both Bennion-like liberalism and McConkie-like conservatism have been represented, at various times in the twentieth century, in Mormon sermons, books, and lesson manuals. The respective positions—and combinations of them—have found support from prophets, apostles, and leaders and followers at every level of the Church. Though exchanges between adherents of the contrasting attitudes have sometimes been sharp, diversity has usually been accommodated, sometimes even celebrated.[68] If Church literature or leaders in one generation leaned too far in one direction, those with other ideas could comfort themselves with the hope that correctives would eventually appear. This "healthy tension" helps account for the combined progressivism and stable traditionalism one can find in Mormon history, and helps explain its unusual staying power, noticed by such careful outside observers as Thomas O'Dea. However, the ascendent conservativism discernible in the Mormon leadership for the past several decades may recently have produced an ally so commanding as to assure its long-range dominance. In the new LDS edition of the King James Version (1979), strongly conservative views reflected in the various supplements have received incalculable prestige by being printed and bound with the Holy Bible.

"As the generations roll on," said Apostle Boyd K. Packer to a 1982

---

68. Characteristic of this Mormon sentiment is a 1911 letter written by future General Authority Levi Edgar Young to a participant in an ideological skirmish at Brigham Young University. Embarrassed by an editorial in the Church-owned *Deseret Evening News,* which categorically denounced the theory of biological evolution, Young wrote, "I think the article . . . was the most ridiculous thing I have ever read. Let me apologize for the Church for such an article. It made me heart sick. . . . You and I may differ radically on many things pertaining to religion and science, but we are living in the age of differences, when men put their contributions together to make for *truth.* So God bless you in your work . . . our differences will make us both better and broader" (Young to Prof. Ralph Chamberlin, March 12, 1911, David C. Chamberlin collection).

general conference of the Church, the new editions of the LDS scriptures "will be regarded . . . as the crowning achievement in the administration of [Church] President Spencer W. Kimball."[69] Students of Mormonism have not seemed to take Elder Packer's historical assessment too seriously. This is understandable, because the dramatic events of Kimball's administration included a revelation allowing blacks to hold the priesthood, and it is difficult to imagine any change having as much impact on the Church's future unless leaders were to reconsider, say, their policies on women. Still, Elder Packer should not be ignored. Although the project was not really President Kimball's, the new LDS edition of the scriptures, the form of which was crucially influenced by Bruce McConkie and by Boyd Packer himself, will continue to guide the Mormon mind for the indefinite future.

That the producers of the LDS Bible embraced the King James Version has been considered earlier. Also significant in molding Mormon conceptions are the new Bible's chapter headings, six-hundred page topical index, intricate cross-reference system, and Bible dictionary. These supplements disclaim any official doctrinal validity, but they have already become important media through which Latter-day Saints decipher the meaning of scripture.

Although ordinary readers are not often conscious of their influence, summaries of chapters or passages, explanations of difficult readings, explicit commentary, and other marginal annotations have long had significant impact on Christian interpretations of biblical texts. Before Gutenberg, marginalia regularly intruded even into the texts themselves, thus becoming a part of the canon and helping to account for the thousands of discrepancies in extant Greek and Hebrew manuscripts. Marginal notations are equally crucial to the history of the printed Bible. They have been fiercely contested from the time of William Tyndale's first printed English New Testament (1525), which drew the ire of British authorities because its notes and text reflected the influence of Luther's German edition.[70] Under shift-

69. *Ensign* 12 (November 1982): 53. The new edition of the KJV was quickly followed by a companion edition of the jointly bound Book of Mormon, D&C, and *PGP*.

70. Allen Wikgren, "The English Bible," in *The Interpreter's Bible,* 12 vols. (Nashville: Abingdon, 1952), 1:87. Luther's German translation, like Calvin's French, contained a great deal of theological commentary. Luther in particular insisted on absolute attention to Christ. If Christ was not explicitly mentioned in the text of even Old Testament passages, then, he felt, the reader must go beyond the "grammar," or literal meaning, to the inner spiritual meaning visible only through eyes of faith.

ing pressures, various Bibles of the sixteenth century alternately included and excluded marginal notes. By 1560, after a good deal of Bible burning, the great Geneva Bible appeared "with most profitable annotations upon all the hard places."[71] These Calvinist notes, expositions, and alternative translations contributed greatly to the preferred status of the version among Protestant people but offended Catholics and royalty because of their doctrinal slant.

By July 1604 a list of rules of procedure for a new translation of the Bible had been provided. These rules specified that no marginal notes were to be used except for necessary explanations of the Hebrew or Greek. When the Bible was published in 1611, however, it was found that the translators and editors could not help themselves: running titles and prefatory chapter summaries were included, many showing their Genevan heritage. Despite the rules of procedure, this 1611 Bible also contained approximately seventeen thousand cross-references and other notations, some of them interpretive. As anticipated, criticism was severe and led to several revisions.

In these subsequent editions of the (implicitly) Authorized Version, explanatory notes and almost indiscriminate cross-references multiplied. Bishop Ussher's chronology was added in Lloyd's 1701 edition, and by the time of Blayney's 1769 edition, the notes and references totaled about sixty-five thousand.[72] Later evolutions of such references were found inadequate or misleading by Mormon authorities, who during the twentieth century had become increasingly committed to the Authorized Version as their official Bible. The Latter-day Saints naturally wished for notes and references that reflected their own perspectives and connected with their other scriptures. Leaders took steps in the early 1970s to produce their own

71. Lloyd E. Berry, ed., *The Geneva Bible: A Facsimile of the 1560 Edition* (Madison: University of Wisconsin Press, 1969). The body of marginal commentary exceeded three hundred thousand words and constituted a self-contained theological library for common readers. Greatly influenced by Luther's commentary in the German Bible, the prefaces to every single Old Testament book in the Geneva Bible explicitly focused on the life and person of Christ. Excluding the Bible itself, the Genevan commentary was the only literature common to all people. Its influence on the popular religious imagination was considerably more direct than the less widely circulated sermons and spiritual autobiographies (Stout, "Word and Order," in *The Bible in America*, ed. Hatch and Noll, pp. 21–25.)

72. Wikgren, "The English Bible," pp. 94–95.

edition of the KJV that would fill such desires, completing the effort in 1979.[73]

The notes, chapter summaries, and other supplements to the LDS Bible do not, of course, influence contemporary readers so deeply as such helps affected Christian devotees in the sixteenth and seventeenth centuries. Among other things, the Bible no longer dominates the literary diet of common readers. But certainly the supplements have a significant impact on popular Mormon understanding. When studying the Old or New Testaments, Mormon classes are more apt than not to refer to the supplements. A glance at their theological orientation is thus warranted.

The new Bible boasts seven major features distinguishing it from other editions of the KJV: (1) new chapter headings, (2) an LDS-oriented Bible dictionary, (3) an LDS-oriented topical index, (4) cross-references to all other Mormon scriptures, (5) excerpts from Joseph Smith's "inspired translation," (6) a creative, simplifed footnote system, and (7) a gazetteer and twenty-four newly created maps. The last two items are not often directly relevant to theological interpretation,[74] but the topical guide, Bible dictionary, and selection of longer Joseph Smith Translation passages form an 813-page appendix—more than half the number of pages in the biblical text itself, and in smaller print at that. Additionally, interpretive summaries preceding each chapter are generally three to six lines each. Notes, cross-references, and shorter Joseph Smith Translation readings constitute roughly 20 percent of the typical page in the New Testament, somewhat less in the Old Testament. In all, an enormous amount of theologically colored reference material accompanies the biblical text.

The cross-references and topical guide are thoroughly interwoven with the Book of Mormon, the Doctrine and Covenants, and the Pearl of Great Price. This by itself represents a controlling interpre-

73. Matthews, "The New Publications of the Standard Works—1979, 1981," *BYU Studies* 22 (Fall 1982): 387–88.

74. Even the notes specifying clearer renditions of Hebrew or Greek terms are, however, sometimes influenced by theological concerns. In Genesis 1:1, for example, the Hebrew word (*bara*) behind the English "created" is clarified in the notes as meaning "shaped, fashioned, created." This would, perhaps, be a useful footnote in any English Bible, but in a Mormon context it is intended to reinforce Joseph Smith's arguments against a creation *ex nihilo*.

tive scheme, for its intent is not simply to suggest connected themes for religious reflection (which both Lowell Bennion and Bruce McConkie would have encouraged) but also to demonstrate "in a unique way . . . that [the Bible and the specifically Mormon scriptures] teach the same doctrine."[75]

As we have noticed, the idea that all scriptures honored by Latter-day Saints "teach the same doctrine," despite the differing times and circumstances during which they originated, enjoys a long tradition in Mormon history. Some imposition of twentieth-century Mormon views upon the biblical texts was all but inevitable because relating the Bible to specifically LDS scriptures was a major motivation for producing the new editions. However, as I have argued, Mormon scriptural understandings are not monolithic. Hence what is most interesting for present purposes is not the mere fact that Mormon theology is proffered in the new biblical supplements but, rather, the kind of Mormon theology expressed. The interpretations adopted in these supplements are far closer to Bruce McConkie's views—in many cases they *are* McConkie's views—than to Lowell Bennion's. Because a thorough exploration of the supplements would require a separate essay, we will consider here only a few representative examples from the new Bible dictionary and the summaries preceding each chapter of the biblical text.

Although it is not self-evident how much of the published version of the dictionary was the work of an individual and how much the reworking of a supporting committee, the chief compiler was Professor Robert J. Matthews, former dean of religious education at Brigham Young University and longtime associate of Bruce R. McConkie.[76] The dictionary is not fundamentally a new work but an adaptation of the *Cambridge Bible Dictionary* appended to a popular King James Bible published by Cambridge University Press. Like the other LDS supplements, it denies itself official status, though this fact is not particularly prominent in the minds of Church members. By attending to the alterations made in its Cambridge model, one can discern a hermeneutic that, by implication, is considered normative by those who produced it.

75. Matthews, "New Publications," p. 391.

76. Lavina Fielding Anderson, "Church Publishes First LDS Edition of the Bible," *Ensign* 9 (October 1979): 17.

As Matthews and other participants have noted, the changes introduced by the committee are often deliberately doctrinal in nature.[77] Much like the cross-references and topical index, many entries are not purely attempts to convey the biblical meaning of a concept but conscious expressions of modern Mormon theology. This is so because the *Cambridge Bible Dictionary* was "prepared by scholars who did not have the benefit of latter-day revelation." The LDS dictionary's analysis of "Baptism" is thus supported primarily by proofs from modern revelation rather than from biblical texts. Similarly, entries on the "Fall," "Zion," "Urim and Thummim," "Adam," and hundreds of others reflect contemporary LDS conceptions. In other words, the new "Bible dictionary" is not really a Bible dictionary but a dictionary of LDS theology, conservatively construed, using biblical terms.

A second and related trait of the dictionary is the tendency to harmonize. Because many Mormons perceive the gospel as the same in all ages, it follows that all biblical writings (in their original forms) must agree on essentials. Hence the new dictionary explains (as the *Cambridge Bible Dictionary* does not) that the pessimism of Ecclesiastes is not actually pessimism but the referring to things only as they appear "from a worldly point of view," that is, "under the sun." The classic Hebrew description of *Sheol* and the finality of death in Ecclesiastes 9:5 and 9:10 "should not," says the dictionary, be taken "as theological pronouncements on the condition of the soul after death; rather, they are observations by the Preacher about how things appear to men on the earth 'under the sun.' " The dictionary implies that because Ecclesiastes is inspired, its author's view about the afterlife must be compatible with the rest of the Bible and with modern Mormonism.

Sometimes the dictionary attempts to steer a middle course between current scholarship on the one hand and tradition and modern revelation on the other. Under "Pentateuch," for instance, the editors write, "The Pentateuch was written by Moses, although it is evident that he used several documentary sources . . . besides a divine revelation to him." They go on to say that "it is also evident that scribes and

---

77. Matthews, "New Publications," p. 393; Matthews, "Using the New Bible Dictionary," p. 48; William James Mortimer, "The Coming Forth of the LDS Edition of Scripture," *Ensign* 13 (August 1983): 37.

copyists have left their traces upon the Pentateuch as we have it today; for example, the explanation of Moses' supposed death."

The dictionary is often careful on attributing authorship, as when it treats the Book of Joshua or Jonah. However, even on this subject there is a decided tilt. The entry for "Pauline Epistles," for example, does not question Paul's authorship of any of the fourteen New Testament epistles traditionally ascribed to him except for Hebrews, where the dictionary gently allows for a possible exception, though asserting that "the ideas are certainly Paul's."

Despite some efforts at holding modern scholarship together with tradition or modern revelation, the dictionary's theological thrust often reflects a certain fundamentalist literalism. In a statement consonant with Bruce McConkie's views, but one that would not have pleased such Mormon stalwarts as B. H. Roberts, James Talmage, John Widtsoe, David O. McKay, or Lowell Bennion, the entry under "Death" reads: "Latter-day revelation teaches that there was no death on this earth for any forms of life before the fall of Adam." Because the dictionary also provides a chronological table for Old Testament events, and because this table shows Adam's Fall occurring at 4,000 B.C.E. (p. 635), the implication is that no death for any forms of life existed on earth before this date. No entry exists for "fossil."

A fifth tendency of the editors has been the effort to rid the new dictionary of what were apparently considered embarrassments. The *Cambridge Bible Dictionary,* for example, gives the meaning of the name "Abel" as "breath, vanity." Other dictionaries suggest "transitoriness" or "vapor." Presumably because the etymology was seen as unflattering to the righteous Abel, the Mormon dictionary omits the explanation without replacing it. Unlike other biblical names, no meaning is offered for Abel.

A final proclivity of the dictionary is the pronounced effort to preserve the historicity of biblical books. An example is the listing "Job." The entry here follows the Cambridge text for the most part but deletes the line "The book [of Job] should not be regarded as literal history." It is possible the committee excised the line because it properly did not want to imply that Mormonism has an official position on the historicity of Job. But as the dictionary is not official anyway, one suspects the omission means the committee thought Latter-day Saints should view the story of the Book of Job as historical, a position contradictory to other assumptions of Mormon theology.[78] To Lowell Bennion, and to Mormonism's First Presidency in an earlier generation, the historicity of Job is irrelevent, no more important than the historicity of the prodigal son in Jesus' parable.[79]

Like the Bible dictionary, the summaries that precede each chapter of the biblical text have a distinct theological point of view. Although they are succinct and many are purely descriptive, others actually serve, as one committee member put it, "as a commentary to each chapter." They were authored by Bruce R. McConkie.[80]

A few examples will suggest how Elder McConkie interprets the text. The chapter summary for Romans 4 includes the anomalous sentence "Man is justified by faith, righteous works, and grace." Now, it is true that the Apostle Paul did have more to say about the importance of "works" than is sometimes acknowledged by those in the Augustinian tradition, but this does not occur in the fourth chapter of the Epistle to the Romans. Paul might have been as perplexed to learn Mormons had thus summarized this passage of his letter as he would be to discover that evangelical hands had paraphrased his "work out your own salvation with fear and trembling" (Phil. 2:12) with "you must be even more careful to do the good things that result from being saved."[81] The LDS chapter heading is thus not so much an accurate summary of the contents of Romans 4 as it is a reflection of Elder McConkie's urge to harmonize Paul's theology with other Pauline passages or with his understanding of Joseph Smith's revision or his perception of Mormon theology more generally.

Similarly, the author of Revelations 3 may or may not have had the Mormon "celestial kingdom" quite so clearly in mind as the chapter heading suggests. Without qualification, the chapter summaries equate the "truth" that "shall spring out of the earth" (Ps. 85) with the Book of Mormon; the stick of Judah and the stick of Joseph (Ezek. 37) with the future Bible and Book of Mormon, respectively; and the "branches" in Jacob's blessing of Joseph (Gen. 49) with the

78. Conservative LDS literature has often argued that Job is historical. See, e.g., *Old Testament: 1 Kings–Malachi,* Religion 302, Student Manual for Institutes of Religion (SLC: Church of Jesus Christ of Latter-day Saints, 1981–1982), pp. 28–29.

79. See chap. 4, n. 78 and the paragraph in the text that it documents.

80. Matthews, "New Publications," p. 390; Anderson, "Church Publishes First LDS Edition of the Bible," p. 16.

81. The Living Bible.

Nephites and Lamanites. Some readers of the Bible have been surprised to learn through the chapter summaries that Nah. 1, Zeph. 1, and Zech. 3, 12, and 14 all refer to the second coming of Jesus.

An Unintended Posture?

Throughout the twentieth century, Protestant fundamentalists have been urged to read the Bible itself, without the distractions of outside commentaries (which are "the words of men" rather than "the words of God"). However, the Bible is a formidable compilation of ancient and foreign documents, difficult to understand in many places. To help reduce this problem, fundamentalist leaders published in 1909 the *Scofield Reference Bible,* one of the most influential study Bibles ever produced.

In now well-documented ways, the Scofield Bible (and more recently the Ryrie Bible) have, using the King James text, shaped the conceptions of millions of devout, conservative Christians. So utterly have the notes and divisions of this Bible given a distinctive dispensationalist cast to biblical history and theology that many readers can imagine no other way to comprehend the texts. Yet as Timothy Weber notes, "There is something incongruous about fundamentalists who say that they can read the Bible by themselves, then pore over Scofield's notes in order to discover what the text really means."[82]

Latter-day Saints also are urged to depend primarily on the scriptures rather than on works about the scriptures. Like the readers of the Scofield Bible, many of them are unaware of alternatives to the ways in which their new edition fashions their conceptions. But for the foreseeable future—so long as English-speaking Mormonism re-

---

82. "The Two-Edged Sword: The Fundamentalist Use of the Bible," in *The Bible in America,* ed. Hatch and Noll, pp. 112–14; Marsden, *Fundamentalism,* p. 119; Sandeen, *The Roots of Fundamentalism,* pp. 61, 165, 191, 222–24, 233. Biblical scholar James Barr estimates from his own teaching experience that "in many conservative evangelical student groups, as they were in the early 1950s, perhaps a half, and among those who had been brought up in conservative evangelical homes a larger proportion, were accustomed to the Scofield Bible and regarded its interpretations as normal, often being surprised to discover that any other interpretation is possible" (*Fundamentalism,* p. 191). The Scofield KJV continues to be among the best selling of a considerable array of Bibles at Oxford University Press (letter from Senior Editor Cynthia Read to author, March 15, 1989).

lies on its present official edition—the biblical supplements and the King James text will color Mormon assumptions. Through this medium, and without recognizing their distinctive intonations, Latter-day Saints will hear the voices of Bruce McConkie and J. Reuben Clark above those of Lowell Bennion and David O. McKay. From among the many expressions of Mormon faith articulated throughout its history, one particular expression will have the unofficial—perhaps even the inadvertent—but nevertheless the implied support of The Church of Jesus Christ of Latter-day Saints.

Summary: The Ambiguities of a New Religious Tradition

When I was a boy, I was fascinated by celestial constellations and their interpretations by ancient cultures. I delighted in images of the Archer and the Hunter and Lions and Bulls and Crabs, drawn by artists against pictures of the night sky, using the stars as suggestive reference points. The trouble was, when I faced the real night, or pictures of the stars without the artists' impositions, I had considerable difficulty discerning the images. I didn't see a lion when I looked at the constellation Leo, and I didn't see a bull when gazing at Taurus. I did manage to make a sort of pot out of the Big Dipper, but that was about all.

In some ways scholars and their readers face analogous circumstances. As a historian, I have tried to abstract from a broad and complex expanse a few points of reference by which fellow travelers can map their way. I hope the effort helps, but the particular references I have chosen and the way I have connected them will not likely satisfy all readers.

If the foregoing study aspired to be a fully fleshed rather than a skeletal interpretation of Mormon biblical usage, it would have to consider many issues it ignores or treats in passing. One obvious candidate would be popular cultural uses of the holy texts. Under such a heading, one might include scripture's talismanic value (like other Christians, Mormons have their own lore about the soldier whose pocket scripture providentially stopped a bullet), its social roles (the very citation of scripture, almost irrespective of its content, is sometimes enough to identify one as a member of an approved circle), its oracular uses (such as the occasional practice of randomly opening scriptural volumes and adopting the first passage encountered as a guide for some pressing personal problem),[1] or even its somnolent potential (with or without his tongue in his cheek, Church President Heber J. Grant once noted at a general Church conference that the repetition of scripture was an aid to sleep).

One could treat seriously the fascinating genre of popular LDS literature about the Bible, such as Cleon Skousen's *The First Two-Thousand Years* and its sequels. Richard Mouw's taxonomy of biblical usage might be further explored, expanded, or subdivided. We could consider the therapeutic, solace-giving properties assigned to scripture, as distinct from its devotional aspects. We could look more intently on the Bible's regulatory role, or its hortatory functions, or its symbolic dimensions, or its utility as a weapon against theological rivals.

Apart from strictly popular usage, leaders other than those I have treated need scrutiny, so that idiosyncrasies and generalities may more carefully be distinguished. Mormon women need to be measured against men, different regions of the United States against one another, and American Saints against those outside this country. Admonitions by Church officials need to be compared to actual practice. Time-focused studies should be accomplished for every era of Mormon history. Particularly interesting would be a detailed comparison between the LDS and RLDS churches.

But these diverse tasks await other hands. My goal has been more modest: to sketch, through pivotal figures, the main developing lines of LDS biblical usage, and to compare those lines to those of other American religionists. The project was launched against a backdrop of partially conflicting scholarly assessments of Mormonism's essential nature. It seemed to me that Mormonism represents a particu-

1. The archetypal instance of this practice is probably St. Augustine (*Confessions*, 8:12), but it or related practices occur regularly in Protestant fundamentalist circles (Ammerman, *Bible Believers,* pp. 53–56), and occasionally among Mormons (miscellaneous interviews with author) and Catholics (see the account by Thomas Merton, who indulges in the practice, which he implies he has learned from co-believers, though he quickly labels his behavior superstitious [*The Seven-Story Mountain* (1948; reprint, San Diego: Harvest Books, 1978), p. 334]).

larly important case for exploring American social and religious boundaries. It also seemed that many issues in LDS history skillfully treated by previous writers—whether concerning visions, the Book of Mormon, polygamy, "the kingdom," economics, millennialism, priesthood, developing theology, Mormon self-consciousness, social practices, attitudes toward women or Jews, church structure, or many other things—ultimately depended in crucial ways on diffuse and often unconscious understandings of the Bible for their very existence and meaning. Mormon biblical usage thus invited direct consideration.

After giving the subject some attention, one easily sees why scholars have drawn differing conclusions on whether the Latter-day Saints are insiders or outsiders in American culture. The conflicts, I now think, do not result merely from the inevitable myopia of individual observers, nor from the difficult fact of an ever-changing nation and a constantly developing Mormonism. They derive also from an ambiguity inherent in Mormonism itself, planted deeply there by Joseph Smith. Indeed, the paradoxical tendency of the Saints to employ the Bible sometimes like other Americans and sometimes as outsiders is a recurrent theme of this study.

But this somewhat confusing tendency ought not frustrate us, for it is part of what makes Mormonism unusually important to the student of religion. What Jonathan Z. Smith asserted about the study of Judaism in his pathbreaking *Imagining Religion* is so equally true of Mormonism that one can exchange the "isms" without greatly damaging the insight:

> The interest of the historian of religion in [Mormonism] cannot depend on apologetic, historical, or demographic reasons. That is to say, the interest in [Mormonism] for the imagination of religion cannot be merely because it is "there," because it has played some role in our collective invention of western civilization, or because some students of religion happen to be [Mormons]. Rather it is because of the peculiar position of [Mormonism] within the larger framework of the imagining of western religion: close, yet distant; similar, yet strange; . . . commonplace, yet exotic. This tension between the familiar and the unfamiliar, at the very heart of the imagining of [Mormonism], has enormous cognitive power. It invites, it requires comparison. [Mormonism] is foreign enough for comparison and interpretation to be necessary; it is close enough for comparison and interpretation to be possible. By

virtue of its tensive situation between the near and the far, [Mormonism] provides an important test case for central methodological issues such as definition and comparison besides illuminating the larger issues of imagination, self-consciousness, and choice crucial to the academic study of religion.[2]

The pressure of various historical contexts has brought to the surface a great many similarities in the perspectives of the Saints and their approximate contemporaries. Yet this of itself does not tell us enough, for one could say the same of the biblical uses of American Jews, Catholics, or Protestants. No matter how numerous and obvious these similarities—and they became more numerous and obvious in the twentieth century—Mormon habits emerged from the unique soil mixed and nurtured by their founding prophet. This soil produced differences that color all the similarities. The differences are even sufficiently controlling to induce sympathy for Jan Shipps's contention that Mormonism represents a distinct religious tradition.

But if Shipps's discerning eye has taught us much, she still must be read in conjunction with Klaus Hansen, Thomas Alexander, and the several others who have probed the profound changes making twentieth-century (American) Mormonism, far more than its nineteenth-century counterpart, resemble American middle-class culture. Equally important, Shipps's thesis must be integrated with the work of Laurence Moore, who asserts that Mormon identity originally rested on a highly "schizophrenic" set of relations with the American experiment.

Moore argues that what separated early Mormons from their opponents was partly an elaborated fiction, used by both sides for their own ends. Opponents sought to draw the Saints outside the circle of legitimate Christian society and thus to isolate and dispose of them. The treatment was often brutal, but Mormons found ways to appropriate such opposition, making it the fertilizer by which they thrived. The very hardships induced dedication and resilience, and clarified identity. As Joseph Smith put it, "The Lord has constituted me so curiously that I glory in persecutions." But in making the most of their hard lot as an oppressed minority, Mormons ironically fit a pattern that was quintessentially American. Outsiders, in some

2. Jonathan Z. Smith, *Imagining Religion: From Babylon to Jonestown* (Chicago: University of Chicago Press, 1982), p. xii.

fashion, were as much insiders as those who thought they were in control.[3]

In my judgment, Moore occasionally exaggerates his point, makes the process he describes seem more deliberate than it was, and even comes close to suggesting the Saints deserved the unconscionable treatment they received. Nevertheless, Moore's insights are important because they shed light on Mormon and American self-consciousness and unself-consciousness, and because they further undermine historians' addiction to handling Mormons, Spiritualists, blacks (before treating blacks more thoughtfully became an academic-political necessity), and all manner of shunned minorities as if they were no more than eccentric footnotes to the real story of America's religious past. My look at the Mormons does not intend to undercut these contributions, but it does, I hope, complement them. Moore arrived at his conclusions by focusing on polemical sources. He properly noted that the intention of these sources was not often to clarify but, rather, to attack and debunk or to persuade and mythify. He says that the problem of judging Mormon typicality within American culture is rooted in such sources.[4] Through this method he is able to make us see more clearly the nature of Mormonism's relation to the broader society, a relationship he says was largely based on and fostered by participants' rhetoric.

I have approached the problem from a different angle. I have suggested that no conversation about Mormon cultural typicality is secure without careful attention to Mormon biblical usage, which provides essential common ground for comparing similarities and differences with the larger body of American religionists. Such an approach does not disdain the social, political, theological, or rhetorical traits that other scholars have used as bases for comparison, but it does point to a dimension that makes a difference to the whole discussion. It helps one notice, first, that assertions about Mormonism's being a new religion have both truth and ambiguity to them, and

3. Shipps, *Mormonism: The Story of a New Religious Tradition;* Hansen, *Mormonism and the American Experience;* Alexander, *Mormonism in Transition;* Moore, *Religious Outsiders and the Making of Americans,* pp. 25–47. On Joseph Smith and other Mormons making use of their attackers' hostility, see Roberts, *History of the Church,* 5:157; Hill, *Joseph Smith,* pp. 343, 392; many examples in *TS* and other early Mormon periodicals.

4. *Religious Outsiders,* p. 27.

second, that the ambiguity of Mormonism vis-à-vis American culture goes far deeper than the fictions of nineteenth-century rhetoric. More than any other single factor, Mormon biblical usage lays bare and symbolizes the nature and basis of the ambiguity. Moreover, although this ambiguity was altered and obscured by the cultural accommodations made at the beginning of the twentieth century, it did not wholly disappear merely because of them. From the time of Joseph Smith, Mormons have remained Bible-believing Christians, but with a fundamental, uneven, and evolving difference.[5]

A certain tension existed between Joseph Smith and the Bible. The Prophet's mind was demonstrably saturated in biblical language, images, and themes, and in some ways he "out-Bibled" the traditional biblicists who surrounded him. Yet the limitations he put on biblical authority were substantial, singular, and progressive. Although he continued to understand himself and his people as Bible loyalists and, indeed, as embodiments of biblical prophecy, he increasingly found the relatively rigid biblical perceptions of his audiences to confine his own cosmic vision uncomfortably.

Related tensions are equally crucial. On the one hand were Smith's tendencies toward literalism and his inherited assumptions about "verbal inspiration." On the other were his own prophetic experiences, which invaded and altered his earlier assumptions. These experiences, though inconsistently applied, suggested scripture was provisional, subject to improvement and expansion. It was not just that revelation was filtered through human capacities, as many Bible-believers allowed; it was that revelation involved an active human participation, even dimensions of experimentation, as Smith's biblical revision and Doctrine and Covenants section 9 attest. Sometimes, at least, the exchange included a kind of divine–human dialectic.

Joseph Smith differed from evangelical Protestants in rejecting the

5. From a sociological perspective, this difference may be most appropriately gauged not by a linear, unidirectional, Troeltsch-like picture of sect-to-church development (cf. Leone, *The Roots of Modern Mormonism*) but by a modified model more recently proposed by Armand Mauss. Mauss suggests that to survive as an independent people, groups like the Mormons have swung pendulum-like from being so different from the host culture that they have been in danger of obliteration, to being so similar that they have been in danger of assimilation, and then partially back again (Mauss, "Assimilation and Ambivalence: The Mormon Reaction to Americanization" *Dialogue* 22 [Spring 1989]: 30–67).

Bible as a sufficient religious guide. He differed from Catholics and Episcopalians and Unitarians in rejecting churchly tradition or human scholarship as adequate substitutes or supplements for that insufficiency. He differed from contemporaneous visionaries in his notions of revelation and scripture and by producing the remarkable, biblically conditioned Book of Mormon. And he differed from *everyone* by instigating distinctive social and religious practices, justified and fundamentally inspired by his biblical views.

It likely never occurred to Joseph Smith that he was anything but a Christian, just as Paul of Tarsus may not have considered himself an apostate from the religion of Israel.[6] And certainly Smith and his followers remained Christians in their devotion to Jesus Christ. But as the Prophet combined his vision of "the ancient pattern of things" with a nineteenth-century style and certain antebellum assumptions, something original formed. A new type of Christianity—Mormon Christianity—was born.

Smith's followers inherited these tensions. After their Prophet's death, Latter-day Saints maintained their basic loyalty to the Bible and continued to feel they alone were the truest Bible believers. Yet as the nineteenth century wore on, some leaders increasingly restricted biblical authority, insisting not only on the primacy of living prophets but also on the importance of common sense and the truths revealed by science and human experience. Brigham Young went beyond allowing for biblical errors of translation and transmission; he dismissed parts of the Bible as uninspired folktales. And if some biblical assertion did not seem to square with Mormon predilections, individual Saints were always aware of their private safety net: "We believe the Bible to be the word of God *as far as it is translated correctly.*" The insistence on the fallibility of the biblical texts and translations was, of course, a legitimate perspective. But partly because of this theoretical protection, most Mormons were not forced to think very deeply about the theological diversity in the Bible itself and in their own exclusively Mormon scriptures.

The distinctive tension between the Bible and the Saints is even more apparent when one compares general Protestant views, against which, because of their cultural dominance, Mormonism defined it-

---

6. A. Leland Jamison, "Religions on the Christian Perimeter," in *The Shaping of American Religion,* ed. James Ward Smith and A. Leland Jamison, p. 214.

self in the nineteenth century. Compared to contemporaneous evangelicals, Mormons both elevated and lowered the Bible's status. Because they believed themselves so vividly to recapitulate biblical narratives and because they saw the process of revelation occur right before them, biblical reality and biblical authority were renewed for them. However, the proximity and foibles of their own prophets reminded them of the fallibility of all mortals, and it was comparatively easy for them to recognize the limitations of even biblical writers. Hence, the Mormon "difference" persisted.

It is a commonplace that during the decades surrounding the turn of the twentieth century the Mormons surrendered their most distinctive practices, especially polygamy and theocracy and the propensity for social, political, and economic isolation. Consequently, some have argued, Mormonism became "merely one more slightly idiosyncratic form of Christianity." The Saints underwent "bourgeoisification."[7] Incontestably, much accommodation did occur, but fundamental differences also remained. In the late nineteenth and early twentieth centuries, the Saints and their religious peers faced a common enemy (or opportunity) in the form of higher criticism. This new challenge had unprecedented implications. Because they did not depend solely on the Bible for religious authority, the Mormons had the potential to respond nondefensively. With this potential, they possessed resources apart from Protestants and more nearly like Catholics, who leaned on tradition more than on scripture, and Jews, among whom—even in Orthodox circles—the Torah was usually held to have no meaning until the people of God gathered to debate and discover it.[8]

7. This perception is asserted in many periodical pieces. For a convenient summary, see Jan Shipps, "From Satyr to Saint," (paper presented at the annual meeting of the Organization of American Historians, Chicago, 1973; copy in LDS Church Archives). Also, Hansen, *Mormonism and the American Experience.*

8. Such a fact illustrates the danger of facilely applying constructs such as "fundamentalist" across religious boundaries.

It is notable that the considerable interest Mormons have shown in Judaism has not provoked a serious contemplation of Jewish attitudes toward the Bible. Despite an array of Jewish perspectives as diverse as Mormon views, many core ideas seem to invite cross-fertilization. Among them, Jews' appreciation for oral tradition, their conception of scholarship as a form of worship, their extreme respect for commentary and the rights of scholarly consensus, their broad notions of what constitutes holy writing, their explicit awareness of levels of authority and sacredness in various texts, and their dynamic flexibility of interpretation (Jonathan Rosenbaum, "Judaism: Torah and Tradi-

Among a minority of Saints, this potential was realized; among the majority, it was not. In this, they were no different from other Americans, though the Saints, like the Jews, had distinctive reasons for reacting as they did, including the implied threat to the Book of Mormon and to modern revelation generally. Because these groups all believed fundamentally in the Bible and were addressing a similar force, they responded in similar, though proportionately contrasting and chronologically staggered, ways. But this does not mean that Mormon biblical usage suddenly became essentially like that of other Christians. Higher criticism changed the nature and tone of scriptural allegiance for some, but the Mormon relationship with the Bible remained on its distinctive foundation.

Both continuities and evolutions in LDS biblical usage are visible during the course of Mormon history. The most basic continuity is the perpetuation of the underlying tension between the fundamental Mormon acceptance of the Bible as the Word of God and the restrictions placed on biblical authority by the existence of living prophets, additional scriptures, and modern scholarship. Many contemporary Saints are scarcely aware of this tension, simply assuming that, inconsequential details aside, all Bible theology is perfectly compatible with itself and with twentieth-century LDS conceptions. Others see more significant discrepancies but attribute them to corruptions in the biblical texts. Others yet give broad leeway to the human element in both ancient and contemporary scripture.

Additional continuities for one side of the Mormon tradition include an enduring interest in eschatology and predictive prophecy. Typological and dispensational perspectives are still pronounced, as well as a strong tendency toward literalism.[9] Millions of Latter-day Saints, like millions of other Christians, remain unfazed by issues of historical biblical criticism.

But changes, too, have occurred. Liberal views among Mormon leaders are less visible now than formerly. The experimental, adven-

tion," in *The Holy Book,* ed. Denny and Taylor; Gilbert S. Rosenthal, *Contemporary Judaism: Patterns of Survival* [New York: Human Sciences Press, 1986], passim; Abraham Karp, *The Jewish Way of Life and Thought* [New York: KTAV, 1981], pp. 187–93).

9. I do not intend these assessments to be pejorative. The tendency toward literalism has marked advantages as well as liabilities. For one scholar's simultaneous gratitude for and despair over Mormon literalism, see Cummings, "Quintessential Mormonism: Literal-Mindedness as a Way of Life."

turous aspects of the scriptural approaches of nineteenth-century Mormonism, which struggled against the confining hegemony of evangelical orthodoxy, have faded. By the turn of the twentieth century these dimensions began gradually to be displaced by a growing conservatism, which reacted against an increasingly secular culture. Interest in serious scholarship, substantial if embattled and modest in the first half of the twentieth century, is proportionately weaker now. Indeed, scholarship is valued often merely for apologetics. And, ironically, the King James Version has evolved from the common translation, inherited from antebellum Protestantism, into the official Mormon Bible—precisely as Jacobean language has grown increasingly obscure and as other Americans have gradually adopted more current versions. Although understandable from a world-religions perspective, profound implications for both biblical accessibility and for how Mormons conceive of revelation inheres in this evolution.

The biblical proof-texts currently used to prove the truth of the Book of Mormon and the Latter-day Saint Restoration seem to have been in use from the earliest days of Mormonism, but many passages have been discarded.[10] When compared to the preoccupations of their nineteenth-century counterparts, the millenarian interests of most contemporary Mormons are muted. One side of the tradition shows no concern at all with such matters.

Modern Mormons do not know the Bible as their ancestors did. This is also true of other Bible-believing groups, of course, for few twentieth-century people read the Bible and little else. But in Mormonism the shift is further explained by the fact that the more accessible and distinctly LDS Book of Mormon may have overtaken the relatively obscure Old Testament and much of the New Testament (excepting the Gospels) in the everyday consciousness of many Church members.[11] To the earliest Saints, the messages of Jeremiah

10. See Grant R. Underwood, "The Old Testament in the New Dispensation," in *A Symposium on the Old Testament* (SLC: Church of Jesus Christ of Latter-day Saints, 1983), pp. 178–79.

11. Except for brief proof-texts and favorite poetic passages like the Twenty-third Psalm, modern Saints are not deeply familiar with the Old Testament once they pass Genesis and the first twenty chapters of Exodus, nor with the New Testament after the Gospel of St. John. This is true despite the regular Sunday school rotation of study, which dictates that the Old Testament, the New Testament, the Book of Mormon, and the Doctrine and Covenants be studied one out of every four years.

It remains to be seen whether Church President Ezra Taft Benson's stress on the

and Micah were as familiar as the words of Nephi or Alma are today. The heroes of the first Mormons were Abraham and Joshua rather than Captain Moroni or the sons of Helaman. Phrases like "the horsemen of Israel and the chariots thereof" (2 Kings 2:12) came more easily to mind than "when ye are in the service of your fellow beings ye are only in the service of your God" (Mosiah 2:17).[12]

Additionally, of course, much more diversity exists among today's millions of Mormons than existed among the thousands of a century ago, though variety has been apparent all along. For a minority of modern Saints, the principles of higher criticism have fundamentally altered (not usually eliminated) their faith in the Bible and in revelation generally. Dispensational schemes of human history have faded in relevance for a large part of the LDS community.

In 1977 James Barr damned the evangelical study of the Bible as puerile, self-contradictory, anti-intellectual, and almost worse than worthless.[13] If his language was occasionally intemperate, many of his arguments were cogent. Although conservative American Protestants have always nurtured a deep attachment to the Bible, they have not often been up-to-date in their scholarship. Before the mid-twentieth century, Moses Stuart, Benjamin Warfield, J. Gresham Machen, and Princeton Seminary as a whole were exceptions to the general pattern. However, as historian Mark Noll observes, a "renaissance" in evangelical biblical study has blossomed since World War II. As with Roman Catholics, the choice for thoughtful conservative Protestants is no longer simply between what some of them have perceived as the spiritual sterility of the academic world and the intellectual vacuity of their own dominant positions.[14]

Book of Mormon in the late 1980s will have a lasting effect on Mormon reading patterns. Since the end of the nineteenth century, Mormonism has shifted away from the strong preference among its first generations for the Bible. Still, the ambiguities in these shifts are prominent. At least through 1985, when Elder Benson was sustained as Church president, Mormon leaders tended over the pulpit to cite the Bible substantially more often than the Doctrine and Covenants, and the D&C far more often than the Book of Mormon (Dean R. Zimmerman, "Research Report: Referencs to Latter-day Commentary on the Sciptures, 1830–1974," [unpublished compilation, LDS Church Archives, n.d.]; no listed compiler, "Teachings of the Living Prophets, Jan. 1974–Nov. 1985," [unpublished, LDS Church Archives, n.d.).

12. Cf. Underwood, "Joseph Smith's Use."

13. *Fundamentalism*, pp. 40–89, 120–59, passim.

14. Noll is frank in his criticism of evangelical Bible studies, but the evidence he marshals for substantial progress is persuasive. An example is the more than thirty

One cannot point to a similar biblical-studies renaissance among the Mormons. This is not, of course, because the Saints are incapable of the task. In the second half of the twentieth century they have produced a "Great Awakening" in historical scholarship and at least the uneven beginnings of a movement for serious Book of Mormon scholarship. The causes for their lack in biblical fields may probably be explained in part by in-house political and economic causes.[15]

One consequence of this lack is that Mormons have no developed theory or doctrine of scripture adequate for a modern world. Lowell Bennion's efforts are a thoughtful beginning by a nonspecialist but, naturally, they do not enjoy official stature. Nor does any current manual or textbook recommended for official Church usage adopt or encourage a consideration of Bennion's work or anything analogous to it.

The reluctance to assign official status to most theological efforts has a long Mormon heritage and possesses what many Saints consider the virtue of restricting Mormon creedalism; individual Saints are free to believe as they wish. Yet the Church's constant urging to "study the scriptures"—without any serious discussion of scripture's nature, and coupled with what are implied to be the normative views of the 1979 biblical supplements and the recent generation of religious educational publications based not on informed scholarship but on dogmatic concerns—insures a minimum of competent thought about a quintessential aspect of Mormonism. Latter-day Saints continue to adhere to an article of faith encountered earlier: "We believe the Bible to be the Word of God as far as it is translated correctly. . . ." But in what sense is the correctly translated Bible "the Word of God"? For Mormons, there has never been an official answer. There are only predominant attitudes.

different series of commentaries kept in print by Grand Rapids publishers alone, some of which are of high quality ("Evangelicals and the Study of the Bible," pp. 108–9, 197 n.20). By contrast, one cannot cite a single good-quality commentary by Mormon authors on either the complete Old or New Testament, much less the entire Bible.

15. Perhaps because of past suspicions concerning higher criticism, competent and serious LDS biblical scholars, unlike, say, Roman Catholics, generally receive no official encouragement from the Church itself, unless the scholarship serves apologetic or devotional ends. Sensitive areas are studiously avoided by many scholars. And, unlike historians, Mormon biblical students have relatively few employment opportunities outside Church-owned facilities. Furthermore, LDS scholars may tend to think they can make more distinctive contributions in areas that are more specifically Mormon than in the widely explored field of biblical studies.

These attitudes run in several directions. Richard Bushman perhaps overgeneralized one of them with his penetrating observation that "Mormonism was history, not philosophy." That is, it was "the power of Joseph Smith to breathe new life into the ancient sacred stories, and to make a sacred story out of his own life, [that] was the source of his extraordinary influence."[16] In this light, the Bible is important not primarily for the specifics of its doctrine or its ethics but for its deepest message that God lives and is acting in human history to lift humankind to a better existence. This may indeed be the Bible's deepest or most enduring meaning for many Mormons, and it is a meaning at work even when the covers of scriptural books are closed. The majority of Mormons remain in a hermeneutical Eden, innocent of a conscious philosophy of interpretation. The Bible as story also relates to the devotional dimensions of biblical usage, which I have not so much focused on as taken for granted.

But whenever Latter-day Saints *study* the Bible, whenever they show deliberate interest in it, or write or read Church manuals about it, or quote it to one another for edification, or proselytize or define their faith by it, then other perspectives become at least as apparent. In these realms, the predominant attitudes of the most recent generation of Saints are not revealed by the writings of biblical specialists but are archetypified in the approaches of Lowell Bennion (liberal, ethically concerned, informed by but not preoccupied with modern scholarship) and Bruce McConkie (fundamentalistic, doctrinally oriented, oblivious or hostile to modern perspectives). These two attitudes represent the "left" and "right" hermeneutical boundaries of the main body of active Latter-day Saints. The positions have analogues in other Christian faiths, and can even be seen as part of the "great divide" to which Robert Wuthnow points in discussing the restructuring of American religion.[17] Yet in Mormonism the positions exist in a theological and historical and scriptural tradition too distinctive to be considered generically "liberal" and "conservative."

Since the time of Joseph Smith, the Mormon use of scripture has combined a traditional faith in the Bible with more "conservative" elements (like a more than occasional extra dose of literalism), some

16. *Joseph Smith and the Beginnings of Mormonism,* pp. 187–88.
17. Wuthnow, *The Restructuring of American Religion: Society and Faith Since World War II* (Princeton: Princeton University Press, 1988).

liberal components (such as Joseph Smith's Bushnell-like insistence on the limitations of human language), and, at least in an American context, some radical ingredients (an open canon, an oral scripture, the subjugation of biblical assertions to experimental truth or the pronouncements of living authorities). This peculiar recipe links the Saints sometimes with Catholics, sometimes with Jews, sometimes with more exotic groups like the Jehovah's Witnesses, and sometimes with others of the world's religions. It links them often with evangelical Protestants. Yet taken as a whole, the combination constitutes the "difference" in the Mormon use of the Bible. Despite the broad terrain the Saints continue to share with others devoted to scripture, that enduring difference should provide an essential clue to scholars who attempt to locate Mormonism on their evolving maps of religion in America.

Select Bibliography

The following is a listing of materials bearing most directly upon this study. Much of the literature not central to Mormons and the Bible, but closely related to it, is cited only in the footnotes, particularly in cases where the book or article has been mentioned only once. The notes thus serve as a more comprehensive secondary bibliography, topically arranged.

Primary Sources

Chapters 1 and 2

The principal works written, spoken, or dictated by Joseph Smith are collected in the following: Andrew F. Ehat and Lyndon W. Cook, eds., *The Words of Joseph Smith* (Provo, UT: Religious Studies Center, Brigham Young University, 1980); Scott H. Faulring, ed., *An American Prophet's Record: The Diaries and Journals of Joseph Smith* (SLC: Signature Books in association with Smith Research Associates, 1987); and Dean C. Jessee, ed., *The Personal Writings of Joseph Smith* (SLC: Deseret Book, 1984). Also important, though published too late to be of use in this study, are Dean C. Jessee, ed., *The Papers of Joseph Smith: Volume 1, Autobiographical and Historical Writings* (SLC: Deseret Book, 1989), and the two projected related volumes to follow. B. H. Roberts, ed., *History of the Church of Jesus Christ of Latter-day Saints: History of Joseph Smith, the Prophet, by Himself*, 2d rev. ed., 7 vols. (SLC: Deseret Book, 1957), contains much material attributed to Smith, though it is a primary source only in the sense explained in my chapter 2. Joseph Fielding Smith, ed., *The Teachings of the Prophet Joseph Smith* (SLC: Deseret Book, 1976), makes often useful selections from the previous source. Scriptures issued through Smith's hand include the Book of Mormon (see especially the *Book of Mormon Critical Text,* 2d ed., 3 vols. [Provo, UT: F.A.R.M.S., 1987]), the Pearl of Great Price (in various forms), the Doctrine and Covenants (in various forms) and Joseph Smith's "Inspired Translation" of the Bible, published as *The Holy Scriptures* (Independence, MO: Herald, 1974; orig. 1867).

Chapter 3

The Library-Archives of the LDS Church Historical Department in Salt Lake City house thousands of pages of journals, letters, and miscellaneous manuscripts of Brigham Young. Dean Jessee has collected significant correspondence in *"My Dear Son": Letters of Brigham Young to His Sons* (SLC: Deseret Book, 1974). About half of Young's eight hundred recorded sermons were published, mostly in the *Journal of Discourses,* 26 vols. (Liverpool: F. D. Richards [and others], 1855–1886). Most of the others are gathered in Eldon J. Watson, ed., *A Chronological Compilation of Known Addresses of Brigham Young,* 6 vols. (n. p., 1979–1984), also in the Church Archives.

The primary works of Orson Pratt used in this study include *The Bible & Polygamy: Does the Bible Sanction Polygamy? A Discussion Between Professor Orson Pratt and Rev. Doctor J. P. Newman* (SLC: Deseret News Steam Printing Establishment, 1874); the *Journal of Discourses* (see Young above); *The Seer* (a newpaper edited and published by Pratt in Washington, DC, and Liverpool, England, January 1853–August 1854); Eldon J. Watson, comp., *The Orson Pratt Journals* (SLC: n.p., 1975); and various proselytizing pamphlets preserved in the LDS Church Archives.

Chapter 4

B. H. Roberts's most directly relevant writings are *Defense of the Faith and the Saints* (SLC: Deseret News Press, 1907); *The Gospel* (SLC: Contributor Co., 1888); *New Witnesses for God, Vols. I and II* (SLC: Deseret News Press, 1909); *The Second Coming of the Messiah and Events to Precede It* (Independence, MO.: Mission of the LDS Church, 1919?); *The Seventy's Course in Theology* (SLC: Deseret Book, 1907–1912); *Studies of the Book of Mormon,* ed. Brigham D. Madsen (Urbana: University of Illinois Press, 1985); "The Truth, the Way, and the Life," (unpublished manuscript, underground copy [original inaccessible in LDS Church Archives], n.d.); and various sermons and essays. Roberts's letters and papers are in the Marriott Library at the University of Utah, and in the LDS Church Archives. His personal library is also largely preserved at the Church Archives.

Joseph Fielding Smith's essential position becomes clear through his *Answers to Gospel Questions,* ed. Bruce R. McConkie, 5 vols. (SLC: Deseret Book, 1957–1966); *Doctrines of Salvation,* comp. Bruce R. McConkie, 3 vols. (SLC: Bookcraft, 1954–1956); *Man: His Origin and Destiny* (SLC: Deseret, 1954); *Seek Ye Earnestly* (SLC: Deseret Book, 1970); *The Signs of the Times* (SLC: Deseret Book, 1964); and miscellaneous sermons.

Although William Chamberlin's philosophical books and privately published and unpublished essays (e.g., "An Essay on Nature" [Provo, UT: n.p., 1915]; "The Development of the Ethical Ideal with Special Reference to the Ethics of the Hebrews" [n.p., n.d.]), bear indirectly on our subject, he published comparatively little specifically on biblical hermeneutics, and was influential instead largely through his teaching. His most relevant essays are cited in notes to the text. Although the book is partially a secondary source, Ralph Chamberlin quotes heavily from his brother's published and unpublished writings in *Life and Philosophy of W. H. Chamberlin* (SLC: Deseret News Press, 1925). Chamberlin's personal papers are located in the Utah State Historical Society Library, in the Marriott Library at the University of Utah, and in the private collection of his grandaughter, Mrs. Frances Stewart. I have used photocopies of the latter collection in the possession of Chamberlin's grandnephew, David C. Chamberlin, Hillsboro, Oregon.

Chapter 5

J. Reuben Clark's main books are *Our Lord of The Gospels* (SLC: Deseret Book, 1954) and *Why the King James Version* (SLC: Deseret Book, 1956). Other important primary material is found in David H. Yarn, ed., *J. Reuben Clark: Selected Papers* (Provo, UT: Brigham Young University Press, 1984), and sermons published in various Church periodicals. The bulk of Clark's personal papers are found in the Harold B. Lee Library, Brigham Young University.

Chapter 6

Bruce R. McConkie's books include *Doctrinal New Testament Commentary* (DNTC), 3 vols. (SLC: Bookcraft, 1970–1974); *Mormon Doctrine* (SLC: Bookcraft, 1966); a triology entitled *The Promised Messiah, The Mortal Messiah* (4 vols.), and *The Millennial Messiah* (SLC: Deseret Book, 1978–1982); and *A New Witness for the Articles of Faith* (SLC: Deseret Book, 1985). His published speeches especially relevant for this study are "The Bible, a Sealed Book," in *A Symposium on the New Testament,* Supplement (SLC: Church of Jesus Christ of Latter-day Saints, 1984); "The Seven Deadly Heresies," (*BYU Speeches of the Year,* June 1, 1980); "Ten Keys to Understanding Isaiah," *Ensign* 3 (October 1973); and "Understanding the Book of Revelation," *Ensign* 5 (September 1975).

Lowell Bennion's principal books explicitly entailing a philosophy of scripture are *The Best of Lowell L. Bennion: Selected Writings, 1928–1988,* ed.

Eugene England (SLC: Deseret Book, 1988), which includes a nearly exhaustive bibliography of Bennion's published and unpublished writings; *The Book of Mormon: A Guide to Christian Living* (SLC: Deseret Book, 1985); *Do Justly and Love Mercy: Moral Issues for Mormons* (Centerville, UT: Canon Press, 1988); *I Believe* (SLC: Deseret Book, 1983); *Teachings of the New Testament* (SLC: Deseret Book, 1956); *Understanding the Scriptures* (SLC: Deseret Book, 1981); and *The Unknown Testament* (SLC: Deseret Book, 1988). Other relevant sources include Lowell L. Bennion Oral History (typescript; SLC: James Moyle Oral History Program, LDS Church Archives, 1985); "A Saint for All Seasons: an Interview with Lowell L. Bennion," *Sunstone* 10 (February 1985): 6–17; and various other published and unpublished interviews, sermons, and essays.

Secondary Works

Books

Ahlstrom, Sydney E. *A Religious History of the American People*. 2 vols. Garden City, NY: Image Books, 1975.

Alexander, Thomas. *Mormonism in Transition*. Urbana: University of Illinois Press, 1986.

Allen, James B., and Glen M. Leonard. *The Story of the Latter-day Saints*. SLC: Deseret Book, 1976.

Ammerman, Nancy Tatom. *Bible Believers: Fundamentalists in the Modern World*. New Brunswick: Rutgers University Press, 1987.

Anderson, Richard L. *Understanding Paul*. SLC: Deseret Book, 1983.

Arbaugh, George Bartholomew. *Revelation in Mormonism*. Chicago: University of Chicago Press, 1932.

Arrington, Leonard J. *Brigham Young: American Moses*. New York: Knopf, 1985.

———, ed. *The Presidents of the Church*. SLC: Deseret Book, 1986.

Arrington, Leonard J., and Davis Bitton, *The Mormon Experience: A History of the Latter-day Saints* (New York: Knopf, 1979).

Barr, James. *Fundamentalism*. London: SCM Press, 1977.

———. *Beyond Fundamentalism: Biblical Foundations for Evangelical Christianity*. Philadelphia: Westminster Press, 1984.

Bozeman, Theodore Dwight. *Protestants in an Age of Science: The Baconian Ideal and Antebellum American Religious Thought*. Chapel Hill: University of North Carolina Press, 1977.

Brodie, Fawn. *No Man Knows My History: The Life of Joseph Smith, the Mormon Prophet*. New York: Knopf, 1971.

Brown, Jerry W. *The Rise of Biblical Criticism in America, 1800–1870: The*

New England Scholars. Middletown, CT: Wesleyan University Press, 1969.

Bruce, F. F. *The English Bible: A History of Translations from the Earliest English Versions to the New English Bible.* Rev. ed. New York: Oxford University Press, 1970.

Burtchaell, James T. *Catholic Theories of Biblical Inspiration Since 1810.* Cambridge: Cambridge University Press, 1969.

Bush, T. Russ, and Tom J. Nettles. *Baptists and the Bible: The Baptist Doctrines of Biblical Importance and Religious Authority in Historical Perspective.* Chicago: Moody Press, 1980.

Bushman, Richard L. *Joseph Smith and the Beginnings of Mormonism.* Urbana: University of Illinois Press, 1984.

Carson, D. A. *The King James Version Debate.* Grand Rapids, MI: Baker Book House, 1979.

Denny, Frederick M., and Rodney L. Taylor, eds. *The Holy Book in Comparative Perspective.* Columbia: University of South Carolina Press, 1985.

Durham, Reed C., comp. *Revelation and Scripture.* N.p. 1971.

England, Breck. *The Life and Thought of Orson Pratt.* SLC: University of Utah Press, 1985.

Fogarty, Gerald P. *American Catholic Biblical Scholarship: A History from the Early Republic to Vatican II.* San Francisco: Harper & Row, 1989.

Fox, Frank W. *J. Reuben Clark: The Public Years.* Provo, UT, and SLC: Brigham Young University Press and Deseret Book, 1980.

Gates, Susa Young, with Leah D. Widtsoe. *The Life Story of Brigham Young,* New York: Macmillan, 1934.

Gileadi, Avraham. *The Book of Isaiah: A New Translation, with Interpretive Keys from the Book of Mormon.* SLC: Deseret Book, 1988.

Grant, Robert M. *A Short History of the Interpretation of the Bible.* New York: Macmillan, 1963.

Hansen, Klaus. *Mormonism and the American Experience.* Chicago: University of Chicago Press, 1981.

Hatch, Nathan O., and Mark A. Noll, eds. *The Bible in America: Essays in Cultural History.* New York: Oxford University Press, 1982.

Hill, Donna. *Joseph Smith: the First Mormon.* Garden City, NY: Doubleday, 1977.

Hovenkamp, Herbert. *Science and Religion in America, 1800–1860.* Philadelphia: University of Pennsylvania Press, 1978.

Howard, Richard. *Restoration Scriptures: A Study of Their Textual Development.* Independence, MO.: Herald, 1969.

Hutchison, William R. *The Modernist Impulse in American Protestantism.* Cambridge: Harvard University Press, 1976.

Leone, Mark P. *The Roots of Modern Mormonism.* Cambridge: Harvard University Press, 1979.

Ludlow, Victor L. *Isaiah: Prophet, Seer, and Poet.* SLC: Deseret Book, 1982.

Madsen, Truman. *Defender of the Faith: The B. H. Roberts Story.* SLC: Bookcraft, 1980.

Malan, Robert H. *B. H. Roberts: A Biography.* SLC: Deseret Book, 1966.

Marini, Stephen A. *Radical Sects of Revolutionary New England.* Cambridge: Harvard University Press, 1982.

Marsden, George M. *Fundamentalism and American Culture: The Shaping of Twentieth Century Evangelicalism, 1870–1925.* New York: Oxford University Press, 1980.

Matthews, Robert J. *"A Plainer Translation": Joseph Smith's Translation of the Bible—A History and Commentary.* Provo, UT: Brigham Young University Press, 1975.

McConkie, Joseph Fielding. *True and Faithful: The Life Story of Joseph Fielding Smith.* SLC: Bookcraft, 1971.

McDonald, H. D. *Theories of Revelation: An Historical Study 1700–1960.* Grand Rapids, MI: Baker Book House, 1979.

McMurrin, Sterling M. *The Theological Foundations of the Mormon Religion.* SLC: University of Utah Press, 1965.

Moore, R. Laurence. *Religious Outsiders and the Making of Americans.* New York: Oxford University Press, 1986.

Nibley, Hugh. *Old Testament and Related Studies.* Edited by John W. Welch, Gary P. Gilliam, and Don E. Norton. SLC: Deseret Book, 1986.

Noll, Mark A. *Between Faith and Criticism: Evangelicals, Scholarship, and the Bible in America.* San Francisco: Harper & Row, 1986.

———, et al., eds. *Eerdmans' Handbook to Christianity in America.* Grand Rapids, MI: Eerdmans, 1983.

———. "Evangelicals and the Study of the Bible." In *Evangelicalism and Modern America,* edited by George Marsden, pp. 103–21. Grand Rapids, MI: Eerdmans, 1984.

Nyman, Monte S., and Robert L. Millet, eds. *The Joseph Smith Translation: The Restoration of Plain and Precious Things.* Provo, UT: Religious Studies Center, BYU, 1985.

Pals, Daniel L. *The Victorian "Lives" of Jesus.* San Antonio: Trinity University Press, 1982.

Phy, Allene S., ed. *The Bible and Popular Culture in America.* Philadelphia: Fortress Press, and Chico, CA: Scholars Press, 1985.

Quinn, D. Michael. *J. Reuben Clark: the Church Years.* Provo, UT: Brigham Young University Press, 1983.

Rasmussen, Ellis T. "The New LDS Edition of the King James Version of the Bible: Its Development and Significance." In *Church Educational Sys-*

tem *Religious Educators' Symposium on the Old Testament,* pp. 27–30. N.p. 1979.

Roberts, Brigham Henry. *A Comprehensive History of The Church of Jesus Christ of Latter-day Saints.* 6 vols. SLC: Deseret News Press, 1930.

Rogers, Jack B., and Donald K. McKim. *The Authority and Interpretation of the Bible: An Historical Approach.* San Francisco: Harper & Row, 1979.

Sandeen, Ernest R., ed. *The Bible and Social Reform.* Philadelphia: Fortress Press, and Chico, CA: Scholars Press, 1982.

————. *The Roots of Fundamentalism: British and American Millenarianism, 1800–1930.* Chicago: University of Chicago Press, 1970.

Shepherd, Gordon, and Gary Shepherd. *A Kingdom Transformed: Themes in the Development of Mormonism.* SLC: University of Utah Press, 1984.

Shipps, Jan. *Mormonism: The Story of a New Religious Tradition.* Urbana: University of Illinois Press, 1985.

Sivan, Gabriel. *The Bible and Civilization.* New York: Quadrangle/New York Times Book Co., 1973.

Smith, James Ward, and A. Leland Jamison. *The Shaping of American Religion.* Princeton: Princeton University Press, 1961.

Smith, Joseph Fielding, Jr., and John J. Stewart. *The Life of Joseph Fielding Smith, Tenth President of the Church.* SLC: Deseret Book, 1972.

Smith, Lucy. *Biographical Sketches of Joseph Smith, the Prophet, and His Progenitors for Many Generations.* Reprint. New York: Arno Press, 1969.

Snell, Heber C. *Ancient Israel: Its Story and Meaning.* SLC: Stevens & Wallis, 1948.

Sperling, S. David. "Judaism and Modern Biblical Research." In *Biblical Studies: Meeting Ground of Jews and Christians.* Edited by Lawrence Boadt, Helga Croner, and Leon Klenicki, pp. 19–44. New York: Paulist Press, 1980.

Sperling, S. D., and B. A. Levine. *History of Jewish Biblical Scholarship in North America.* San Francisco: Harper & Row, forthcoming.

Stendahl, Krister. "The Sermon on the Mount and Third Nephi." In *Reflections on Mormonism: Judaeo-Christian Parallels.* Edited by Truman G. Madsen. Provo, UT: Religious Studies Center, BYU, 1978.

Talmage, James E. *The Articles of Faith.* SLC: Deseret News Press, 1899.

————. *Jesus the Christ.* SLC: Deseret News Press, 1915.

Talmage, John Russell. *The Talmage Story.* SLC: Bookcraft, 1972.

Underwood, Grant. "Joseph Smith's Use of the Old Testament." In *The Old Testament and the Latter-day Saints: The Sperry Symposium,* pp. 381–413. SLC: Randall Book, 1986.

———. "The Old Testament in the New Dispensation." In *A Symposium on the Old Testament,* pp. 169–72. SLC: Church of Jesus Christ of Latter-day Saints, 1983.

Whittaker, David. "By Study and Also By Faith: The Book of Daniel in Early Mormon Thought." In *Essays in Honor of Hugh Nibley.* Edited by John Lundquist and Stephen D. Ricks. SLC: F.A.R.M.S. and Deseret Book, 1990): 155–201.

Yarn, David H. *Young Reuben: The Early Life of J. Reuben Clark, Jr.* Provo, UT: Brigham Young University Press, 1973.

Theses and Dissertations

Bishop, Gary L. "The Tradition of Isaiah in The Book of Mormon." Master's thesis, BYU, 1974.

Durham, Reed Conwell. "A History of Joseph Smith's Revision of the Bible." Ph.D. diss., BYU, 1965.

Hill, Marvin S. "The Role of Christian Primitivism in the Origin and Development of the Mormon Kingdom, 1830–1844." Ph.D. diss., University of Chicago, 1968.

Irving, Gordon Ivor. "Mormonism and the Bible, 1832–1838." Senior honors thesis, University of Utah, 1972.

LeCheminant, Dale. "John A. Widtsoe—Rational Apologist." Ph.D. diss., University of Utah, 1977.

Lowe, Jay R. "A Study of the General Conferences of the Church of Jesus Christ of Latter-day Saints, 1830–1901." Ph.D. diss., BYU, 1972.

Lyon, Thomas Edgar. "Orson Pratt: Early Mormon Leader." Master's thesis, University of Chicago, 1932.

Persons, William R. "An Analysis of Changes in the Introduction and Utilization of Revelation in the Church of Jesus Christ of Latter-day Saints." Th.D. diss., Iliff School of Theology, 1964.

Rasmussen, Ellis T. "Textual Parallels to the Doctrine and Covenants and Book of Commandments as Found in the Bible." Master's thesis, BYU, 1951.

Riley, William L. "A Comparison of Passages from Isaiah and Other Old Testament Prophets in Ethan Smith's 'View of the Hebrews' and the Book of Mormon." Master's thesis, BYU, 1971.

Smutz, Lois Jean. "Textual Parallels to the Doctrine and Covenants (Sections 65–133) as Found in the Bible." Master's thesis, BYU, 1974.

Thacker, Brandon. "Inspired Revisions: The Challenges of Translating Scripture." Honors thesis, BYU, 1982.

Walters, Wesley, "The Use of the Old Testament in the Book of Mormon." Master's thesis, Covenant Theological Seminary, 1981.

Wernick, Nissim, "A Critical Analysis of the *Book of Abraham* in Light of Extra-Canonical Jewish Writings." Ph.D. diss., BYU, 1968.

Whittaker, David J. "Early Mormon Pamphleteering." Ph.D. diss., BYU, 1982.

Articles

Adams, Larry L. "A Computer Analysis of the Isaiah Authorship Problem." *BYU Studies* 15 (Autumn 1974): 95–102.

Alexander, Thomas G. "The Reconstruction of Mormon Doctrine: From Joseph Smith to Progressive Theology. *Sunstone* 5 (July/August 1980): 24–33.

Arrington, Leonard. "The Intellectual Tradition of the Latter-day Saints." *Dialogue* 4 (Spring 1969): 23–24.

Ashment, Edward H. "The Facsimiles of the Book of Abraham: A Reappraisal." *Sunstone* 4 (December 1979): 33–48.

Barney, Kevin, L. "The Joseph Smith Translation and Ancient Texts of the Bible." *Dialogue* 19 (Fall 1986): 85–102.

Bennion, Lowell L. "Reflections on the Restoration." *Dialogue* 18 (Fall 1985): 160–67.

Bergera, Gary James. "The Orson Pratt-Brigham Young Controversies: Conflict Within the Quorums, 1853 to 1868." *Dialogue* 13 (Summer 1980): 7–49.

Buerger, David John. "Speaking with Authority: The Theological Influence of Elder Bruce R. McConkie." *Sunstone* 10 (March 1985): 8–13.

Charles, Melodie Moench (see also Moench, Melodie). "The Mormon Christianizing of the Old Testament." *Sunstone* 5 (November/December 1980): 35–39.

Christensen, Harold, and Kenneth L. Cannon. "The Fundamentalist Emphasis at Brigham Young University: 1935–1973." *Journal for the Scientific Study of Religion* 17 (March 1978): 53–57.

Crawley, Peter. "The Passage of Mormon Primitivism." *Dialogue* 13 (Winter 1980): 26–37.

Cummings, Richard. "Quintessential Mormonism: Literal-Mindedness as a Way of Life." *Dialogue* 15 (Winter 1982): 92–102.

Ericksen, Ephraim E. "William H. Chamberlin: Pioneer Mormon Philosopher." *Western Humanities Review* 8 (Autumn 1954): 277–85.

Gunn, Jon. "Ezekiel, Dr. Sperry, and the Stick of Ephraim." *Dialogue* 2 (Winter 1967): 137–40.

Hoekema, Anthony A. "Ten Questions to Ask the Mormons." *Christianity Today,* January 19, 1968, pp. 378–82.

Howard, Richard P. "A Tentative Approach to the Book of Abraham."
    Dialogue 3 (Summer 1968): 88–92.
Hutchinson, Anthony A. "The Joseph Smith Revision and the Synoptic Prob-
    lem: An Alternative View." *John Whitmer Historical Association Jour-
    nal* 5 (1985): 47–53.
————. "LDS Approaches to the Holy Bible." *Dialogue* 15 (Spring 1982):
    99–125.
————. "A Mormon Midrash? LDS Creation Narratives Reconsidered." *Dia-
    logue* 21 (Winter 1988): 11–74.
Irving, Gordon. "The Mormons and the Bible in the 1830s." *BYU Studies* 13
    (Summer 1973): 473–88.
Jeffrey, Duane. "Seers, Savants, and Evolution: The Uncomfortable Inter-
    face." *Dialogue* 3 (Autumn/Winter 1974): 41–75.
Jessee, Dean C. "The Reliability of Joseph Smith's History." *Journal of Mor-
    mon History* 3 (1976): 23–46.
Keller, Jeffrey E. "Discussion Continued: The Sequel to the Roberts/Smith/
    Talmage Affair." *Dialogue* 15 (Spring 1982): 79–98.
Kenny, Scott. "Mormons, Genesis, and Higher Criticism." *Sunstone* 3
    (November/December 1977): 8–12.
Kirkland, Boyd. "Of Gods, Mortals, and Devils." *Sunstone* 10 (December
    1985): 6–12.
"The Lutherans: Fractured Fellowship." *Christianity Today,* November 5,
    1976, pp. 81–84.
Lyon, T. Edgar. "Doctrinal Development of the Church During the Nauvoo
    Sojourn, 1839–1846." *BYUS* 15 (Summer 1975): 435–46.
Matthews, Robert J. "The Bible and Its Role in the Restoration." *Ensign* 9
    (August 1979): 42–47.
————. "The New Publications of the Standard Works." *BYU Studies* 22
    (Fall 1982): 387–424.
————. "Plain and Precious Things Restored." *Ensign* 12 (July 1982): 15–
    20.
————. "Using the New Bible Dictionary in the LDS Edition." *Ensign* 12
    (June 1982): 47–50.
Millet, Robert L. "Joseph Smith's Translation of the Bible and the Synoptic
    Problem." *John Whitmer Historical Association Journal* 5 (1985): 41–
    46.
Moench, Melodie (See also Charles, Melodie Moench). "Joseph Smith:
    Prophet, Priest and King." Task Papers in LDS History, no. 25. SLC:
    LDS Historical Department, 1978.
————. "Nineteenth-Century Mormons: The New Israel." *Dialogue* 12
    (Spring 1979): 42–56.

Ostler, Blake T. "The Book of Mormon as a Modern Expansion of an Ancient Source." *Dialogue* 20 (Spring 1987): 66–124.

"Presbyterians and Biblical Authority" (multiple authors; see related articles under various titles). Special issue. *Journal of Presbyterian History* 59 (Summer 1981): 95–285.

Robson, Kent. "The Bible, the Church, and Its Scholars." *Dialogue* 2 (Spring 1967): 85–90.

Russell, William D. "Recent Shifts in the RLDS Conception of Scripture." *Sunstone Review* 2 (August 1982): 19–20.

Sandberg, Karl C. "Knowing Brother Joseph Again: The Book of Abraham and Joseph Smith as Translator." *Dialogue* 22 (Winter 1989): 19–37.

Sherlock, Richard. "A Turbulent Spectrum: Mormon Reactions to the Darwinist Legacy." *Journal of Mormon History* 5 (1978): 33–59.

———. "Campus in Crisis: BYU: 1911." *Sunstone* 4 (January/February 1979): 10–16.

———. "Faith and History: The Snell Controversy." *Dialogue* 12 (Spring 1979): 27–41.

———. " 'We Can See No Advantage to a Continuation of the Discussion': The Roberts/Smith/Talmage Affair." *Dialogue* 13 (Fall 1980): 63–78.

Smith, Timothy L. "The Book of Mormon in a Biblical Culture." *Journal of Mormon History* 7 (1980): 3–21.

Snow, Marcellus S. "The Challenge of Theological Translation: The New German Versions of the Standard Works." *Dialogue* 17 (Summer 1984): 133–49.

Sorenson, John. "The 'Brass Plates' and Biblical Scholarship." *Dialogue* 10 (Autumn 1977): 31–39.

Swensen, Russel. "Mormons at the University of Chicago Divinity School." *Dialogue* 7 (Summer 1972): 37–47.

Tanner, Sandra. "The Bible and Mormon Doctrine." SLC: Modern Microfilm, 1971.

Thorp, Malcolm R. "James E. Talmage and the Tradition of Victorian Lives of Jesus." *Sunstone* 12 (January 1988): 8–13.

Tvedtnes, John. "Hebraisms in the Book of Mormon: A Preliminary Survey." *BYU Studies* 11 (Autumn 1970): 50–60.

Underwood, Grant. "Book of Mormon Usage in Early LDS Theology." *Dialogue* 17 (Autumn 1984): 35–74.

Urrutia, Benjamin. "The Structure of Genesis, Chapter 1." *Dialogue* 8 (Autumn/Winter 1974): 142–43.

Walton, Michael T. "Professor Seixas, the Hebrew Bible, and the Book of Abraham: Joseph's Study of Hebrew and the Translation of the Book of Abraham Examined." *Sunstone* 6 (March/April 1981): 41–43.

————. "Mormonism: The Talmudic Phase?" *Sunstone* 5 (September/October 1980): 18–20.

Welsh, John. "Chiasmus in the Book of Mormon." *BYU Studies* 10 (Autumn 1969): 69–84.

————, and David Whittaker. " 'We Believe . . .': Development of the Articles of Faith." *Ensign* 9 (September 1979): 50–55.

Whittaker, David. "Orson Pratt: Early Advocate of the Book of Mormon." *Ensign* 14 (April 1984): 54–57.

————. "Orson Pratt: Prolific Pamphleteer." *Dialogue* 15 (Autumn 1982): 27–41.

Zucker, Lewis, "Joseph Smith as a Student of Hebrew." *Dialogue* 3 (Summer 1968): 41–55.

Index

Abbott, Lymon, 108, 117, 134
Abelard, Peter, 200
Adam (and Eve), 93, 104, 109, 137, 179
Alexander, Thomas, 218
Alexandrian text of New Testament, 166–67
America as chosen nation, 6, 11, 98, 100–101
Anglicans. *See* Episcopalians
Antinomian controversy, xii, 151
Anselm, Saint, 200
Apocrypha, 50, 62, 99
Arrington, Leonard J., 137
Article of Faith #8, 157, 221, 226
Augsburg Confession, 184
Augustine, 216n.1
Authorized Version. *See* King James Bible
Authorship, concept of, 58–60

Babel, Tower of, 32, 134
Baptists, Northern, 144, 182
Baptists, Southern, xii, 145, 182
Barr, James, 33
Bayle, Pierre, 107
Beecher, Lyman, 82, 154
Bennion, Adam S., 138
Bennion, Lowell L., xv, 194–205, 226; accepts suprahuman inspiration, 200, 201; advocates reason and inspiration as mutual checks, 200; asserts integrity of Old Testament independent of modern revelation, 201; biographical information on, 196–97; capacity for verbal combat, 196–97n.40; as conscience of modern Mormonism, 195; criteria for scriptural interpretation, 200; defines liberalism, 198n.44; dimensions of religion for, 198–99; dislikes "Christianizing" of Old Testament, 201; founds Institute of Religion, 196; great attention to Old Testament and Jesus, 198; hermeneutic contrasted with McConkie's, 197–205; hermeneutic summarized, 203–4; historicity of Job irrelevant for, 212; influence of, 195–96, 214; not trained as biblical scholar, 182, 197; as pragmatic exegete, 197; primacy of ethics over theology, science, or history, 199–200, 204; refuses employment at BYU, 139; religion and ethics distinct for, 198–99; selective use of scriptures, 200n.48; as teacher of Bruce McConkie, 194; use of non-Christian scriptures, 197n.41; views on higher criticism, 203,

Bennion, Lowell L. (*continued*)
    203n.63; as Weberian type, 184;
    writings of, 195–96
Benson, Ezra Taft, 224–25n.11
Beza, Theodore, 166
Bible: American Standard Version of,
    157, 160; attacked, 4, 46; authority of,
    xx, 6, 8, 9, 45, 109, 220–28, and
    passim; and Book of Mormon, 25–32,
    42, 141; cited more frequently than
    other scriptures by Mormon leaders,
    224–25n.11; condescension toward,
    127–28; contains fables, 80, 92, 100;
    cultural use of, xiii, 198, 204n.66,
    215–16; culture and, 3–4n.1, 3–10,
    and passim; democratic use of, 7–8,
    39; devotional use of (*see* pietistic use
    of); distinctive regional use of, 216;
    distribution of, 4, 175–76n.67;
    doctrinal use of, xiii, 94, 98, 191, 198–
    200, 204nn.66–67, 227; ethical use of,
    201, 203, 227; evangelical
    paraphrasing colors theology of, 212;
    Geneva, xii, 149–51, 207; geology
    and, 89–91; hortatory functions of,
    216; influence of annotations in, 149–
    50, 206, 207–13, 207n.71; inspiration
    of, 98–99; knowledge of, xii;
    moralistic use of, xiii, 198–200,
    204n.66; "Mormonization" of, 208–
    14; as myth, 92, 98, 133, 134; oracular
    uses of, 216, 216n.1; pietistic use of,
    xiii, 98, 198, 204n.66, 216, 227;
    popular uses of, 215–16; preferred
    over Book of Mormon by earliest
    generations of Mormons, 44–45, 83,
    88; proof texting of, 88, 224, passim;
    proselytizing use of, xiii, 38, 45; public
    use of, xiii; regulatory role of, 216;
    sanctions polygamy, 84–87; selective
    use of, 46, 80, 88, 95; social roles of,
    215–16; somnolent potential of, 216;
    stature of in antebellum America, 3–
    10; subordinated to other authorities,
    74, 79–81, 86, 88, 89, 92–93, 96;
    talismanic use of, 215; tensions

between Joseph Smith and, 220; as
    theological weapon, 216; therapeutic
    properties of, 216; transmission
    difficulties of, 95, 102, 116, 118, 165–
    68, 221, 223; unequal value of various
    books of, 80, 193, 200n.48, 202;
    versions of, xi–xii, 148–81; women's
    uses distinguished from men's, xix–xx,
    216. *See also* Alexandrian text of New
    Testament; Apocrypha; Bibliolatry;
    Book of Mormon; Byzantine text of
    New Testament; Douay Bible; Higher
    criticism; Inerrancy; Joseph Smith
    Translation of Bible; King James
    Bible; LDS Edition of Bible; New
    Testament; Old Testament;
    Relevation/revelations; Revised
    Standard Version of Bible; Revised
    Version of Bible; Scripture; Syrian
    text of the Bible; *Textus Receptus;*
    Vulgate Bible
Biblical criticism. *See* Higher criticism;
    Textual criticism
Bibliolatry, 133
Bitton, Davis, x, 137
Book of Abraham, 69–70, 69n.66
Book of Mormon: affirms Bible, 27;
    allegedly addresses nineteenth-century
    concerns, 43–45; biblical style of, 11,
    26–32, 221; cited, xviii, 40; enduring
    importance of for contemporary
    Mormonism, 56n.35; given new
    subtitle, xx; improving scholarship on,
    226; influences author's perspectives,
    xviii; and Joseph Smith Translation of
    Bible, 51, 52, 53, 54, 55, 56; makes
    Joseph Smith unique, 41; obliterates
    distinction between Old and New
    Testaments, 35–38; produced in brief
    time, 25; scholarship on, 37n.67;
    sections in common with Bible, 16–
    17; specifies "conditions of void,"
    xviii; subject to higher criticism, 114;
    as supplement to Bible, 78;
    theological differences with Old
    Testament, 35–37; as threat to

traditional scripture, 26; used less than Bible by early Mormons, 44; verifies the Bible, 12–13, 120–21, 212–13. *See also* Bible

Book of Moses, 48, 70

Bowne, Borden Parker, 130–31

Boyd, George, 162n.38

Briggs, Charles, 108, 119

Brigham Young University, 142–43; hurt by Chamberlin–Peterson affair, 139; religion department, 143

Brodie, Fawn, vii, 12, 56, 72

Broughton, Hugh, 150–51

Brown, Hugh B., 185

Bryan, William Jennings, 137

Buddha, 118

Burgon, John W., 162

Bushman, Richard L., 227

Bushnell, Horace, 24, 108, 228

BYU. *See* Brigham Young University

Byzantine text of New Testament, 166, 167

Cambridge Bible Dictionary, 209, 211

Canon/canonization: limitations of canonized statements, 133; malleability of canonized texts, 95; noncanonized scripture, x; open, 40, 88, 95, 99, 228; problems of, x, 9, 88, 192; written vs. oral, x, 41

Case, Shirley Jackson, 140

Catholic Biblical Association, 146

Catholic Biblical Quarterly, 146

Catholics/Catholicism, xi, 8, 11, 39, 101, 157; conflict with Protestants over biblical versions, 149, 154–56; as cultural "outsiders," 9, 154–55; higher criticism and, 107, 145–46; likened to Mormons, 118–19, 145–46, 222, 228; progress in scholarship among, 145–46, 226n.15; struggle to adopt a vernacular version, 179. *See also Divino Afflante Spiritu;* Douay Bible; *Lamentabili; Pascendi Dominici Gregis;* Leo XIII, Pope; Pius XII, Pope; *Providentissimus Deus;* Vatican II

Chamberlin, Ralph, 134

Chamberlin, William H., xiv, 103, 129–34, 145, 194; biographical information on, 129–31; controversy surrounding teachings of, 134, 137–38; defended by David O. McKay, 138; influence of, 130; not a general authority, 130; opposite of Joseph Fielding Smith, 129; reality of God for, 132–33; rehired after dismissal, 138; repercussions of dismissal of, 137–39; views of warmly received by students, 134

Christian Primitivism, 11, 46, 71, 95; doctrinal emphasis of, 97; Mormonism a part of yet distinct within, 18, 40, 68; New Testament emphasis of, 6

Clark, J. Reuben, xv, xix, 104n.2, 149, 158–74, 188; appropriates Protestant arguments for KJV, 149, 161; arguments of against RSV summarized, 161; biographical information on, 158–59; disagrees with David O. McKay about KJV, 169; distrusted intellectuals, 171; influence of, 174, 214; misconstrues Joseph Smith's revelations, 163–64; perceptions of revelation, 163–64; supported Joseph Fielding Smith, 143

Codex/codices (Greek) of the Bible, 167

Confucius, 118

Congregationalists/congregationalism, xii, 10, 108

Conservatives/conservativism, xviii, xviiin.21, 109; ascendance in Mormonism, 146–47, 185, 205, 213–14, 224; in selecting biblical versions, 148

Context, importance of various types of for biblical interpretation, 201

Correlation movement, 185

Cotton, John, 82

Cowdery, Oliver, 23n.29, 25, 49

Creeds, relative paucity of in Mormonism, 184–85

"Culture Mormons," 139, 183

Day, Dorothy, 195
"Deconstruction," xv
Deists/deism, 4, 26
Deutero-Isaiah, 111, 129, 142
Devil. *See* Satan
Dispensationalism, 11, 117, 223; and
    Mormon restoration, 18; traced to
    John Nelson Darby, 176n.70; as a way
    to structure history, 71, 225
Divino Afflante Spiritu, 146
Doctrine and Covenants, 21–25, 21n.25,
    52; not all sections of in KJV idiom,
    177; perceived to contain exact words
    of God, 163; portions of by multiple
    authorship, 23–24n.29; portions of
    resulting from Joseph Smith's biblical
    translation, 62
Documentary hypothesis of Genesis,
    111, 128
Douay Bible, 155, 168

Edersheim, Alfred, 136
Eichorn, J. G., 108
Elliot, Charles, 99
Enoch, 48–49, 51, 54; Book of, 99
Episcopalians, 182, 221
Erasmus, 165, 166
Eriksen, E. E., 139–40
Essays and Reviews, 107
Estienne, Robert, 166
Ethical monotheism, 198
Evangelicals/evangelicalism, xii;
    apologists for, 101; assumed Bible's
    clarity and finality, 39; attuned to
    Bible's cultural role, xi; canon closed
    for, 99; contrasted with Mormons, 11,
    15, 99–100, 102, 220–22; differ from
    Mormons in selecting biblical
    translations, 148; indignant about
    polygamy, 85–86; paraphrase edition
    of Bible colors theology, 212; progress
    in scholarship among, 225; "scientific"
    apologists for Bible among, 89. *See
    also* Fundamentalists/fundamentalism
Evolution: accepted by some who
    rejected higher criticism, 105–6,

106n.5, 114–15; accepted in Europe
    more easily than in America, 107;
    construed as evil, 129; embraced by
    James E. Talmage, 136–37; embraced
    by John A. Widtsoe, 136; ignored by
    Brigham Young, 91; more easily
    popularized than higher criticism,
    104–5; no official Mormon position
    on, 137; not confronted by Orson
    Pratt, 89; rejected by Bruce
    McConkie, 191; rejected by Joseph
    Fielding Smith, 122; relative
    importance of as challenge to faith,
    xiv, 104–5; taught by William H.
    Chamberlin, 134; threat to Genesis,
    104–5
Exodus, Mormon compared to biblical,
    75–77

Farrar, Frederic W., 136
Finney, Charles, 8, 19, 20, 41, 56, 82
Fiske, John, 114
Folk magic, xi
Franklin, Benjamin, 151
Fundamentalists/fundamentalism, xii,
    137; accuse Mormons of not believing
    in Bible, xx; among Catholics, 107;
    among Jehovah's Witnesses, 143–44;
    forsake literalism to protect inerrancy,
    33; flourishes in Mormonism, 144;
    Islamic, 194; Jewish, 194; as relative
    term, 182n.1; and *Scofield Reference
    Bible,* 213n.82; sects within
    Mormonism, 183; view of revelation,
    194. *See also* Evangelicals/
    evangelicalism

Garden of Eden, 135
"Gathering," the Mormon, 77
Geike, Cunningham, 136
General Authorities, xxviii
Geneva Bible. *See* Bible: Geneva
Geography. *See* Utah compared to Israel
Geology, Bible and, 89–91
Gladden, Washington, 108
God: evolving conceptions of, 131–32;

goals of for humankind, 47, 131;
Orson Pratt's conception of, 93
Goethe, Johann Wolfgang, xvi
Goodspeed, Edgar, 142
Gore, Charles, 107
Grant, Heber J., 216
Gutenberg, Johann, 206

Hammurabi, 127
Hansen, Klaus, viii, 218
Harris, Martin, 20, 21
Harvard University, 38, 135
Hengel, Martin, 128n.61
Higher criticism, xii–xiii, xiv, 102, 103–
47; Bennion's use of, 203, 203n.63;
Brigham Young and, 91; Catholics
and, 107; Chamberlin's use of, 131–34;
conclusions illustrated, 61; seen as
conspiracy, 125; criticized, 115–17,
119, 127–28, 128n.61; declared a
failure, 118–19, 128–29; deeper
challenge than evolution, 104–6; did
not flourish until after Civil War, xii,
xiv; divergent responses to, 103, 134–
39; early Mormon responses to, 109–
11; European background of, 99, 106–
7; as influence on LDS attachment to
KJV, 149, 156; introduced to America,
8–9, 38; less easily popularized than
evolution, 105; majority of Mormons
unaffected by, 111, 223; misleading
term, 124, 124n.52; and Mormon
historiography, 104n.2; no official LDS
response toward, 137; perceived as
anti-semitism, 121; potential
acceptance of by Mormons, 110;
potential rejection of by Mormons,
109–10; promoted by Widstoe, 135–
36; rejected by some who accepted
evolution, 104–6, 106n.5, 135–37
Hindus/Hinduism, 179. *See also*
Vendanga commentaries; Vedas
Historical criticism. *See* Higher criticism
Historiography, Mormon, vii–ix, xiii–xx,
103, 216–220, 226
Hitchcock, Edward, 90

Hodge, A. A., 108, 115
Hooker, Thomas, 82
Hort, F. J. A., 166–67
Howison, George, 114

Immanence, in William Chamberlin's
theology, 130. *See also* Modernists/
Modernism
Inerrancy, 54n.29, 99–100, 107, 108, 116,
144; fundamentalists value over
literalism; McConkie's views on, 187,
193–94; original autographs used to
protect, 194; trials over issue of, 138;
rejected by Brigham Young, 96;
rejected by Joseph Smith, 34, 43;
rejected by Mormons, 116, 116n.27,
201–2, 221–22; views on among
Catholics, 146
inspiration, verbal, 126, 163–64, 193–94
"Iron Rod Saints," 183–84. *See also*
Conservatives/conservatism; "Liahona
Saints"; Liberals/liberalism
Irving, Gordon, 34
Isaiah, Deutero-. *See* Deutero-Isaiah
Islam, ix, 178–79. *See also* Mohammed;
Qur'an
Ivins, Anthony W., 137

Jasher, Book of, 99
Jehovah's Witnesses, 143–44, 228
Jessee, Dean, 59
Jesus Christ, 35, 51, 104; Book of
Mormon identifies as Christ, 27; as
champion of women's rights, 136;
controversy over virgin birth of, 189;
as culmination of God's revelation,
132; divinity of as reflected in various
translations, 180–81; Joseph Smith
honors as divine redeemer, 39, 42;
portrayed as focus of Old Testament,
71; portrayed as merely mortal, 115
Jewish Theological Seminary, 145
Jews/Judaism, 5, 27, 148; accused of
expunging sacred texts, 36n.65;
assigning priority to Talmud over
Bible, 8; attached to KJV, 179–80;

Jews/Judaism (*continued*)
  construing higher criticism as anti-
    semitic, 121; as cultural outsiders, 9;
    disturbed by "Christianizing" of Old
    Testament, 201; likened to Mormons,
    182, 222–23n.8, 228; response to
    higher criticism of compared to that of
    Mormons, 145; Talmud cited in
    support of inerrant Bible, 194
Job, historicity of considered, 137, 211–
  12
Jonah, historicity of considered, 137
Joseph Smith Translation of Bible, 18,
  34, 43, 46–51, 64, 95; incompleteness
  of, 49, 51, 153; as influence on LDS
  attachment to KJV, 149, 153–54, 163;
  portions of included in LDS edition of
  Bible, 208

Kimball, Spencer W., 206
King James I, 149, 173–74
King James Bible: affects American
  speech, 5; as beautiful literature, 149,
  151, 157, 168–70; Blayney's edition
  of, 207; commands loyalty of Jews,
  179–80; "common" distinguished from
  "official" usage of, xv, 149, 151–52,
  158, 177, 224; criticism of, 150, 207;
  difficulties of for youth, 170; as factor
  in founding of Catholic parochial
  schools, 156; history of annotation in,
  207; imperfections of, 16–18, 46–47,
  151; implications of allegiance to, 149;
  influence of on Mormon revelations,
  14–19, 21–32, 51–55, 62, 63, 71;
  influences Mormon perceptions, 213–
  14; Koine Greek behind, 170;
  language of affects modern LDS
  conceptions, 176, 176n.69; language
  of assumed to be sacred, 14; LDS
  Edition of, xv, 148–49, 205–13;
  Lloyd's edition of, 207; Mormons
  inherit from Protestants, 148;
  popularity of, 175, 175n.67; presents
  Mormons with dilemma, 180; reverent
  preface to, 173–74; revised by Joseph

Smith, 46–61; seventeenth-century
  criticisms of, 150; As *the* American
  Bible, 155; translators of forsee
  criticism, 150, 207; translators of not
  inspired, 152, 156, 172; competes with
  Geneva Translation, xii, 150–51. *See
  also* Bible; LDS Edition of Bible
Koran. *See* Qur'an

Lamentabili, 146
Language: limitations of, 24, 95; as
  "objective," 179; as sacred, 178–79; as
  vehicle of numinous, 178
LDS Edition of Bible, xv, 182–83; Bible
  dictionary, 209–12; chapter headings,
  212–13; features of, 208; gives
  prestige to KJV, 178; impact of
  annotations in, 209–10, 213–14;
  implied theology of, 209–13;
  McConkie's influence on annotations,
  209–14; producers of, 206, 209;
  unofficial nature of supplements in,
  209. *See also* King James Bible: LDS
  Edition of
Lee, Harold B., 141, 177
Leeser, Isaac, 179
Leo XII, Pope, 107
Leo XIII, Pope, 145
Leone, Mark, viii
"Liahona Saints," 183–84. *See also*
  Conservatives/Conservativism; "Iron
  Rod Saints"; Liberals/Liberalism
Liberals/liberalism: Brigham Young as
  liberal, 90; comparative usefulness of
  term, xviii, xviiin.21; declining
  visibility in Mormonism, 185, 223;
  "liberalized literalism," 117; in
  Mormon scriptural approaches, 148;
  as relative terms, 182n.1; supported
  by LDS leaders and laity, 205
Life, Mormon perception of purpose of,
  47, 131
Lindsell, Harold, xiii
Literalism, 33–35, 87, 108, 109; in Book
  of Mormon, 33, 34; Chamberlin
  rejects, 133–34; helps distinguish LDS

from RLDS, 34–35;
"hyperliteralism," 87; in James
Talmage, 136; in John A. Widstoe,
135; in Joseph Fielding Smith, 125; in
Joseph Smith's use of Bible, 33–35,
42, 65, 71, 220; "liberalized
literalism," 117; meaning of, 33–34; in
the Mormon First Presidency, 137;
and nature of Joseph Smith's visions,
19, 23–24n.29; 42; Orson Pratt's, 84,
87; remains strong in Mormonism,
223; selective, 33, 38, 65, 95, 97, 122;
subordinate to inerrancy among
fundamentalists, 33
Loisy, Alfred, 107
Lower criticism. *See* Textual criticism
Lucifer. *See* Satan
Luther, Martin, 7, 38n.69, 193, 206
Lutheran Church–Missouri Synod, xii
Lux Mundi, 107
Lynd, Robert and Helen, 144

Machen, J. Gresham, 167, 225
McConkie, Bruce R., xv, xix; basic
allegiance to Bible, 192; biographical
information on, 187–88; concern for
millennial events, 199–200;
disagreements with Mormon leaders,
190; dismisses some biblical books,
193; disparages higher criticism, 188–
89; doctrine before ethics, 191, 204;
extraordinary enthusiasm for
scriptural study, 188; importance of
King James Bible for, 189; influence
of, 185–87, 190, 214; influences new
LDS Edition of Bible, 206, 209, 212–
13; interest in theology, 185–87; keys
for scriptural interpretation, 189–90;
limits biblical authority, 192–93;
minimizes worth of learning biblical
languages, 189; motives of, 190–91;
not trained as biblical scholar, 182,
185; perspectives on Bible, 187–94;
prefers New Testament over Old
Testament, 197; ranks methods for
scriptural study, 189; reasons for

influence of, 186; rejects evolution,
191, 211; rejects inerrancy in Bible
but not in modern revelation, 201–2;
self-reliant interpretations of, 188;
supported Joseph Fielding Smith, 143;
views salvation as possible without
Bible, 193; as student of Lowell
Bennion, 193, 197; views biblical
books as unevenly inspired, 193; as
Weberian type, 184; writings of, 186–
87
McKay, David O., 138, 141, 169, 170,
175, 185, 211, 214
McMurrin, Sterling, 139, 141
Margolis, Max, 179
Matthews, Robert J., 209
Mauss, Armand, 220n.5
Mercersburg Theology. *See* Nevin,
John W.
Merrill, Joseph F., 141
Methodists/Methodism, 76, 78
Middlekauf, Robert, 75
Millenarians, 33n.55. *See also*
Millennialism; Millennium
Millennium: conditions during, 49;
prophesied by Moroni, 16. *See also*
Millenarians; Millennialism
Millennialism: Brigham Young's
participation in, 95; Joseph Smith's
concern for, 11, 42, 71; McConkie's
concern for, 199, 213; Mormon
interest in, 46, 68, 95; Orson Pratt's
interest in, 84, 95; subordinate to
biblical usage in understanding Saints,
xi; waning interest in, 224. *See also*
Millenarian; Millennium
Miracles, 26; actuality of among
Mormons, 33, 76, 84, 101, 111, 117,
121; miraculous dimensions of Bible
heightened by Joseph Smith, 52; other
names for, 162; secondary importance
of, 133; skepticism about challenged,
111, 117, 119, 127; subject to critical
thought, 4, 135–36
Modernists/modernism, xii, 108–9,
124n.51, 130, 204

Morgenstern, Julian, 145
Mohammed, 118, 178, 180. *See also*
   Islam; Qur'an
Moody, Dwight L., 129
Moore, Laurence, viii–ix. 218–
   19
Mormons/Mormonism: ambiguity of
   towards American culture, 217, 219–
   20; and American culture, vii, ixn.6,
   148, 178, 192, 217–20, 228; anti-
   intellectual tendencies of, 109–10;
   biblical usage of crucial for
   understanding, ix–xi, 217, 219–20;
   compatible with Bible, 87–88, 92, 95–
   97; continuities of scriptural usage
   summarized, 223; contrasts between
   nineteenth- and twentieth-century
   expressions of, 158, 218, 222; creedal
   or creedless?, 184–85; differences
   with American culture influence all
   similarities, 218, 228; distinctive
   scriptural usage of summarized, 227–
   28; diversity celebrated in, 205,
   205n.68; diversity of scriptural views
   in, 74, 81, 87–89, 92–97, 103–47
   passim, 170–71, 177–78, 209;
   evolutions in biblical usage
   summarized, 223–25; as history rather
   than philosophy, 227; inherent
   ambiguity of, 217; as new type of
   Christianity, 221; persecution of, 75,
   218–19; reasons for modest biblical
   scholarship by, 226, 226n.15; respect
   for learning and intellect, 110;
   sociological model accounting for
   change in, 220n.5; as "true Israel," 18,
   49, 67–69, 75–77, 98, 100–101. *See
   also* Historiography, Mormon
Moroni, 16, 17, 18, 19, 46
Moses, 47–48, 77, 91, 109, 111. *See also*
   Book of Moses
Mountain Meadows Massacre, 124
Mouw, Richard, xiii, 198, 204n.66, 67,
   216
Muslims. *See* Islam; Mohammed; Qur'an
Myth, 92, 98, 134

Neo-orthodoxy, 109
Nevin, John W., 9, 39, 101
Newman, J. P., 85–87
New Testament, 25, 39, 40, 71;
   appropriated by Mormons, 69; books
   missing from, 48; changes in Joseph
   Smith Translation, 50; distinction
   between Old and New Testaments
   erased, 35–36, 71; increasing
   prominence after 1820, 6, 68; more
   than an appropriation of Old
   Testament, 24; Old Testament viewed
   through New Testament lens, 37–38,
   42; preferred by Brigham Young, 80,
   97, 97n.49; said to result from
   apostolic journals, 64. *See also* Bible;
   Old Testament; Scripture
Niebuhr, Reinhold, 191
Niebuhr, H. Richard, 191
Noah and flood: historicity of
   questioned, 134
Noll, Mark, 225

Objectivity, xv–xviii, 215
O'Dea, Thomas, 197, 205
Old Testament, 24, 25, 42, 47, 80;
   changes in Joseph Smith Translation,
   50; "Christianization" of, 6, 35–39,
   71, 206n.70, 207n.71; integrity of
   independant of modern revelation,
   201; Joseph Smith's interest in, 18, 40;
   as link to polygamy, 65; more obscure
   than Book of Mormon, 224–25,
   224n.11; preferred by Orson Pratt, 97,
   97n.49; public dominance of before
   1820, 6; suspect morality of heroes in,
   4; typological use of, 66–69
Oral scripture, 63, 228

Packer, Boyd K., 205–6
Pascendi Dominici Gregis, 146
Penrose, Charles W., 137
Personalism, 131
Petersen, Mark E., 143, 160, 161
Peterson, Henry, 134
Peterson, Joseph, 134

Phelps, Wiliam W., 44

Pius XII, Pope, 146

Plenary inspiration, 98–99, 109. *See also* Inspiration, verbal

Poll, Richard, 183

Polygamy, vii, 74, 77, 124; defended on scriptural grounds, 84–86; Pratt-Newman debate, 84–86; subordinate to Bible for understanding Saints, xi; surrendered, 222; typology and, 66

Pope Pius XII, 146

Pratt, Orson, xiv, 13, 74, 81–89, 91, 92–94; as apologist for Joseph Smith, 12; author of synthetical works, 185; debates polygamy with Newman, 84–86; enthusiastic about Joseph Smith Translation, 153; importance of, 81–82; interpretation of biblical prophecies, 84; not restricted to KJV, 152; Old Testament orientation of, 83; one of original apostles, 82; prefers Old Testament, 97, 97n.49; successful in proselytizing with Bible, 45

Pratt, Parley, 47, 76, 80, 185

Presbyterians/Presbyterianism, 10, 108, 119

Priesthood, xxvii, 25, 43

Primitivism. *See* Christian Primitivism

Progressivism. *See* Modernists/modernism

Prophets, Mormon, xxviii–xxix; primacy of living over scripture, 57, 61, 72, 80, 81, 96–97, 102, 220–21. *See also individual prophets*

Providentissimus Deus, 145

Pseudepigrapha, 99

Puritans/Puritanism, vii, viii, 4, 6, 66, 68, 75–76, 82

Qur'an, 8, 179. *See also* Islam; Mohammed

Reformers/Reformation, 6, 39, 103, 118. *See also* Luther, Martin

Reimarus, Hermann, 107

Religion, transitory forms of, 131–33

Renan, Ernest, 116

RLDS Church, 35, 49, 153, 216

Restoration, 17, 18, 69

Revelation/revelations, x, xvi, 23, 23n.29, 57, 58; contrasting conceptions of, 183; as divine–human dialectic, 220; fundamentalist view of, 194; misunderstanding of Joseph Smith's, 149, 163; provisional nature of, 43–73 passim, 80–81, 92, 110, 126, 131–32, 134, 163–64, 220; transcends history, 127; twentieth-century example of, 127; verbal, 163, 193–94. *See also* Bible; Book of Abraham; Book of Mormon; Book of Moses; Inerrancy; New Testament; Old Testament; Prophets, Mormon; Scripture; Smith, Joseph; Visionaries contrasted with Joseph Smith

Revised Standard Version of Bible, 159–74 passim; appearance of, 159–60; public resistance to, 159–60; resistance to among Mormons, 160–61; reverent preface to, 172–73; as vehicle of humanism, 161, 165

Revised Version of Bible, 157, 160

Revivals/revivalism, 7, 19–20, 82–83

Reynolds, George, 111

Richards, Stephen L., 174

Rigdon, Sidney, 45, 46n.12, 47

Rischen, Moses, vii

Roberts, Brigham H., xiv, xix, 103, 143; accepts evolution, 114, 211; affirms miracles, 116; approves of textual criticism, 156; assessed as Bible scholar, 113; author of synthetical works, 185; biographical information on, 112–13; and higher criticism, 113–15, 117–22; hostile to conclusions of many higher critics, 115; literary works, 113; preeminent intellectual in Mormon history, xiv, 106, 106n.6, 112–13; rejects inerrancy, 116; respect

Roberts, Brigham H. (*continued*)
  for science, 113–14; temporarily alone
  in confronting higher criticism, 112
Roman Catholics. *See* Catholics
Royce, Josiah, 130

Satan, 109, 122
Schechter, Solomon, 121, 145
Science, 89, 93–94, 99, 114; Brigham
  Young and, 89–91; compatible with
  revelation, 135; corrects scripture,
  133; difficulties between scripture
  and, 100; embraced by Mormonism,
  110, 113–14; geology and Genesis,
  89–91; harmonizes with Bible, 100;
  relationship with religion inverted,
  104; subordinate to scripture, 126;
  undermines Genesis, 8. *See also*
  Evolution; Geology, Bible and
Scofield Reference Bible, 213, 213n.82
Scottish Common Sense philosophy, 89, 90
Scripture, xvii; contradictions in, 96;
  eisegesis of, 13–14, 96, 97; human
  elements in, 115–16; inadequate
  hermeneutic among Mormons, 202;
  limitations of, 201–2; nature of, ix–x,
  43, 63–64, 87, 90; nature of for Bruce
  McConkie, 193–94; nature of for
  Joseph Smith, 220; nature of for
  Lowell Bennion, 200–201; nature of
  for William Chamberlin, 130–134; not
  sole source of God's Word, 43, 88;
  oral, x, 43, 63, 64; private, x, 64;
  provisional nature of, chapter 2
  passim, 72, 80–81, 92, 110, 126, 131–
  132, 134, 163–64, 220; as record of
  religious experience, 131–32;
  revelation and, x; subordinate to
  science, 131; temporary, x. *See also*
  Bible; Book of Abraham; Book of
  Mormon; Doctrine and Covenants;
  Joseph Smith Translation of Bible;
  New Testament; Old Testament;
  Qur'an; Revelation/revelations; Vedas
Scrivener, F. H. A., 162
Semler, Johann, 107

Septuagint, 30–31
Shipps, Jan, ix, 218
Silliman, Benjamin, 89–90
Sinaiticus, Codex, 167
Skousen, Cleon, 216
Slaves/slavery, vii, 6, 85, 100
Smith, Emma, 31
Smith, George Albert, 152
Smith, Jonathan Z., 217
Smith, Joseph Fielding, xiv, 103, 122–29,
  136; attacks Heber Snell's book, 140–
  41; biographical information on, 122–
  23; continuing influence of, 143;
  criticizes higher critics, 127–29;
  disparages textual criticism, 156;
  heightens Mormon devotion to
  scripture, 123–24; hostile to higher
  criticism, 122, 124–29, 156, 160; ill-
  prepared as biblical critic, 128; insists
  on legitimacy of miracles, 127;
  interested in theology, 185; legitimizes
  KJV, 175
Smith, Joseph, Jr., vii, xiii, xn.9, xvii,
  xix, 11–73; as Bible-like martyr, 75,
  88; biblical usage of summarized, 220–
  21; as a Christian, 42, 221; early
  exposure to Bible, 13–15; first vision
  of, 13–15; influence of KJV on, 14–73
  passim, 151–52; KJV not official for,
  151–52; on limitations of human
  language, 23–24, 134; "out-Bibles"
  contemporaneous biblicists, 220;
  revelation and, xvii, 13–32, 56–65,
  163–64 (*see also* Revelation/
  revelations); and scriptural literalism,
  32–35; sincerity of, 12; tensions
  between Bible and, 220; use of
  Hebrew language, 69–70, 72–73
Smith, Joseph, Sr., 10
Smith, Lucy Mack, 10, 12, 18–19, 20
Smith, Timothy, vii
Snell, Heber C., 140–41
Socrates, 127
Sola Scriptura, 7–9, 101, 102
Southern Baptists. *See* Baptists,
  Southern

Spencer, Herbert, 114
Sperry, Sidney, 142–43
Spinoza, Baruch, 106
Stephanus. *See* Estienne, Robert
Stauss, David Friedrich, 116, 119
Stuart, Moses, 9, 90, 101, 225
Supernatural rationalists, 200
Swensen, Russel, 138, 162n.38
Swing, David, 108
Syrian text of the Bible, 166

Talmage, James E., 136–37, 189, 211
Talmud, 194
Tanner, George, 162n.38, 170
Targum, 32
Taylor, John, 152, 177
Textual criticism, 118, 165–68
Textus Receptus, 165, 166
Theocracy, xi, 74, 77
Tree of Life, 183
Truth: assumptions about clarity of, 34,
    80n.11, 89–90, 97, 100; immutability
    of, 11, 80n.11, 97 (*see also* Scottish
    Common Sense philosophy);
    mutability of, 131; relation of to
    scripture and revelation, x
Tübingen critics, 107, 124, 127, 136
Tyndale, William, 206
Types/typology, 11, 66–69, 67n.60, 83–
    84, 223; Mormons as antitype of
    Israel, 75–77; Mormons recapitulate
    biblical events, 75–77, 95, 97, 100
Types, Weberian, xv, 184

Underwood, Grant, 88
Union Theological Seminary, 108
Unitarians/Unitarianism, xii, 11, 40, 108,
    221
Ussher's historical chronology, 207, 211
Utah compared to Israel, 76

Vatican II, 146. *See also* Catholics/
    Catholicism
Vaticanus, Codex, 167
Vedanga commentaries, 179. *See also*
    Hindus/Hinduism; Vedas
Vedas, 63, 182. *See also* Hindus/
    Hinduism; Vedanga commentaries
Visionaries contrasted with Joseph
    Smith, 11, 16, 20–22, 41, 221
Vulgate Bible, 165

Warfield, Benjamin B., 108, 115, 167,
    225
Weber, Max, 195
Webster, Noah, 151
Westcott, B. F., 166–67
Wellhausen, Julius, 107
West, Franklin L., 140
Westminster Confession, 184
White, Andrew, 126
Why the King James Version, 160, 174
Widtsoe, John A., 135, 141, 185, 196,
    211
Wise, Isaac, 121
Women and the Bible, xix–xx, 216
Woods, Leonard, 99
Wright, David P., 141, 141–42n.91
Wuthnow, Robert, 227

Young, Brigham, xiv, 35, 74, 121, 221;
    allegiance to Bible, 77–79; asserts
    Joseph Smith's influence on Book of
    Mormon, 37; childhood of, 77–78;
    dismisses portions of Bible as
    legendary, 92, 221; and higher
    criticism, 91; limits biblical authority,
    79–81, 221; as modern Moses, 77; not
    limited by KJV, 152; pragmatic use of
    the Bible, 94; prefers New Treatment,
    97, 97n.49
Young, Levi Edgar, 143